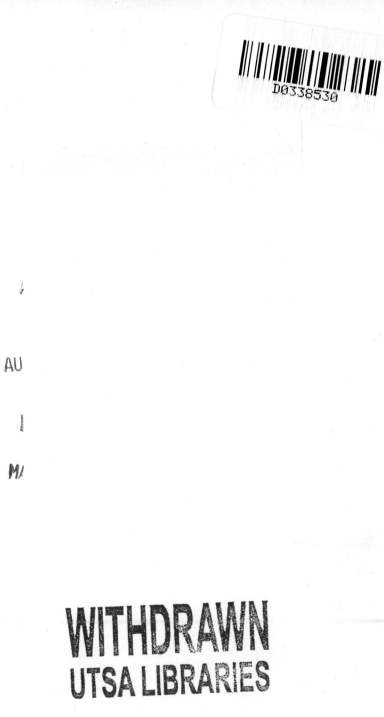

D0338530

AU

l

M

Guidelines for Parole and Sentencing

Guidelines for Parole and Sentencing

A Policy Control Method

Don M. Gottfredson
Rutgers University

Leslie T. Wilkins
State University of
  New York at Albany

Peter B. Hoffman
United States Parole
  Commission

Lexington Books
D. C. Heath and Company
Lexington, Massachusetts
Toronto

Library of Congress Cataloging in Publication Data

Gottfredson, Don M.
   Guidelines for parole and sentencing.

   Includes index.
   1. Parole—United States. 2. Sentences (Criminal procedure)—United
States. I. Wilkins, Leslie T., joint author. II. Hoffman, Peter B., joint
author. III. Title.
HV9304.G68   364.6'2'0973   77-1940
ISBN 0-669-01428-1

Published simultaneously in Canada.

Printed in the United States of America.

International Standard Book Number: 0-669-01428-1

Library of Congress Catalog Card Number: 77-1940

LIBRARY
The University of Texas
At San Antonio

Contents

List of Figures

List of Tables

Acknowledgments

Many people have aided directly or indirectly in the preparation of this book and in the parole decision-making project on which it has drawn. The studies reported could not have been done without the active collaboration of the then United States Board of Parole: Maurice H. Sigler, George J. Reed, William E. Amos, Curtis C. Crawford, Thomas R. Holsclaw, Gerald E. Murch, Paula A. Tennant, and William T. Woodard, Jr.; other members during the study were the late Walter Dunbar, William F. Howland, Jr., Zeigel W. Neff, and Charlotte Paul Reese.

An advisory committee, appointed jointly by the National Institute of Law Enforcement and Criminal Justice and the U.S. Board of Parole, did more than merely advise and made extremely helpful contributions at all stages of the project. This committee included Herbert Solomon, T. Conway Esselstyn, C. Ray Jeffery, Malcolm W. Klein, Charles L. Newman, and Stanton Wheeler. Susan M. Singer, a member of the project staff whose work contributed greatly to this book, later became a member of the advisory committee.

In the course of the studies reported, the late Bernard Wrenn, chief hearing examiner for the U.S. Board of Parole was especially helpful. The cooperation of the late Director J. Edgar Hoover of the Federal Bureau of Investigation in making information resources available to the project was sincerely appreciated. Similarly, Director Norman Carlson provided access to records of the Federal Bureau of Prisons; and Merrill Smith, Chief, Division of Probation, and James McCafferty, Assistant Chief, Division of Procedural Studies and Statistics, Administrative Office of the U.S. Courts, did the same.

Appreciation is also extended to Bridget Stecher for research assistance and to Margaret T. McGuire for preparation of the manuscript. We thank Margaret Zusky, Criminal Justice Editor of Lexington Books, for her patience, help, and active interest in the project.

The parole decision-making project cited frequently in this book was supported by grant number NI-72-017-G to the National Council on Crime and Delinquency by the National Institute of Law Enforcement and Criminal Justice, Law Enforcement Assistance Administration, U.S. Department of Justice, under the Omnibus Crime Control and Safe Streets Act of 1968, as amended. Points of view or opinions stated in this document are those of the authors and do not necessarily reflect the official position or policies of the United States Parole Commission, the Law Enforcement Assistance Administration, or the U.S. Department of Justice.

Similarly, although the interest and contributions of those noted have been much appreciated and we have profited from the wise counsel and active help cited, the responsibility for this book's contents must rest only with the authors.

Guidelines for Parole and Sentencing

1   Guidelines

guideline, *n*., a standard or principle by which to make a
judgment or determine a policy or course of action . . .

Webster's New Twentieth Century Dictionary

Parole boards, judges, and other decision makers in the criminal justice system
are responsible for two related but distinct decision functions regarding offenders or alleged offenders—individual case decisions and policy decisions.
Prominent in both types is the exercise of discretion that is common to all the
principal actors in the drama of the criminal justice process. While the first type
of decision (case) is readily apparent, widely discussed, and argued about, the
second (policy) often is not. Although it is possible for the policy function to be
recognized and explicit, this function (in relation to parole, sentencing, and
other criminal justice decision-making practice) traditionally has been unrecog-
nized, unwritten, implicit, and ill-defined.

The objectives of criminal justice decisions usually have been poorly
articulated. Even when explicitly stated, they often have produced controversy
and frequently have contained conflicting goals. Explicit general policies setting
forth a structure within which individual decisions may be carefully and fairly
made rarely have been available to those making such decisions. When such
statements have been attempted they often have been so vague and devoid of
operational meaning as to be nearly worthless. This lack of explicit policy has
led to widespread criticisms of unbridled discretion, unwarranted decision
disparity, and inequity in the making of case decisions by our sentencing and
paroling authorities and by other criminal justice system workers.

In this book it will be demonstrated that the articulation of decision policy,
through the development of explicit written standards or guidelines, provides a
feasible method of structuring and controlling decision discretion without
removing the ability for individual case consideration. Moreover, it will be
argued that by having made policy explicit, both the agency concerned and the
general public are in a better position to evaluate the rationality and fairness of
both that policy and the case decisions made.

The general purpose of this study was to develop and implement, in close
collaboration with the United States Board of Parole, improved procedures for
parole decision making, including the articulation of explicit policy. The
guideline policy model developed is a self-regulating system for the exercise and
control of discretion in the paroling of confined offenders. It is our belief that

this model has considerable generality for other decision problems in the criminal justice arena.

These guidelines were put to use in practice by the United States Board of Parole[1] as a matter of administrative practice and later were incorporated into a major legislative change of federal parole procedures.[2] Guidelines development stimulated similar work in state paroling jurisdictions[3] and in the courts.[4] (The latter work applied the guidelines concept to sentencing.) Proposed sentencing legislation now in the Congress of the United States includes the guideline concept.[5] Thus, the guidelines themselves and the conceptual framework for policy control that was developed in this study have had a direct implementation in the federal paroling system and a wide impact on thinking in relation to other areas of discretion in criminal justice decision making.

Study Setting

During the three years of this study, the United States Board of Parole was the target of unprecedented criticism from various individuals, the press, and members of the Congress of the United States. Charges of lack of procedural due process, arbitrariness, capriciousness, defensive self-protectiveness, failure to specify reasons for decisions, and working at cross-purposes to rehabilitation were among the complaints.[6] The board, meanwhile, was seeking to address such criticisms and had embarked upon the collaborative study reported in this book. The issue of general policy was particularly related also to plans for a proposed regionalization of the board's functions. Given an explicit statement of general policy, some decision functions might be delegated—a necessary concomitant to regionalization.

The U.S. Board of Parole (now the U.S. Parole Commission) was created by Congress in 1930 and at the time of the study was comprised of eight (now nine) full-time members appointed by the president by and with the advice and consent of the Senate. The Commission has jurisdiction over parole consideration for all eligible prisoners released on parole or mandatory release.[7]

Federal judges, by statute, have broad discretion in sentencing, as do judges in most jurisdictions of the United States. This discretion covers both the type and duration of the sentence, and may include imposition of fines, suspension of the sentences imposed, placement on probation, any period of imprisonment not exceeding the statutory maximum for the offense, or combinations of these sanctions. In adult cases, if the offender is imprisoned for a maximum term of more than one year, then the judge may set a minimum term of one-third of that maximum, a lesser minimum term, or no minimum term. Youth and juvenile cases contain a maximum term, but a judicial minimum term is not permitted. The determination of the actual time to be served in prison is made by the parole board within the constraints of the minimum term (if any) and the maximum term (less institutional good time earned).

Although state sentencing structures and paroling procedures vary markedly among jurisdictions in the United States, many state systems have various similarities to the process described. There usually is an element of indeterminacy, though its extent is widely varied. Common state patterns, for example, include either minima and maxima fixed by statute or the requirement that an offender must serve a fixed proportion of his or her sentence before parole eligibility. Although some crimes are peculiar to the federal system (such as counterfeiting, income tax evasion, or immigration law violations) the federal prisons have a substantial share of persons sentenced for crimes common to state jurisdictions, such as car theft, fraud, burglary, and robbery. Thus, although there are differences in the offender populations of federal and state prisons, there are many similarities as well.

Action Research Collaboration

It is hoped that this study provides an example of truly collaborative research and action with active participation by both the research staff and the practitioners concerned. The nature of the product resulting may be a function of the mechanism for its production. If so, this collaborative stance (the production process) provides a basis for understanding the model developed. It was assumed that the action research worker is not particularly concerned with his own satisfaction in discovery; that is, the work done will mean little if it is not put into effect by others.

The basic philosophy of the research team was that we would carry out research with the paroling authorities, but that we would not carry out research for, to, or upon them. Indeed, we would not conduct research into paroling authorities or their persons but into the problems of the articulation of general paroling policies.

The research staff advised the paroling authority members that there was no wish to impose any particular policy or philosophy upon them. We expected, but did not find (possibly because of the general attitudes just expressed), that they might be initially concerned that the researchers would merely treat them as subjects, reveal differences of opinion or disparities in decision making, subsequently publish the results, and deplore the state of the art. We took the position that in this project there would be no question of changing the persons or personalities of those presently responsible for paroling decisions. That is, the problem of general policy for parole can be dealt with as a problem related to structures, information flow, organization, and procedures, without the decision makers themselves being regarded as the problem.

It seems clear that such collaborative research, related to social action and administrative processes, cannot be value free. Thus, in such action research into parole decision making, the ethical concerns of both the research workers and the paroling authority members will obtrude at many points. Even the idea of guidelines, a central feature of the paroling policy model concept, implies that already some choices have been made. For example, some persons take the view that paroling or sentencing authority discretion is undesirable and should be eliminated. Others have taken the opposite view. Some doubt that discretion can be eliminated either by edict or by procedural rules. Others may see the development of such guidelines as a mere codification of the status quo, with an inherent danger of rigidifying present procedures and impeding their improvement.

There are, indeed, many perspectives, preferences, and ethical concerns involved in decisions as to how much time convicted offenders must serve. There is, however, little disagreement on the critical nature of these decisions. They very markedly affect the lives of individual offenders and, in this regard, there appears to be basic agreement that fairness and rationality in the decision-making process are prime concerns.

Rationality and Fairness

If such decisions are to be made rationally—a probable requirement if they are to "effectively" control or reduce crime—then some knowledge of the likely consequences of alternative choices is an obvious requisite. Such knowledge, however, rarely is available. Rational decision making concerning offenders implies a set of agreed-upon objectives for the decisions, information concerning the person who is the focus of attention, alternatives, and knowledge of the probable outcomes for that person—given selection among the alternative disposition choices. About paroling decisions, as elsewhere in the criminal justice system, objectives rarely are agreed upon except in the most general terms. There usually are much data about the person but little *information* (if that word is defined as that which reduces uncertainty in the decision). Usually, there are alternative placements available, but with an absence of evidence for the effectiveness of any, since data concerning probable outcomes are ordinarily fully lacking.

Although the terms *effectiveness, justice*, and *fairness* are commonly used, there is little agreement among criminal justice functionaries or various publics as to their specific meanings. As used here, the concept of effectiveness refers to the degree of attainment toward specific, measurable objectives (such as the reduction of crime).

The focus of the study reported here is primarily upon the concept of justice and only to a limited degree on the concept of effectiveness. Within the concept of justice, we focus particularly upon a more limited concept of equity.

Whatever meanings are assigned to the concept of justice, it appears that there may be general agreement with the concept of equity as an included but not synonymous concept. Thus, justice must include equity, but equity does not ensure justice. But how is equity to be determined? If it means that similar offenders, in similar circumstances, are given similar sentences, then it is clear that equity is a statistical concept of classification. As decisions become less variable with respect to a given classification of offenders (assuming the agreed-upon relevance of the classification procedures), they may be said to be more equitable. Moreover, the concept of equity or fairness is not identical with that of justice. That is, merely ensuring equity does not necessarily ensure justice, because it would be possible to conclude that while similar persons were treated equally, they were all treated unjustly. That is, the word *justice* must relate not only to fairness but also to some external morally acceptable standards. While articulation of paroling policy cannot guarantee the moral acceptability of such standards, it does make them explicit and open for discussion. Equity, thus, is not the only goal of paroling decisions; and paroling authorities at present typically lack information about offenders which demonstrably is related to goals of changing the offender, deterring him or others, or community protection. Such information can be provided only by follow-up studies to determine the consequences of the decision outcomes, based upon information systems providing careful record keeping concerning the offenders' characteristics, the paroling decisions, and the results in terms of the goals of the criminal justice system. While it is believed that the present studies may provide useful beginning points for study of effectiveness, it must be made clear that the purpose of the present project was to further the articulation of present paroling policies, not to test them.

Assumptions

The concept that a paroling authority may develop guidelines for use in their decision-making processes is in conflict with the belief that paroling authorities require only the individual wisdom of the board member whose determination should be in no way restricted; that is, it is inconsistent with the idea of complete, unbridled discretion for each board member in parole determinations. Similarly, the concept of guidelines conflicts with the belief that paroling (sentencing) authorities should exercise *no* discretion in the timing of or mode of release from prison. Thus, two quite different viewpoints are simultaneously rejected as a beginning point: the belief, on one hand, that release from prison should be fixed by statute, leaving no room to maneuver on the part of the paroling (sentencing) authority and, on the other hand, the belief that the time to be served should be wholly indeterminate, leaving it to expert authority by a parole (sentencing) board to decide how long an offender must serve. The former viewpoint would generally be associated with those who argue for mandatory sentences fixed by the legislature, while the latter would be the extreme limit of a treatment philosophy associated with the concept of indeterminate sentencing.

Placement decisions about offenders are made at every step in the criminal justice process, and there is much current discussion and debate as to the proper and appropriate locus and extent of discretion. Whatever the beliefs that might be held regarding the feasibility and appropriateness of the removal or reduction of discretion in the disposition of offenders along the "decision tree" of these placement decisions, the foundation of the methods adopted in this study is in the concept that discretion should be structured and visible rather than eliminated or controlled externally to the system. Thus, both the unbridled exercise of individual discretion and the complete statutory elimination of discretion are inconsistent with the assumptions underlying this project.

Individual versus Policy Decisions

It already has been asserted that paroling authorities make decisions on two levels—individual case-by-case and general policy decisions which provide a general context in which the individual decisions are made. This assumption is not always readily agreed to by paroling authorities. Members of parole boards (and judges) are sometimes apt to assert that there is no general policy guiding their decisions; rather, they sometimes see the concept of a general policy as in conflict with their own aim of individualized decision making, seeking to ensure that each decision is made on the merits of that individual case. On the other hand, we were inclined to believe that an analysis of a substantial number of decisions might reveal an implicit policy that, if made explicit, could provide an increased degree of control.

The language of statutes cannot differentiate acts to such an extent that it matches by its variety the infinite variety of offender behaviors. No matter how clear the language of the law, some interpretive and discretionary functions have to be performed by someone. At some point the idiosyncratic nature of the act, if not the individuality of the offender, must be considered. Thus, predetermined penalties that are set for categories of behavior attempt to put together two quite different functions—the policy and the individual case determinations. While statutes might, and indeed should, determine many of the general policy issues, it is our belief that the case-by-case issues can be determined only by a system in which the information available can approximately match in complexity the variety of individual behavior. Hence, a policy system is required that has considerable information handling capacities and permits considerable variety of response.

The Action Research Approach

It is hoped that the foregoing discussion gives an indication of the general strategy adopted for this study. As the model developed does not propose to eliminate discretion, it is very important that the ability of the model to adapt to change be considered. It is not our belief that action research can or should attempt to find lasting answers to problems. No matter how excellent any solution, it will become out of date as changes occur in the environment in which it is embedded. All solutions must be temporary ones. No model or method should be considered that does not have built into it the seeds of its own modification; any system must adapt or perish, and this applies whether we are considering organizations or organisms. Thus, we have sought to invent *an evolutionary process*. It is not thought to be sufficient to develop a mechanism, procedure, or simple answer. The kinds of solutions we seek to invent are in the form of "cybernetic systems."

In collaborating with the members of the United States Board of Parole, we sought continuously to keep this single purpose in our sights. In issues concerning the disposition of offenders, changes in underlying philosophy normally would be expected to result in a change in the actions of the criminal justice system. Changes in perceptions of the functions of the criminal law now seem to be making their impact upon thinking in this field. There are conflicting views of the purposes of a paroling authority in sentencing decisions; we seem to be moving away from a rehabilitation and treatment philosophy toward a philosophy that frankly acknowledges the concept of punishment and speaks more often of "just desert" and issues of equity. The point is that an appropriately flexible and sufficiently complex system would not find it difficult to adjust to the change of course of the target.

If we were to examine two missiles, one of which was self-homing and the other designed for discharge from a preprogrammed gun and mounting, we would be able to detect some fundamental differences in the designs. The self-homing missile would have an information detection and processing system actually on board. There would also be systems whereby the information received would be coupled to a decoding device and eventually it would influence the control surfaces of the projectile. The research worker may design "systems" in the course of his research, but these systems must be such that they can become tools of management. Further, the management tools themselves ought to be continuously under review, and the results of such review in relation to any changes in the perception of change of direction of the purpose (target) must determine modifications in the original design of the tool. A system may be designed, but there must also be provided a mechanism to continuously redesign the design.

If we seek to develop an evolutionary process of management control, then there must be some means whereby the system we invent has built into it an informational feedback loop. Moreover, the system must be coupled into the larger environment because it is that which will determine how the smaller system should change its operations in order to stay focused upon the target—as a kind of open system possessing the ability to adapt rapidly.

The Guidelines Model

If our assumption is accepted, that some discretion in decision making is essential, then a central research issue is how to use this discretion within necessary legal and ethical constraints. Thus, we shall discuss structuring and controlling discretion, not eliminating it. We shall discuss issues of equity and argue that this concept implies that similar decisions are to be applied to similarly situated offenders. The characteristics of the offense or offender to be taken into account will next be discussed in the context of efforts to determine the weight given to these concepts (by the paroling authority) in its decisions, which led, as described in chapter 2, to an explicit guidelines model based mainly on the dimensions of the seriousness of the offense and the prognosis for parole. This model, as implemented by the United States Parole Commission, will be described.

The Risk of Recidivism

The expected success or failure of the person considered for parole may be said to be an issue that concerns all parole boards in greater or lesser degree. It was found to be of sufficient importance for decision making by the U.S. Board of Parole that the dimension of risk forms one of the two main dimensions used in the guidelines. Chapter 3 discusses the steps taken in this study to provide the board with an objective, empirically derived measure of risk, called a "salient factor" score.

Sanctioning

The second dimension of the guidelines model explained in chapter 2 is that of the seriousness of the offense for which the person was sent to prison. The methods used to establish a classification of offense seriousness, for use in the guidelines system, are explained in chapter 4. Their purpose was to assist in developing a procedure for more consistent judgments of offense seriousness, thus contributing to more equitable decisions.

Information in Decision Making

Some general problems of information usage for decision making are considered in chapter 5. Some avenues to possible improvement in prediction are first discussed. Next, the relation of the computer to the human decision maker is considered, leading to a discussion of the nature of decision-making. Is it a process? Can we identify or speculate reasonably about types of parole decision makers? If computers are to assist in decision making, must we understand something of the preferences of the decision makers for certain forms of information search and processing?

Implications for Sentencing and Other Criminal Justice Decisions

The problem of disparity in sentencing (which we think is more properly termed unwarranted sentencing variation) is widely regarded as one of the most significant present problems of criminal justice. In chapter 6, this general problem is considered, and alternative proposals for dealing with it are discussed. It is argued that a guidelines model, analogous to that described in chapter 2, can provide a feasible solution through formulation of an explicit sentencing policy identifying the major factors to be considered and the weights to be given them.

We seek in chapter 7 to assess the implications of this research; in looking ahead, in chapter 8, we discuss other potential applications to decision problems in criminal and juvenile justice. We argue that the procedures for the granting of parole have become more open, explicit, and available for public review and criticism; that the system includes the evolutionary process desired to permit periodic review and change; that a general method has been discovered that can reduce disparity in any decision field where considerable discretion obtains.

The guidelines model raises moral issues; indeed, some issues are raised as a result of the fact that the parole guidelines are explicit in identifying information used and its weighting. Some of these concerns are discussed, and it is asserted that some of the moral issues raised may themselves be addressed by simulations making use of proposed models. Finally, some examples of the claimed generality of the guidelines model are discussed.

Appended are studies of information selection and use in parole decision making (app. A); an illustration of a method for providing feedback on paroling policy to a parole board (app. B); and a statistical note. The latter (app. C) is a demonstration, by Lancucki and Tarling, of the relation between the Mean Cost Rating and Kendall's Rank Correlation Coefficient. Although the mean cost rating has been widely used in parole (and other criminological) prediction studies (as in chapter 3) this relation was not previously known and no test for significance of this statistic was available.

The Evolutionary Process

The concept of continuous review is central to the continuous evolutionary process that is desired. Information relating to possible changes in policy, including statistical or other summaries of departures from guidelines, are discussed by the U.S. Parole Commission at scheduled, periodic meetings. Regular meetings specific for this purpose would seem to be required to ensure that the review does not become a mere formality and that the guidelines system does not merely rigidify present policy, militating against change rather than providing a vehicle to guide it.

The research that undergirds the guidelines developed and the guidelines themselves are essentially descriptive, not prescriptive; yet the very term implies prescription. Although they summarize expected paroling decisions on the basis of recent practice and seek to indicate the relative weights given to what apparently are regarded as the most important factors to be considered, they do not tell what either the decisions or the criteria ought to be.

This situation is a consequence of two distinct but complex sets of issues. First, judgments concerning deserved punishment, the proper aims of parole decision making, or the fairness of including various criteria often involve moral or ethical issues. The research may shed light on the present handling of these issues; but whether future changes should be made is a question that must depend on moral judgments. Second, judgments of criteria to be used in parole decision making may be based not only on moral but also on scientific grounds. Thus, whether a given guideline element *should* be included may depend also on the evidence that the factor is or is not related to an aim of those parole decisions, for example, the reduction of recidivism. This is at once an important limitation and, we believe, a major strength.

The strength is given by the circumstance that the development of a guideline system requires the explicit description of paroling policy. Hence, it is open, public, and available for public review and criticism. Indeed, a central feature is its provision for repeated review and revision. This allows for, and indeed invites, subjecting the parole decision-making criteria now in use to rigorous scrutiny with respect to both the moral and effectiveness issues raised. The moral issues may be debated more readily; the effectiveness issues can be tested.

Notes

1. 28 C.F.R. §2.52, 38 Federal Register 222, (November 19, 1973), as amended. Most recently published as 28 C.F.R. §2.20, 41 Federal Register 173, (September 3, 1976).

2. Public Law 94-233, effective May 14, 1976.

3. D.M. Gottfredson, C.A. Cosgrove, L.T. Wilkins, J. Wallerstein and C. Rauh, *Classification for Parole Decision Policy*. Report prepared for the Law Enforcement Assistance Administration, May 1977 (draft).

4. L.T. Wilkins, J.M. Kress, D.M. Gottfredson, J.C. Calpin, and A.M.

Gelman, *Sentencing Guidelines: Structuring Judicial Discretion.* Final report of the Feasibility Study, prepared under Law Enforcement Assistance Administration Grant 74NI-99-0054, draft, October 1976.

5. See U.S. Senate Bill S.2699, cosponsored by Senators Kennedy, Abourezk, Bayh, Fong, Hart, Hruska, McClellan, and Tunney, introduced and referred to the Committee on the Judiciary, November 1975; U.S. Congress Bill H.11655, sponsored by Congressman Rodino, introduced and referred to the Committee on the Judiciary, February 1976; U.S. Senate Bill S.1437, cosponsored by Senators McClellan and Kennedy, introduced and referred to the Committee on the Judiciary, May 1977 (the Criminal Code Reform Act of 1977).

6. See, for example, the *Washington Post*, March 29, 1971, and February 26, 1972; *Harper's Magazine*, November 1971.

7. For a more detailed description of the structure and procedures of the board at the time of the study, see Gottfredson et al. (*The Utilization of Experience in Parole Decision-Making*) Summary Report, Parole Decision-Making Project, National Council on Crime and Delinquency Research Center, Davis, Calif., June 1973.

Making Paroling Policy Explicit: A Matter of Equity

Justice and Fairness

The concept of fairness is not exactly the same as the concept of justice. There is, however, seldom any clear distinction made in the use of the two terms in law. Some dictionaries define *fairness* as lack of injustice, but the absence of injustice is not the same as the presence of justice—thus, *justice* is not defined as fairness but, rather, as "an accord with truth." That is, there seems to be reasonable agreement among authorities of English usage that nothing can be just that is unfair; but fairness is not necessarily justice; or justice includes fairness but is more demanding. It may be that we could claim that this is because *fairness* is a relative term, but justice implies absolute values. This is a convenient distinction and, accordingly—since words have uses rather than meanings—we propose to use the words in this way. Ensuring justice (accord with truth/law) also ensures fairness. In the first case (justice) there is an external criterion. In the second case (fairness) the elements can be in accord with each other but are not necessarily in accord with an external criterion.

By fairness we mean that similar persons are dealt with in similar ways in similar situations. Thus the idea of fairness implies the idea of similarity and of comparison; it cannot relate to the unique individual since, obviously, if every person is unique, there are no grounds for comparisons and, hence, no ways in which it is possible to discuss fairness. Will an individual, then, see his treatment as fair if he sees himself as (in all significant ways) similar to another person who received exactly similar treatment? Not quite, since it would seem to require more than one other person; it would not be unreasonable to claim that both were treated unfairly. As the sample of similar persons increases, however, the idea of similar treatments among that sample becomes more likely to be regarded as fairness.

The moral, or at least metaphysical, idea of fairness thus becomes closely related to statistical concepts of similarity (or variance) and sample size. Any claim on the part of a citizen or another who asserts that the parole board is unfair is implicitly stating that according to his beliefs (knowledge?) similar persons, involved in similar crimes, are receiving different treatments. The factors that are taken into consideration may vary in some degree from one

Adapted from P.B. Hoffman and D.M. Gottfredson, *Paroling Policy Guidelines: A Matter of Equity*, Parole Decision-Making Project, Report Nine (Davis, Calif.: National Council on Crime and Delinquency Research Center, June 1973).

critic to another; some will look with particular care at race (unfairness related to racial characteristics is defined as racism because race is not seen as a reasonable or morally acceptable factor to justify differences in treatment); some will look with particular care at the type of offense, and some at both types of offenses and racial factors. However, the scale and scope of comparison upon which critics may rely are not likely to be wider than the scale and scope of factors that a parole board might consider. By the use of a model that is built upon known elements of comparison (fairness criteria), the board could respond with precision to criticisms. If the board explicitly considers such factors as probability of reconviction, crime seriousness, and behavior in the institutional setting, and ignores race, it will be unlikely to be accused of racial bias.

If a parole board were to have before it, in each case in which a decision is to be made, a chart that indicated the balance among the three or four most obvious factors to be considered, the decision makers could always depart from the calculated figure; but in doing so they would be making a value judgment of further factors not included in the model. If these further factors were made explicit in the decision, a sound case for each decision would seem to be possible. The general policy of the board would not be defended by such a model; but, clearly, the decisions within the model would be fair. The question of justice is one of beliefs; but we can, by the use of research methods and the preparation of models, address the question of fairness. If attention were diverted from individual cases (his case was not fairly determined) to questions of general principles of parole, the understanding and control of the system would, it seems, be increased in great measure. Human attention could then be more thoroughly devoted to humanitarian considerations because the routine comparative work (even although highly complex) could be delegated to models of fairness.

Setting Paroling Policy

The National Advisory Commission on Criminal Justice Standards and Goals recently argued that the most important function of a parole board is to set standards and make explicit policies. It stated the major task of a parole board should be

... the articulation of criteria for making decisions and development of basic policies. This task is to be separated from the specific function of deciding individual parole grant and revocation cases, which may be performed either by the board in smaller states or by a hearing examiner.[1]

The issue of explicit general policy is, of course, related to concerns of individual discretion in decision making; the report cited continues: "While discretion is an essential feature of parole board operations, the central issue is how to handle it appropriately."[2]

These issues have been considered by a number of authors,[3] and a principal suggested method for controlling discretion has been the giving of written reasons for parole denial.

While such reasons may be a start in the right direction, they cannot, by themselves, attend to the issue of equity. The process may identify the criteria used but not the weights given to them. For example, the Model Penal Code lists four primary reasons for parole denial:

1. There is a substantial risk that he will not conform to the conditions of parole; or
2. His release at that time would depreciate the seriousness of his crime or promote disrespect for law; or
3. His release would have a substantially adverse effect on institutional discipline; or
4. His continued correctional treatment, medical care or vocational or other training in the institution will substantially enhance his capacity to lead a law-abiding life when released at a later date.[4]

If parole selection were truly a dichotomous decision (parole/no parole), as it may be in jurisdictions with long minimum sentences, such reasons might suffice. When, however, minimum sentences are short or are not given (as in the federal system), parole selection is, in reality, more of a deferred sentencing decision (a decision of when to release) than a parole/no parole decision. In this case, merely giving reasons for denial does not suffice, as these reasons relate only to the fact of the denial and not to its length (known as a continuance or set-off). Thus, one bank robber who is considered by a parole board may be given a continuance of three years for reasons (1) and (2). Suppose that another similar case were to be given a continuance of five years for the same reasons. Without explicit decision guidelines (which cover not only the criteria used but also the weights to be given to them) a parole board will have little more chance of providing equitable decisions than it does without reasons at all; nor will observers have much more opportunity to challenge these decisions.

One phase of the Parole Decision-Making Project was aimed at identifying the weights given to various criteria in the parole selection decision. It became apparent early in the project that, as other research endeavors had shown, the mere presentation of an experience table (prediction device) was not seen by parole board members as a dramatic aid. A study of criteria used in making paroling decisions, however, (as distinguished from criteria used in predicting parole outcome), in which board members completed a set of subjective rating scales for a sample of actual decisions over a six-month period, indicated that three factors or focal concerns taken together (seriousness of the crime, parole prognosis, and institutional behavior) were primary.[5] Youth Corrections Act cases (which have no minimum sentence and are seen generally within three months of reception) were studied. Using the variable—time to be served before review—as the criterion at the initial decision, it was found that parole board decisions could be predicted fairly accurately by knowledge of their crime seriousness and prognosis ratings. Similarly, at review considerations, parole board decisions (parole or continue) were strongly related to ratings of institutional discipline.

From this knowledge, the development of an explicit indicant of parole selection policy was possible. Concerning initial decisions, a chart with one axis reflecting the concern of offense gravity and another the concern of parole prognosis (risk) could be developed. At each intersection of these axes, an expected decision could be given (in months to be served before review hearing). For example, a low severity/very good risk case might be expected to serve ten months before review; a very high severity/poor risk case might be expected to serve sixty months.

As an aid in actual case decision making, this type of chart could be used in the following manner. After scoring the case on the concerns of severity and prognosis, the parole board member or hearing examiner would check the table to see the expected decision. In practice, a range (say, twenty to twenty-four months) would be appropriate to allow for some variation within broad severity or risk categories. Should the board member or examiner wish to make a decision outside of the expected range, he would be obligated to specify the factors that make that particular case unique (such as unusually good or poor institutional adjustment, credit for time spent on a sentence of another jurisdiction). At review hearings, the decision to parole or continue would be based primarily on institutional performance. That is (with a few specific exceptions),[6] cases with satisfactory institutional performance could expect release at this time.

Parole Board Interest

The United States Board of Parole showed considerable interest in implementation of this model. Very likely, one factor was that the board, under rather heavy criticism for several years, was attempting at this time to develop its own proposal for change, which included regionalization. This proposal called for delegating the routine decision-making power (concerning parole grants and revocations) to an expanded staff of hearing examiners, with the board performing a policy-setting and appellate function. Obviously, decision guidelines of the type noted could enable the board to exercise control more effectively over the decisions of the expanded and decentralized staff proposed.

In any case, the result was that the project staff was requested to develop parole selection policy guidelines, in as objective a format as possible. At this point, the board was told by project staff that it might itself rank-order offense types by seriousness and then, for each risk classification (the determination of which could be aided by a statistical predictive device), decide upon an explicit policy. However, the board expressed doubt about engaging upon this task until it had developed more familiarity with this type of device. Therefore, the project staff was requested to provide sets of policy guidelines (a separate set for youth and adult offenders) based upon the project's coded material reflecting board policy during the preceding two years.[7] Upon approval, these guidelines were to be tested for six months, after which the board would review their use and make any further modifications desired. A plan to enable consideration of guideline modification at regular intervals was also requested.

While the results of the experiment with youth cases provided a set of guidelines based upon subjective ratings, a table based upon more objective measures was desired. Thus, for the parole prognosis axis, an eleven-factor predictive (salient factor) score, developed by the project, was substituted for the subjective ratings. Figure 2-1 displays this device.

The twelve possible scores were combined to form four risk classifications: (9-11) very good, (6-8) good, (4-5) fair, and (0-3) poor. It is important to note that this was one of the initial predictive measures developed by the project and was based upon a relatively small sample. A more powerful device developed subsequently was substituted in October 1973.[8]

For the seriousness of offense scale, a different procedure was necessary. For each of a set of offense ratings (offense behavior descriptions) coded by the

Salient Factors (please check each correct statement):

_A. Commitment offense did not involve auto theft.

_B. Subject had one or more codefendants (whether brought to trial with subject or not).

_C. Subject has no prior (adult or juvenile) incarcerations.

_D. Subject has no other prior sentences (adult or juvenile) (i.e., probation, fine, suspended sentence).

_E. Subject has not served more than eighteen consecutive months during any prior incarceration (adult or juvenile).

_F. Subject has completed the twelfth grade or received G.E.D.

_G. Subject has never had probation or parole revoked (or been committed for a new offense while on probation or parole).

_H. Subject was eighteen years old or older at first conviction (adult or juvenile).

_I. Subject was eighteen years old or older at first commitment (adult or juvenile).

_J. Subject was employed, or a full-time student, for a total of at least six months during the last two years in the community.

_K. Subject plans to reside with his wife and/or children after release.

_ Total number of correct statements = favorable factors = score.

Figure 2-1. Original Salient Factor Score

project,[9] the median time served was calculated. Offense ratings with similar median times served were combined to produce six seriousness level classifications.[10]

The median time served for each seriousness/risk level was then tabulated (separately for youth and adult cases) for the large sample of final decisions (parole/mandatory release/expiration) coded by the project. Smoothing based upon agreement by two project staff members after visual inspection was performed to increase the consistency of these medians, although no attempt to force uniform or linear increments was made. Each median was then bracketed ($\pm x$ months) to provide a discretion range and the guideline table. Table 2-1 displays the adult guidelines. The size of the appropriate range was determined after informal discussions with several board members and hearing examiners and, while arbitrary, is to some extent proportional to the size of the median. As not all offenses were included on this listing, instructions were prepared which explained that the appropriate seriousness level could be determined by comparing the nonlisted offense with those of similar seriousness which were listed. In addition, it was realized that not all offense ratings were specific enough to cover the range of seriousness (for example, vehicle theft for personal use through large-scale vehicle theft for resale). Thus, the instructions indicated that the offense ratings listed were to be used only as a guide but that the hearing panel's determination of the seriousness category should be supported by the description of the offense in the hearing summary prepared. In other words, the seriousness rating is a subjective determination guided by objective indicants.

Actual Use

In October 1972, a pilot project was launched by the United States Board of Parole to test feasibility of regionalization. This project encompassed five institutions in the Northeast (that contain about one-fifth of the total board work load), and had a number of innovative features, including panels of two examiners to conduct institutional hearings, written reasons for parole denial, a two-stage appeal process, and the use of decision guidelines.

For all initial hearings, the panels were instructed to complete an evaluation form that included a severity rating scale and the salient factor score. Should they make a recommendation outside of the guideline table, they were instructed to specify the factors in the case that resulted in this decision.

For review hearings, completion of the evaluation form was required before any continuance (for reasons other than institutional discipline or failure to complete specific institutional programs) was recommended. If a parole grant was recommended, form completion was not necessary. This was designed so that the guidelines would not be exceeded by arbitrary continuances at review hearings. One exception was that, if the previous continuance was thirty months or more, the evaluation form and guideline table had to be completed. This was necessary to deal with the highest offense severity levels where the guidelines might indicate a time to be served longer than possible at the initial hearing (by board policy, continuances were limited to three years at one time). At early review hearings (inmates showing exceptional institutional progress may be recommended by the institution staff for earlier review consideration) the guidelines are consulted also to see whether the exceptional progress justifies the advanced parole date recommended.

Reports from parole board staff were extremely favorable concerning both the guidelines and the other regionalization project features. The need for greater consistency in decision making had long been acknowledged, and the use of the decision guidelines appears to have been accepted as serving this need. One empirical measure of staff interest was that in the first four months of operation, there were only three cases out of 598 initial hearings in which a panel failed to complete the evaluation form.

Guideline Modification

As the danger of rigidity exists with guideline use, as much as the danger of disparity exists without them, it was recognized that procedures for the updating and modification of the guidelines should be developed. Two basic procedures were discussed with the board and agreed upon.

First, the board may at any time vote affirmatively to change parole selection policy by modifying any guideline category or combination of categories. For example, after three months of guideline usage, the board decided to place three additional offense descriptions on the guideline chart. These were Selective Service violation (determined by vote of the board to be a moderate seriousness offense), Mann Act (interstate transportation of women for immoral purposes) with force (determined to be a very high severity offense), and Mann Act without force (determined to be a moderate severity offense). Since the first set of guidelines prepared used offense descriptions developed in another context,[11] at the end of the first six-month period a set of definitions prepared specifically for federal offenders was substituted.[12]

Second, at these policy consideration meetings, (regularly scheduled at six-month intervals) feedback can be provided the board concerning the percentage of decisions falling outside each guideline category and the reasons given for these decisions. This serves two purposes: the reasons for the deviations from the guidelines may be examined to certify their appropriateness, and the percentages of decisions within and outside of the guidelines (and their distribution) for each category can be evaluated to determine whether the width for the category is appropriate. That is, too high a percentage of decisions

Table 2-1
Guidelines for Decision Making (Adult Cases): Average Total Time Served Before Release (Including Jail Time)

Offense Characteristics (Seriousness)

Severity	Offender Characteristics—Salient (Favorable) Factor Score (Probability of Favorable Parole Outcome)			
	(9-11) Very High	*(6-8)* High	*(4-5)* Fair	*(0-3)* Low
Category A: Low Severity Offenses				
Minor theft; walkaway; immigration law violations; alcohol law violations	6-10 months	8-12 months	10-14 months	12-16 months
Category B: Low/Moderate Severity Offenses				
Possess marijuana; possess heavy narcotics, less than or equal to $50; theft, unplanned; forgery or counterfeiting, less than $500; burglary, daytime	8-12 months	12-16 months	16-20 months	20-25 months
Category C: Moderate Severity Offenses				
Vehicle theft; forgery or counterfeiting, greater than $500; sale of marijuana; planned theft; possess heavy narcotics, greater than $50; escape; Mann Act—no force; Selective Service	12-16 months	16-20 months	20-24 months	24-30 months
Category D: High Severity Offenses				
Sell heavy narcotics; burglary, weapon or nighttime; violence, "spur of the moment"; sexual act, force	16-20 months	20-26 months	26-32 months	32-38 months

	26-36 months	36-45 months	45-55 months	55-65 months
Category E: Very High Severity Offenses Armed robbery; criminal act—weapon; sexual act, force, injury; assault, serious bodily harm; Mann Act—force	26-36 months	36-45 months	45-55 months	55-65 months
Category F: Highest Severity Offenses Willful homicide; kidnapping; armed robbery, weapon fired or serious injury	Information not available owing to limited number of cases			

Notes:

1. If an offense behavior can be classified under more than one category, the most serious applicable category is to be used. If an offense behavior involved multiple separate offenses, the seriousness level may be increased.

2. If an offense is not listed, the proper category may be obtained by comparing the seriousness of the offense with those of similar offenses listed.

3. If a continuance is to be recommended, subtract 30 days (one month) to allow for release program division.

outside the guideline range without adequate explanation may indicate that either a wider range is necessary or that the hearing panels are inappropriately exceeding their discretionary limits. On the other hand, a very high percentage of decisions within the guidelines may indicate excessive rigidity. While the guidelines themselves cannot provide answers to these questions of policy, the focus they provide may enable a more rational consideration of these questions.

Implications

The use of explicit decision guidelines for parole selection attunes to a much stressed need for parole boards to formulate a consistent general policy. By articulating the weights given to the major criteria under consideration, it can allow interested publics to assess the rationality and appropriateness of the policy set by their representatives (the parole board). It acknowledges that parole selection in the federal system is actually a deferred sentencing decision which determines the time to be served before release, rather than a dichotomous yes/no decision. For individual case decision making, it provides a method of structuring and controlling discretion without eliminating it. This fits with the issue of fairness or equity. Furthermore, as the factors of seriousness of crime and risk of recidivism will be considered at the initial hearing, subsequent hearings, if any, primarily will consider institutional behavior. This procedure should substantially reduce the present uncertainty felt by inmates as to when they will be actually released (and as to what they must accomplish to obtain this release).

It is important to stress that much work ought to be done in refining the guidelines concept, the scales used, the procedures to be used in their modification. At present, these are admittedly crude. Nevertheless, they appear to be seen as useful.

Federal Parole Guidelines[a]

One of the most troublesome issues in the administration of criminal justice involves the exercise of discretionary power. On one hand, the unguided and unfettered exercise of discretion can lead to arbitrary and capricious decision making, decision inequity, and disparity. Such has been a major criticism of sentencing and parole practices.[13] On the other hand, the rigid application of fixed and mechanical rules (mandatory sentences) can lead to results as undesirable and unjust.[14]

In an effort to balance these considerations and provide more rational,

[a]Adapted from P. Hoffman, *Federal Parole Guidelines: Three Years of Experience,* Report 10, U.S. Board of Parole Research Unit, November 1975.

consistent, and equitable decision making without removing individual case consideration, the United States Board of Parole has promulgated decision-making guidelines that articulate the major elements considered in parole selection and the weights customarily given to them.[15] Briefly, the guideline concept postulates that by articulating the major decision criteria and the customary decision policy associated with the various combinations of major elements, a decision framework can be created that is specific enough to guide and control discretion yet flexible enough to allow deviation from customary policy when warranted by the circumstances of a particular case. Developed during the course of a collaborative three-year study of decision making conducted by the Research Center of the National Council on Crime and Delinquency under a grant from the Law Enforcement Assistance Administration, the board's decision guidelines consider three major elements: the nature (gravity) of the current offense, parole prognosis, and institutional behavior.

The Guideline Matrix

Table 2-2 displays the guidelines for decision making presently used by the Board of Parole for adult cases. Separate guidelines are utilized for youth (table 2-3) and NARA (Narcotic Addict Rehabilitation Act) cases (table 2-4). On the vertical axis, the gravity (severity) of the applicant's present federal offense behavior is considered. Six offense severity categories are listed. For each category, the board has specified a number of offense behavior examples. For instance, the offense behaviors of embezzlement (less than $20,000), theft of motor vehicle, and theft/forgery/fraud ($1,000 to $19,999) are placed in the moderate severity category. Robbery, extortion, and sale of hard drugs are placed in the very high severity category. It is noted that these are merely examples of typical offense behaviors. Board regulations provide that if a specific offense behavior is not listed on the guideline chart, the proper category is to be obtained by comparison with those offense behaviors that are listed. Moreover, particularly aggravating or mitigating factors in a specific case may warrant a higher or lower severity rating (or a decision outside the guidelines), provided the reasons for this action are stated.[16]

On the horizontal axis, four categories of parole prognosis (likelihood of favorable parole outcome) are listed. As an aid in assessing an applicant's parole prognosis, the board utilizes an actuarial device (experience table) termed a *salient factor score.* This device was developed as part of the Parole Decision-Making project cited earlier. In brief, data were collected for a random sample of 2,483 cases released in 1970 by all forms of release (parole/mandatory release/expiration of sentence). For research purposes, the sample was divided into construction ($n = 902$) and validation ($n = 1581$) subsamples. Two-year follow-up from date of release for each individual was obtained through the

Table 2-2
Adult Guidelines for Decision Making: Customary Total Time Served before Release
(Including Jail Time)

Offense Characteristics: Severity of Offense Behavior (Examples)	Offender Characteristics: Parole Prognosis (Salient Factor Score)			
	Very Good (11-9)	Good (8-6)	Fair (5-4)	Poor (3-0)
Low				
Immigration Law Violations				
Minor Theft (Includes larceny and simple possession of stolen property less than $1,000)	6-10 months	8-12 months	10-14 months	12-16 months
Walkaway				
Low Moderate				
Alcohol Law Violations				
Counterfeit Currency (Passing/Possession less than $1,000)				
Drugs:				
Marijuana, Simple Possession (less than $500)	8-12 months	12-16 months	16-20 months	20-25 months
Forgery/Fraud (less than $1,000)				
Income Tax Evasion (less than $10,000)				
Selective Service Act Violations				
Theft From Mail (less than $1,000)				
Moderate				
Bribery of Public Officials				
Counterfeit Currency (Passing/Possession $1,000-$19,999)				
Drugs:				
Marijuana, Possession With Intent to Distribute/Sale (less than $5,000)				
"Soft Drugs," Possession with Intent to Distribute/Sale (less than $500)				

Offense				
Embezzlement (less than $20,000)				
Explosives, Possession/Transportation				
Firearms Act, Possession/Purchase/Sale (single weapon—not sawed-off shotgun or machine gun)				
Income Tax Evasion ($10,000-$50,000)				
Interstate Transportation of Stolen/Forged Securities (less than $20,000)				
Mailing Threatening Communications	12-16 months	16-20 months	20-24 months	24-30 months
Misprision of Felony				
Receiving Stolen Property With Intent to Resell (less than $20,000)				
Smuggling/Transporting of Aliens				
Theft/Forgery/Fraud ($1,000-$19,999)				
Theft of Motor Vehicle (Not Multiple Theft or for Resale)				

High

Offense				
Burglary or Larceny (Other than Embezzlement) from Bank or Post Office				
Counterfeit Currency (Passing/Possession $20,000-$100,000)				
Counterfeiting (Manufacturing)				
Drugs:				
Marijuana, Possession With Intent to Distribute/Sale ($5,000 or more)				
"Soft Drugs," Possession with Intent to Distribute/Sale ($500-$5,000)	16-20 months	20-26 months	26-32 months	32-38 months
Embezzlement ($20,000-$100,000)				
Firearms Act, Possession/Purchase/Sale (sawed-off shotgun[s], machine gun[s], or multiple weapons)				
Interstate Transportation of Stolen/Forged Securities ($20,000-$100,000)				
Mann Act (No Force—Commercial Purposes)				
Organized Vehicle Theft				
Receiving Stolen Property ($20,000-$100,000)				
Theft/Forgery/Fraud ($20,000-$100,000)				

Table 2-2 (cont.)

Offense Characteristics: Severity of Offense Behavior (Examples)	Offender Characteristics: Parole Prognosis (Salient Factor Score)			
	Very Good (11-9)	Good (8-6)	Fair (5-4)	Poor (3-0)
Very High				
Robbery (Weapon or Threat)				
Drugs:				
"Hard Drugs," Possession with Intent to Distribute/Sale (No Prior Conviction for Sale of "Hard Drugs")	26-36 months	36-45 months	45-55 months	55-65 months
"Soft Drugs," Possession with Intent to Distribute/Sale (over $5,000)				
Extortion				
Mann Act (Force)				
Sexual Act (Force)				
Greatest				
Aggravated Felony (e.g., Robbery, Sexual Act/Aggravated Assault)—Weapon Fired or Personal Injury	(Greater than above—however, specific ranges are not given due to the limited number of cases and the extreme variations in severity possible within the category)			
Aircraft Hijacking				
Drugs:				
"Hard Drugs" (Possession with Intent to Distribute/Sale) for Profit (Prior Conviction[s] for Sale of "Hard Drugs")				
Espionage				
Explosives (Detonation)				
Kidnapping				
Willful Homicide				

Notes:

1. These guidelines are predicated upon good institutional conduct and program performance.
2. If an offense behavior is not listed, the proper category may be obtained by comparing the severity of the offense behavior with those of similar offense behaviors listed.
3. If an offense behavior can be classified under more than one category, the most serious applicable category is to be used.
4. If an offense behavior involved multiple separate offenses, the severity level may be increased.
5. If a continuance is to be given, allow 30 days (1 month) for release program provision.
6. "Hard Drugs" include heroin, cocaine, morphine or opiate derivatives, and synthetic opiate substitutes.

Table 2-3
Youth Guidelines for Decision Making: Customary Total Time Served before Release
(Including Jail Time)

Offense Characteristics: Severity of Offense Behavior (Examples)	Offender Characteristics: Parole Prognosis (Salient Factor Score)			
	Very Good (11-9)	Good (8-6)	Fair (5-4)	Poor (3-0)
Low				
Immigration Law Violations	6-10 months	8-12 months	10-14 months	12-16 months
Minor Theft (Including larceny and simple possession of stolen property less than $1,000)				
Walkaway				
Low Moderate				
Alcohol Law Violation	8-12 months	12-16 months	16-20 months	20-25 months
Counterfeit Currency (Passing/Possession less than $1,000)				
Drugs:				
Marijuana, Simple Possession (less than $500)				
Forgery/Fraud (less than $1,000)				
Income Tax Evasion (less than $10,000)				
Selective Service Act Violations				
Theft From Mail (less than $1,000)				
Moderate				
Bribery of Public Officials				
Counterfeit Currency (Passing/Possession $1,000-$19,999)				
Drugs:				
Marijuana, Possession With Intent to Distribute/Sale (less than $5,000)				
"Soft Drugs," Possession with Intent to Distribute/Sale (less than $500)				

Table 2-3 (cont.)

Offense Characteristics: Severity of Offense Behavior (Examples)	Offender Characteristics: Parole Prognosis (Salient Factor Score)			
	Very Good (11-9)	Good (8-6)	Fair (5-4)	Poor (3-0)
Embezzlement (less than $20,000) Explosives, Possession/Transportation Firearm Act, Possession/Purchase/Sale (single weapon— not sawed-off shotgun or machine gun) Income Tax Evasion ($10,000-$50,000) Interstate Transportation of Stolen/Forged Securities (less than $20,000) Mailing Threatening Communications Misprision of Felony Receiving Stolen Property With Intent to Resell (less than $20,C00) Smuggling/Transporting of Aliens Theft/Forgery/Fraud ($1,000-$19,999) Theft of Motor Vehicle (Not Multiple Theft or for Resale)	9-13 months	13-17 months	17-21 months	21-26 months
High Burglary or Larceny (Other than Embezzlement) from Bank or Post Office Counterfeit Currency (Passing/Possession $20,000-$100,000) Counterfeiting (Manufacturing) Drugs: Marijuana, Possession With Intent To Distribute/Sale ($5,000 or more) "Soft Drugs," Possession with Intent to Distribute/Sale ($500-$6,000) Embezzlement ($20,000-$100,000) Firearms Act, Possession/Purchase/Sale (sawed-off shotgun[s], machine gun[s], or multiple weapons) Interstate Transportation of Stolen/Forged Securities ($20,000-$100,000) Mann Act (No Force—Commercial Purposes) Organized Vehicle Theft Receiving Stolen Property ($20,000-$100,000) Theft/Forgery/Fraud ($20,000-$100,000)	12-16 months	16-20 months	20-24 months	24-28 months

Very High

Robbery (Weapon or Threat)

Drugs:
"Hard Drugs," Possession with Intent to Distribute/Sale (No Prior Conviction for Sale of "Hard Drugs")
"Soft Drugs," Possession with Intent to Distribute/Sale (over $5,000)

Extortion

Mann Act (Force)

Sexual Act (Force)

Greatest

Aggravated Felony (e.g., Robbery, Sexual Act/Aggravated Assault)—Weapon Fired or Personal Injury

Aircraft Hijacking

Drugs:
"Hard Drugs," (Possession with Intent to Distribute/Sale) for Profit (prior Conviction[s] for Sale of "Hard Drugs")

Espionage

Explosive (Detonation)

Kidnapping

Willful Homicide

	20-27 months	27-32 months	32-36 months	36-42 months

(Greater than above—however, specific ranges are not given due to the limited number of cases and the extreme variations in severity possible within the category)

Notes:

1. These guidelines are predicated upon good institutional conduct and program performance.

2. If an offense behavior is not listed, the proper category may be obtained by comparing the severity of the offense behavior with those of similar offense behaviors listed.

3. If an offense behavior can be classified under more than one category, the most serious applicable category is to be used.

4. If an offense behavior involved multiple separate offenses, the severity level may be increased.

5. If a continuance is to be given, allow 30 days (1 month) for release program provision.

6. "Hard Drugs" include heroin, cocaine, morphine or opiate derivatives, and synthetic opiate substitutes.

Table 2-4
NARA Guidelines for Decision Making: Customary Total Time Served before Release
(Including Jail Time)

Offense Characteristics: Severity of Offense Behavior (Examples)	Offender Characteristics: Parole Prognosis (Salient Factor Score)			
	Very Good (11-9)	Good (8-6)	Fair (5-4)	Poor (3-0)
Low				
Immigration Law Violations				
Minor Theft (Includes larceny and simple possession of stolen property less than $1,000)	6-12 months			12-18 months
Walkaway				
Low Moderate				
Alcohol Law Violations				
Counterfeit Currency (Passing/Possession less than $1,000)				
Drugs:				
Marijuana, Simple Possession (less than $500)	6-12 months			12-18 months
Forgery/Fraud (less than $1,000)				
Income Tax Evasion (less than $10,000)				
Selective Service Act Violations				
Theft From Mail (less than $1,000)				
Moderate				
Bribery of Public Officials				
Counterfeit Currency (Passing/Possession $1,000-$19,999)				
Drugs:				
Marijuana, Possession With Intent to Distribute/Sale (less than $5,000)				
"Soft Drugs," Possession with Intent to Distribute/Sale (less than $500)				

	12-18 months	18-24 months
Embezzlement (less than $20,000)		
Explosives, Possession/Transportation		
Firearms Act, Possession/Purchase/Sale (single weapon— not sawed-off shotgun or machine gun)		
Income Tax Evasion ($10,000-$50,000)		
Interstate Transportation of Stolen/Forged Securities (less than $20,000)		
Mailing Threatening Communications		
Misprision of Felony		
Receiving Stolen Property With Intent to Resell (less than $20,000)		
Smuggling/Transporting of Aliens		
Theft/Forgery/Fraud ($1,000-$19,999)		
Theft of Motor Vehicle (Not Multiple Theft or for Resale)		

High

	12-18	18-24
Burglary or Larceny (Other than Embezzlement) from Bank or Post Office		
Counterfeit Currency (Passing/Possession $20,000-$100,000)		
Counterfeiting (Manufacturing)		
Drugs:		
Marijuana, Possession With Intent to Distribute/Sale ($5,000 or more)		
"Soft Drugs," Possession with Intent to Distribute/Sale ($500-$5,000)		
Embezzlement ($20,000-$100,000)		
Firearms Act, Possession/Purchase/Sale (sawed-off shotgun[s], machine gun[s], or multiple weapons)		
Interstate Transportation of Stolen/Forged Securities ($20,000-$100,000)		
Mann Act (No Force—Commercial Purposes)		
Organized Vehicle Theft		
Receiving Stolen Property ($20,000-$100,000)		
Theft/Forgery/Fraud ($20,000-$100,000)		

Table 2-4 (cont.)

Offense Characteristics: Severity of Offense Behavior (Examples)	Offender Characteristics: Parole Prognosis (Salient Factor Score)			
	Very Good (11-9)	Good (8-6)	Fair (5-4)	Poor (3-0)
Very High				
Robbery (Weapon or Threat)				
Drugs:				
"Hard Drugs," Possession with Intent to Distribute/Sale (No Prior Conviction for Sale of "Hard Drugs")	20-26 months		26-32 months	
"Soft Drugs," Possession with Intent to Distribute/Sale (over $5,000)				
Extortion				
Mann Act (Force)				
Sexual Act (Force)				
Greatest	(Greater than above—however, specific ranges are not given due to the limited number of cases and the extreme variations in severity possible within the category)			
Aggravated Felony (e.g., Robbery, Sexual Act/Aggravated Assault)—Weapon Fired or Personal Injury				
Aircraft Hijacking				
Drugs:				
"Hard Drugs," (Possession with Intent to Distribute/Sale) for Profit (Prior Conviction[s] for Sale of "Hard Drugs")				
Espionage				
Explosives (Detonation)				
Kidnapping				
Willful Homicide				

Notes:

1. These guidelines are predicated upon good institutional conduct and program performance.

2. If an offense behavior is not listed, the proper category may be obtained by comparing the severity of the offense behavior with those of similar offense behaviors listed.

3. If an offense behavior can be classified under more than one category, the most serious applicable category is to be used.

4. If an offense behavior involved multiple separate offenses, the severity level may be increased.

5. If a continuance is to be given, allow 30 days (1 month) for release program provision.

6. "Hard Drugs" include heroin, cocain, morphine or opiate derivatives, and synthetic opiate substitutes.

cooperation of the Federal Bureau of Investigation, which provided "rap sheet" copies for the required study subjects. A criterion measure of favorable outcome (no new conviction resulting in a sentence of sixty days or more and no return to prison for parole violation within two years of date of release) was established. From the set of over sixty background variables collected, nine items found to be significantly related to parole outcome on the construction subsample were selected and combined to produce a device scoring from zero to eleven points (the higher the score, the more favorable the parole prognosis estimate). This device was then tested on the validation subsample.[17] Table 2-5 displays the nine items forming the salient factor score presently in use.[18]

Board regulations specify that this device is to be used as an actuarial aid. Thus, when the circumstances warrant, the board representatives hearing a case may use their clinical judgment to override the salient factor score, provided they specify the basis for their action. In this manner, the board has endeavored to combine the advantages of both clinical and actuarial methods in making parole prognosis determinations.

Given the offense rating and parole prognosis estimate, one may refer back to table 2-2 to find the customary or policy range specified for the particular case. For example, the guideline range for an adult offender with a moderate offense severity rating (for example, auto theft) and a salient factor score of 9 to 11 (very good parole prognosis) is 12 to 16 months. On the other hand, the guideline range for an applicant with a very high severity offense behavior (for example, extortion) and a salient factor score of 0 to 3 (poor parole prognosis) is 55 to 65 months. There are no guideline ranges noted for offense behaviors listed in the greatest severity category. This is because of the small number of cases encountered and the extreme variations in severity possible within the category. Thus, for greatest severity cases, decisions must be based upon extrapolation from the time ranges provided in "very high" offense category cases.

In using these guidelines, the board presumes, as already noted, that the applicant will have maintained a satisfactory record of institutional conduct and program achievement (the third major dimension). Applicants who have demonstrated exceptionally good institutional program achievement may be considered for release earlier than the specified guideline range. On the other hand, applicants whose institutional conduct is rated as unsatisfactory are likely to be held longer than the range specified.

Case Decision Making

In actual case decision making, a guideline evaluation worksheet listing the offense rating, salient factor score, and guideline range is completed at each initial parole selection hearing. The board representatives hearing the case must

Table 2-5
Salient Factor Score
(Effective October, 1973)

Item A	____
No prior convictions (adult or juvenile) = 2	
One or two prior convictions = 1	
Three or more prior convictions = 0	
Item B	____
No prior incarcerations (adult or juvenile) = 2	
One or two prior incarcerations = 1	
Three or more prior incarcerations = 0	
Item C	____
Age at first commitment (adult or juvenile) 18 years or older = 1	
Otherwise = 0	
Item D	____
Commitment offense did not involve auto theft = 1	
Otherwise = 0	
Item E	____
Never had parole revoked or been committed for a new offense while on parole = 1	
Otherwise = 0	
Item F	____
No history of heroin or opiate dependence = 1	
Otherwise = 0	
Item G	____
Has completed 12th grade or received GED = 1	
Otherwise = 0	
Item H	____
Verified employment (or full-time school attendance) for a total of at least 6 months during the last 2 years in the community = 1	
Otherwise = 0	
Item I	____
Release plan to live with spouse and/or children = 1	
Otherwise = 0	
Total Score	____

then determine whether a decision within or outside the guideline range is appropriate. If the board representatives feel that a decision outside the guideline range (either above or below) is warranted, they may render such a decision provided that their reasons for departure from customary policy are stated. Analysis of 5,993 initial board hearings conducted during the first half of 1975 (January through June) indicates that 16.2 percent of decisions were outside the guidelines (8.7 percent below the guidelines and 7.5 percent above the guidelines). The remaining decisions (83.8 percent) were considered as within the guidelines. It is to be noted that these figures consider only discretionary decisions as outside the guidelines. Since the board may not parole a case below the judicially set minimum sentence (if any) nor may it hold a prisoner past his maximum sentence (mandatory release date), there are certain cases in which the board's discretion is limited by the sentence structure (a minimum sentence longer than the guideline range or a maximum sentence shorter than the guideline range). For purposes of this analysis, decisions controlled by the limits of the sentence were counted as within the guidelines.

Among the reasons cited for decisions below the guidelines were mitigating offense factors, exceptional institutional program achievement, clinical judgment that the applicant was a better parole risk than indicated by the salient factor score, credit for time spent in state custody on other (concurrent) charges, and serious medical problems. Reasons given for decisions above the guidelines included aggravating offense factors, unsatisfactory institutional conduct, failure to complete specific institutional programs, and clinical judgment that an applicant was a poorer parole risk than indicated by the predictive score.

At an initial parole hearing, an applicant may either be granted parole, denied parole and scheduled for a review hearing during a specific month (subject to board policy that no prisoner be continued without review for more than three years), or denied parole and continued to the expiration of his term (provided no more than three years remain until his mandatory release date). Given guideline usage at initial hearings, it is not surprising that a large majority of review hearings scheduled result in parole grants. During the first half of 1975, 3,290 regularly scheduled review considerations were conducted. Approximately 81 percent resulted in parole, 11 percent resulted in further continuances with disciplinary infractions cited, and 8 percent resulted in further continuances for other reasons.

Provision of Written Reasons for Denial

During a parole consideration hearing, the applicant's offense rating, salient factor score, and guideline range will be discussed with him by the board representatives, in addition to the other elements considered. Moreover, in each case in which parole is denied, the applicant will receive a brief written statement of reasons within fifteen working days from the date of the hearing. Thus, an applicant who is denied parole receives a written statement containing his offense severity rating, an item-by-item breakdown of his salient factor score, the guideline range, and the board's finding as to whether or not a departure from customary policy is warranted in his particular case. In addition, if the decision is outside of the guideline range, the basis for this decision is stated.

Similarly, if the applicant's offense behavior is not clear from reference to the guideline chart, the basis for this rating will be provided. This may be seen from the following case examples.

Case 1 (Forgery–$10,000)

Your offense behavior has been rated as *moderate* severity. You have a salient factor score of *six (6)* (a copy of the item-by-item breakdown is attached). You have been in custody a total of *12 months*. Guidelines established by the Board which consider the above factors indicate a range of *16-20* months to be served before release for *adult* cases with good institutional conduct and program achievement. After careful consideration of all relevant factors and information presented, it is found that a decision outside of the guidelines at this consideration is not warranted. Continue for review hearing in six months (12 months + 6 months = 18 months [within the 16-20 month range]).

Case 2 (Multiple Auto Theft)

Your offense behavior has been rated as *high severity because your offense involved multiple auto thefts.* You have a salient factor score of *four (4)* (a copy of the item-by-item breakdown is attached). You have been in custody a total of *25 months*. Guidelines established by the board which consider the above factors indicate a range of *26-32 months* to be served before release for *adult* cases with good institutional conduct and program achievement. After careful consideration of all relevant factors and information presented, it is found that a decision *above* the guidelines is warranted because:

1. *Your offense was part of a large-scale and ongoing criminal conspiracy.*

2. *You have two recent and serious institutional disciplinary infractions.*

Continue for review hearing in twelve months (25 months + 12 months = 37 months [5 months above the guideline range]).

This format for the provision of written reasons has generally won acceptance in judicial review. In fact, one court has recently commented (*Tougas v. Keohane*),

This statement applying the published Parole Board guidelines to this petitioner is adequate notice of the reasons for denial of parole. A review of the published guidelines in light of notice given petitioner reveals with specificity why parole was denied. Petitioner could hardly ask for a more objective and informative evaluation of his parole suitability status.[19]

Guideline Revision

As a danger of rigidity may exist with guideline usage, just as the problem of disparity exists without it, board policy provides that guideline usage is to be monitored and that the guidelines themselves are to be reviewed at regular intervals to consider possible revision.[20] In this manner the board may judge whether the degree to which the guidelines are being adhered to is appropriate as well as examine the sufficiency of the reasons given for departure from the guidelines. Moreover, the board can consider whether any changes in the severity scale, salient factor score, or time ranges themselves are appropriate and, if so, accomplish the desired modifications.

Summary

Guideline usage began in October 1972, as part of a pilot project in what is now the board's northeastern region, and was extended to all federal parole selection decisions at the end of 1973. In the three years since first established, the guideline system has withstood the test of various court challenges (see, for example, *Battle v. Norton,*[21] *Silvern v. Sigler,*[22] *Wiley v. U.S. Board of Parole*).[23] A guideline model has been specifically incorporated in a parole reform bill recently passed by the United States Congress.[24] Several state parole boards have adopted somewhat similar systems for structuring discretionary power[25] and an LEAA-funded research project to investigate the appropriateness of the parole guideline concept for other state systems also has been undertaken.[26]

Obviously, the establishment of the board's guidelines does not eliminate or even attempt to eliminate all discretion. Rather, it represents an attempt to achieve a balance between the evils of completely unstructured discretion and those of a totally fixed and mechanical approach. In relation to individual case decision making, the guideline method is designed to promote more rational and consistent decisions while still allowing for individual case consideration. On a broader level, by articulating the primary decision criteria, the guideline system is intended to promote openness and enable public assessment[27] of the rationality and appropriateness of the board's general paroling policy.

Notes

1. National Advisory Commission on Criminal Justice Standards and Goals. *Report on the Task Force on Corrections: Summary Report on Corrections* (Texas: Office of the Governor, Criminal Justice Council, 1972), p. 39 (working draft).

2. Ibid.

3. F.L. Bixby, "A New Role for Parole Boards," *Federal Probation* 34:2 (June 1970):24-28; see also: K.C. Davis, *Discretionary Justice* (Baton Rouge: Louisiana State University Press, 1969); F. Remington et al., *Criminal Justice Administration* (Indianapolis: Bobbs-Merrill, 1969).

4. American Law Institute, Model Penal Code (1962), §305.9, p. 290.

5. See appendix B.

6. Long-term sentence cases involve serious offenses in which the initial continuance (limited to three years by board policy) is deemed insufficient.

7. For a description of sampling and coding procedures, see Susan M. Singer and D.M. Gottfredson, *Development of a Data Base for Parole Decision-Making*, Parole Decision-Making Project, Report 1 (Davis, Calif.: National Council on Crime and Delinquency Research Center, June 1973).

8. For a description of the construction and validation of this device, see chapter 3.

9. For coding definitions and procedures, see D.M. Gottfredson and Susan M. Singer, *Parole Decision-Making Coding Manual*, Parole Decision-Making Project, Report 2 (Davis, Calif.: National Council on Crime and Delinquency Research Center, June 1973).

10. Not all offense ratings were used. Some were deemed to lack the specificity needed for inclusion.

11. These offense ratings were developed by D.M. Gottfredson and K.B. Ballard, Jr., in an unpublished study which employed correctional administrators, clinical workers, and paroling authorities in a decision game that provided the basis for scaling. The items used were developed in an unpublished study by Martin Warren and Ernest Reimer in the California Department of Corrections.

12. Current paroling policy guidelines are shown in the following section of this chapter.

13. See generally: Davis, *Discretionary Justice*; W. Gaylin, *Partial Justice* (New York: Alfred A. Knopf, 1974); M.E. Frankel, *Criminal Sentences: Law Without Order* (New York: Hill and Wang, 1973).

14. Davis, *Discretionary Justice*, pp. 17-21; Gaylin, *Criminal Sentences*, pp. 190-194, 219-221.

15. 28 C.F.R. §2.52, 38 Federal Register 222 (November 19, 1973) as amended. (Most recently published as 28 C.F.R. §2.20, 40 Federal Register 173 [September 5, 1975] pp. 41333-41337.) For related board regulations, see 28 C.F.R. §§2.1-2.58.

16. 28 C.F.R. §2.20 (c & d), ibid., p. 41333. (See also, *Grattan v. Sigler*, No. 75-2042 [C.A. 9, August 1975]; *Lupo v. Norton*, 371 F. Supp. 156 [D. Conn. 1974]; *Manos v. U.S.B.P.*, Civil Action No. 75-461 [M.D. Penn., June 19, 1975]).

17. See chapter 3.

18. Effective October 6, 1975, the slightly revised salient factor score shown was implemented. Prior to this date, item F read "no history of heroin, cocaine, or barbituate dependence."

19. Civil Action No. 75-86 (D. Ariz, June 11, 1975).

20. 28 C.F.R. §2.20 (f), p. 41333.

21. 365 F. Supp. 925 (D. Conn. 1973).

22. Civil Action No. 74-391 (D. D.C. September 13, 1974).

23. 380 F. Supp. 1194 (M.D. Penn. 1974).

24. Public Law 94-233, effective May 14, 1976.

25. The California Adult Authority, as well as the paroling authorities of Minnesota and Oregon.

26. Grant 75-NI-99-0004. This project is entitled "Classification for Parole Decision Policy," awarded to the Criminal Justice Research Center by the Law Enforcement Assistance Administration, D.M. Gottfredson and L.T. Wilkins, codirectors.

27. The paroling policy guidelines are published for public comment under the provisions of the Administrative Procedures Act (5 U.S.C., §553 [b] [3]).

The Risk Dimension: A Salient Factor Score

Introduction

An actuarial device (experience table) called a salient factor score (described in chapter 2) is now being used by the members and hearing examiners of the United States Parole Commission in actual case decision making as an aid in the assessment of an applicant's parole prognosis. This chapter describes the construction and validation of this instrument.

Sampling and Data Collection Procedure

Three samples were used. Sample A (N = 902), the construction sample, consists of a 25 percent sample of all persons released from federal prisons by parole, mandatory release, or expiration of sentence during the first six months of 1970.[1] Sample B (N = 919), used as a validation sample, consists of an additional 25 percent sample of persons released during the same period. Sample C (N = 662), used as an additional validation sample, consists of a similar 20 percent sample of persons released during the second six months of 1970. All three samples were drawn by including all cases whose prison identification numbers ended in selected digits.[2] As prison identification numbers are assigned sequentially, this method is assumed to reasonably represent random allocation.

A staff of research clerks completed a code sheet[3] containing more than sixty items of background data for each individual in the sample from the prison-parole file. These items included information about the present offense, prior criminal record, age, education, employment record, past and projected living arrangements, and prison conduct. In addition, information about performance after release was coded. A two-year follow up period from date of release was utilized for each individual. If the subject was released with parole (or mandatory release) supervision, follow-up information was obtained from the prison-parole file. If the subject was released without supervision or if supervision was terminated prior to the end of the follow-up period, followup information was obtained from the subject's "rap sheet," provided through the cooperation of the Federal Bureau of Investigation.

Adapted, in part, from P.B. Hoffman and J.L. Beck, Report 2, United States Board of Parole Research Unit, April 1974; also published as "Parole Decision-Making: A Salient Factor Score," *Journal of Criminal Justice*, vol. 2, no. 3, Fall 1974. Reprinted with permission.

Criterion Measure

A primary outcome criterion measure agreed upon by project and parole board staff is defined as follows.

Within Two (2) Years from Date of Release[4]

Favorable Outcome: No new conviction resulting in a sentence of sixty days or more;

No return to prison for technical violation; and

No outstanding absconder warrant.

Unfavorable Outcome: A new conviction resulting in a sentence of sixty days or more;

A return to prison for technical violation; or

An outstanding absconder warrant.

The utilization of this criterion measure, similar to that used in the Uniform Parole Reports program,[5] enabled the evaluation of outcome for all cases, whether released with or without parole (or mandatory release) supervision, with a uniform two-year follow-up period for each individual.[6]

Selection of the Predictive Method

A recent and rather comprehensive study by Simon,[7] which compared the predictive power of a number of mathematical methods for combining predictive items, indicates that the method commonly known among criminological researchers in the United States as the Burgess method,[8] using a number of equally weighted dichotomous items, tends to predict as well on validation samples as the newer and more mathematically sophisticated methods (such as multiple regression or configural analysis). A smaller but similar study by Wilbanks and Hindelang[9] produced a similar conclusion. That is, while the more sophisticated methods produce a higher correlation on the construction sample, there tends to be considerably greater shrinkage[10] when applied to a validation sample. As the purpose of a predictive device, by definition, is to predict to future samples, it is the validation results that are important. Given this equality in predictive power, the Burgess method was chosen because of its simplicity and ease of calculation in field usage. As Mannheim and Wilkins[11] have pointed out, errors resulting from inaccurate coding or incorrect mathematical tabulation in the application of an actuarial device produce the same effect as error inherent in the instrument itself. As the Burgess method requires only dichotomous (or in this case, trichotomous) coding and simple addition, the probability of coding or tabulation error is reduced.

Prior Studies

Parole prediction studies date back to 1923, when Warner collected data from the files of 680 prisoners of the Massachusetts State Reformatory.[12] When he compared discriminations of success and violation with the criteria used by the board of parole, he concluded that there was little relation between the board's criteria and the behavior of the men after release. He was the first investigator to note that the success rate of those committed for a sexual crime was higher than those committed for larceny and breaking and entering, sugesting Burgess's later generalization that "those guilty of crimes that shock society are less likely to violate parole."

In the same year Hart maintained that fifteen of Warner's factors plus twenty others could be used to improve prediction.[13] He suggested that all significant factors ought to be combined into a single prognostic score for each person.

In 1928, Burgess studied the records for 3,000 men paroled at least two-and-one-half years previously from three Illinois penitentiaries.[14] From study of twenty-one items, each divided into several categories, he found differences in the rates of violation. An arbitrary score of one point was assigned to each factor, and a favorable point was given to each man whose rate was below the institutional base rate. The result was a prediction score related to violation rates.

Between 1930 and 1950, Sheldon and Eleanor Glueck published eight volumes on the study and prediction of parole behavior.[15] Using case material from the Concord Reformatory, Massachusetts, they exhaustively investigated the life histories of 510 prisoners whose sentences expired in 1921 and 1922. In order to supplement the unreliable and incomplete file information, they checked many other sources; and in 73 percent of the cases they interviewed exprisoners or their near relatives in order to seek a more accurate description of the parole adjustment achieved.

Following the earliest study by the Gluecks, Vold in 1931 studied records of 1,192 men who had been discharged from the Minnesota prison between 1922 and 1927.[16] He identified predictive attributes by means of the coefficient of mean square contingency, a statistic that had been used by the Gluecks, and compared the efficiency of a Burgess-type technique (using all available predictive factors without weighting) with the Glueck technique (using only the most significant factors, weighting them according to the maximum percentage differences between any subclass with a particular factor and the recidivism expectancy for the entire group). He found little difference in the results and dropped the Glueck procedures, considering them more laborious.

Monachesi, in 1932, studied 1,515 adult and youth cases handled earlier by a Minnesota probation office.[17] He also found that the Burgess and Glueck procedures gave about the same results.

At about the same time, Tibbits studied the records of 3,000 youths paroled from the Illinois State Reformatory at Pontiac,[18] and a "criminal-liability index," was published by Argow.[19]

A major study by the United States Department of Justice in 1931 included analyses of case histories of 100,000 felons, considering some factors associated with parole selection and outcome.[20] A second analysis of 2,593 case histories of men released from federal institutions from 1930 to 1935 represented an attempt to improve selection by the United States Board of Parole. Eighty-two information items were selected and divided into five groups: parental, social, criminal, institutional, and postinstitutional history. It was concluded that while thirty-nine of the items studied had some predictive power, the resulting tables would not produce substantial improvement in federal parole practice.

Ohlin, in 1951, constructed parole experience tables for use in Illinois, based on his study of 4,941 cases.[21] A violation rate was obtained for each subclassification defined by the data items used. Each man was given one favorable point for each favorable subclass into which he fell and one unfavorable for each unfavorable subclass. Taking the difference gave a final score, essentially as in the Burgess method.

At the same time, others studied probationers in a similar vein. Caldwell reported a study of 1,862 federal probationers;[22] and Reiss studied 736 young probationers in Illinois, testing the validity of the table developed using a follow-up sample of 374 persons.[23]

While these studies were progressing, European research workers were similarly at work. Schiedt in 1936 examined the records for a sample of 500 men who were discharged in 1931 from Bavarian prisons.[24] He identified information items associated with outcome and used the Burgess technique. After applying the scale to 100 Bavarian inmates discharged before 1933, Trunk, in the following year, criticized overlapping factors, the absence of any weighting system, and the high proportion of cases for whom no prediction was made.[25] Gerecke, in 1939, sought to improve the system by assigning various values to the factors and by multiplying each point value by one to four according to the "intensity" of the factor in an individual case.[26] The Schiedt scale was applied by Meywerk in 1938 to a sample of 200 Hamburg prisoners examined earlier.[27] Kohnle, in 1938, also applied the scale to 203 boys discharged from German reformatories between 1926 and 1932, of whom two-thirds had been reconvicted subsequently.[28] Some of the items did not hold up in this examination, so they were modified or omitted; nevertheless, he found a number of the remaining factors had some predictive value.

Others developed and applied various point systems. The Swiss criminologist, Frey, in 1951, criticized American prediction studies as suffering from inadequate data for the period of early childhood, for underemphasis on social factors, and for a lack of comprehensive information about the personality as a whole.[29] He also used a point system. Mannheim, in 1948, found a point system useful in the study of juvenile delinquency at Cambridge, England.[30] Similar work continued, meanwhile, in the United States. Dunham, in 1954, summarized his comparisons of recidivists and nonrecidivists at San Quentin.[31] After identifying information that discriminated between recidivists and nonrecidivists, he combined the five significant factors found, according to standard scores, which resulted in a scale further differentiating between the two groups.

Glaser, in 1954, discussed "a reconsideration of some parole prediction factors" along with his results of a study involving 4,448 Illinois inmates paroled between 1940 and 1949.[32] Differential association theory led him to the examination of factors related to "home background," "schooling and employment," "criminal record," and "personal summarization classification." The latter group relates especially to "social types" redefined from those employed earlier by Burgess and by Ohlin. Reiss, in 1949, had proposed a distinction between the usual concept of reliability for an item of information and "net" reliability, where the latter is defined by the proportion of cases in which independent ratings classify the cases under different score groups of a prediction instrument.[33] From his data regarding "social types," Glaser concluded that the low *gross* reliability obtained with one such factor may—in view of higher *net* reliability—"be considered a tolerable price for the extreme selectivity and the unusual stability of this factor, as compared to those of the highly objective factors."

The last two decades have seen an increased use of multivariate statistical techniques for the combination of predictive information into a single experience table or scoring method. Until the mid-1950s, two basic methods mainly were employed for the combination of predictive attributes into a single scoring scheme. These were the technique of Burgess, using many predictive characteristics without weighting, and the technique of the Gluecks, employing only a small number of characteristics, but using a weighting system. In 1954, Kirby used multiple correlation as a technique for the combination of variables, elimination of overlapping items, and differential weighting.[34] Independently, in England, Mannheim and Wilkins had used the same method.[35]

So far as the methods used are concerned, the problem of prediction of parole performance is little different from problems of personnel selection in industry. In a review of selection methods, Bechtoldt asserts that "the stability of predictions for new samples tends to decrease with an increase in the number of predictor variables in the original sample, when the regression weights are determined by least squares."[36] Discussing various methods for assignment of weights, Bechtold points out that,

The simple addition of scores, as in the case of a set of test items, is sufficiently accurate for the combining of large numbers of variates. The rationale for this simple procedure is that, as the number of positively correlated variables increases, the correlations between any two sets of weighted scores approaches unity and the effect of differential weighting tends to disappear. However, if the number of measures to be added together is not large, the dispersions and the intercorrelations of the measures will influence significantly the effective weighting.

He notes also that,

The general solution is to weight the several measures in such a way that the weighted linear composite will conform as closely as possible to the values of the single criterion observations. If the single criterion is a quantitative one, the theoretically best solution under the least squares principle leads to a multiple regression equation. If the criterion is a qualitative variate, the "best" combination in the same sense is provided by Fisher's discriminant function which, for a dichotomous criterion scored zero or one, can be regarded as a regression-equation problem. These techniques take into consideration the intercorrelations of the measures as well as their correlations with the criterion.[37]

Other methods, however, also have been employed. In 1962, Glaser described a method of combining factors which he called a "configuration table."[38] This procedure is similar (but not quite identical with) the procedure proposed by MacNaughton-Smith and called "predictive attribute analysis."[39] The basis for the method proposed by MacNaughton-Smith is a successive partitioning of the sample into subgroups on the basis of the single item found in each subgroup to have the closest association with the criterion. That is, first the single most predictive item is found and then the total sample is divided on that attribute. Each of the two resulting subsamples is studied further, in order to identify, within each, the single best predictor. Then, the two subsamples are further subdivided and the process repeated until no further items significantly associated with the criterion are found. The approach has been used in parole prediction studies by Wilkins,[40] by Grygier,[41] and by Ballard.[42] Glaser's configural analysis method, which he used also in his 1964 study of the federal prison and parole system,[43] also has been used in parole prediction studies by Mannering and Babst,[44] and Babst, Inciardi, and Jaman.[45]

When both linear regression and the configural analysis methods were applied to the same set of Wisconsin data, results of these methods gave similar predictive efficiency.[46] A shortcoming of the latter approach is that the successive partitioning of the sample into subgroups may involve a capitalization on sampling error.[47]

Other configural approaches are given by the methods of cluster analysis. The first used, for parole prediction, was the method called association analysis. This method, developed by Williams and Lambert for studies in plant ecology,[48] has been employed in delinquency prediction by Wilkins and MacNaughton-Smith[49] and by Gottfredson, Ballard, and Lane.[50] The method provides an empirical means for subdividing a heterogeneous population into subgroups that are relatively homogeneous with respect to the attributes studied. It is more properly called a classification, or taxonomic method; unlike other prediction

methods, the criterion classifications (for example, parole performance outcomes) are ignored in establishing the subgrouping. The establishment of the
classifications is not dependent upon the relationships of predictor candidates to
the criterion; the classification may provide, nevertheless, a valid prediction
method.

A combination of association analysis and regression methods was employed
by Gottfredson and Ballard.[51] The purpose of the study was to determine
whether predictive efficiency might be improved by a sequential method:
classification into homogeneous groups, followed by the use of regression
methods separately for each group. The results supported this approach to
improved prediction, although the numbers in resulting subgroups were small for
the use of multiple regression.

Multiple regression methods also have been employed in a series of studies
completed in the California Department of Correction and the California Youth
Authority.[52]

This cursory review suggests only a sampling of the large number of parole
prediction studies which provide the background for current efforts. A review of
work up to 1955 is found in a text by Mannheim and Wilkins.[53] A review of
parole prediction studies and a general assessment of the prediction problem was
prepared by Gottfredson in 1967.[54] More recently about forty such studies
were reviewed by Frances Simon in the work cited earlier. Her review includes a
number of citations concerning the comparisons of the efficiency of various
methods for developing the experience tables. Her own study went further with
such comparisons, and it is noteworthy that her exhaustive comparison led to
the conclusion that "all of them work about equally well."[55]

Information Concerning Offenders

Information thought, on the basis of prior studies, likely to be useful for the
experience tables to be developed (as well as for a description of the offenders
appearing before the board for parole consideration) was gathered. The procedures devised for coding the information from case files, and explicit definitions
of the various items employed, are given in project reports.[56] Listed, however,
are the titles of the information categories that were coded.

Identification Number
Federal Bureau of Investigation
  Number
Judicial District
Birth Date
Date Probation Began
Date Sentence Began
Date of Admission

How Committed
Type of Admission
Sentence Procedure
Expires Full Term
Mandatory Release Expected
  with Good Time
Living Arrangement Before
  Commitment

Minimum Parole Eligibility
Date
Aliases
Sex and Ethnic Group
Citizenship
Grade Claimed
Marital Status at
Admission
Dependents
Codefendants
Type of Sentence
Weapon in Offense
Assault
Offense Rating
Reason for First Arrest
Age at First Arrest
Age at First Sentence
Age at First Commitment
Longest Time Free Since
First Commitment
Longest Time Served on
Any Commitment
Prior Prison Commitments
Other Prior Sentences
Sentences with Probations
Prior Incarcerations
Probation or Parole
Revocations
Prior Arrests and
Convictions
Total Arrests
Family Criminal Record

Alcohol
Drugs
Mental Hospital Confinement
Homosexuality
Longest Job in Free Community
Employment in Last Two Years
of Civilian Life
Military Discharge
Beta IQ
Standford Achievement Test
Escape History
Prison Adjustment Indicated in
First Classification Report
Custody Classification Prior
to Parole Board Action
Custody Level Reduced During
Imprisonment
Assaultive Infractions
Prison Punishment
On-the-Job Training
Education Program
Letters and Visits from Family
Number of Parole Hearings
Parole Advisor Obtained
Planned Living Arrangement
Type of Decision
Decision Outcome
Continued to Date
Members
Date of Decision
Projected Release Date
(Parole Only)

Selection of the Predictive Items

The nine items or salient factors included in this instrument were selected from sixty-six variables taken from items or combinations of items included on the coding sheet. Each variable was cross-tabulated with the criterion measure. Those items that predicted favorable (or unfavorable) outcome after release (chi-square at 0.05 level) were singled out for possible inclusion in the instrument. From this pool of items, the final nine were chosen by a process of elimination. Items were excluded, even though predictive, if they were judged to pose ethical problems for use in individual parole selection decisions (for example, prior arrests not leading to conviction), if they did not appear frequently enough to be useful (for example, escape history), or if they appeared to overlap substantially with items already included (for example, longest job held and employment during last two years are highly related). Thus, the nine items selected combine both statistical findings and the judgment of the researchers. Table 3-1 displays the nine items selected.

In a slight departure from the Burgess method, the first two items were classified as trichotomous rather than dichotomous. Thus, they are each scored 0, 1, or 2 (the classification with the highest proportion of favorable outcomes is given the highest number). The remaining items are each scored 0 or 1. This produces a scale with a range of possible scores from 0 to 11. The higher the score, the greater is the proportion of favorable outcomes predicted for that score.

Construction and Validation

This instrument was used to calculate a score for each case in the construction sample (sample A: $N = 902$). A point biserial correlation of 0.318 between scores and outcome resulted. For the first validation sample (sample B: $N = 919$) a point biserial correlation of 0.283 was obtained. On the second validation sample (sample C: $N = 662$), a point biserial correlation of 0.270 was found. Combining the two validation samples ($N = 1,581$) produced a point biserial correlation of 0.277. (It is to be noted that the maximum possible point biserial is not $+ 1.00$ as in the case of Pearson's R, but rather it varies with the proportion of success/failures in the sample. For the three samples mentioned, the maximum point biserial correlation possible, assuming perfect prediction, would be approximately 0.75.) Table 3-2 displays the distribution of scores and outcomes for the construction and combined validation samples. For operational usage in conjunction with decision guidelines these scores were collapsed to form four categories as shown in table 3-3.

An alternative measure of predictive efficiency, the Mean Cost Rating, was calculated on the collapsed scores. Developed by Berkson,[57] the mean cost rating is defined as a measure of cost versus utility. Utility is defined as the proportion of unsuccessful candidates eliminated when a cut-off score is used. Cost is the proportion of successful candidates rejected. The mean cost rating for this instrument produced a coefficient of 0.36 on the construction sample, 0.33 on the first validation sample, 0.32 on the second validation sample, and 0.32 on the combined validation sample.

Operational Use

After presentation first to the research committee of the Board of Parole and then to the full board, this device was adopted for operational use. As noted, the

Table 3-1
Salient Factor Score Items

	Score			x^2	Significance Level
	2	1	0		
%	88.5%	72.5%	60.1%	38.561	0.001
Success	$N = 113$	$N = 222$	$N = 567$		

Item A—Prior Convictions

No prior convictions (adult/juvenile) = 2
One or two prior convictions = 1
Three or more prior convictions = 0

	Score			x^2	Significance Level
	2	1	0		
%	80.9%	66.4%	56.6%	49.924	0.001
Success	$N = 278$	$N = 244$	$N = 380$		

Item B—Prior Incarcerations

No prior incarcerations (adult/juvenile) = 2
One or two prior incarcerations = 1
Three or more prior incarcerations = 0

	Score		x^2	Significance Level
	1	0		
%	71.0%	56.6%	17.083	0.001
Success	$N = 635$	$N = 267$		

Item C—Age at First Commitment

Age at first commitment (adult/juvenile) 18 or older = 1
Otherwise = 0

	Score		x^2	Significance Level
	1	0		
%	72.9%	52.6%	34.304	0.001
Success	$N = 630$	$N = 272$		

Item D—Auto Theft

Commitment offense did not involve auto theft = 1
Otherwise = 0

Table 3-1 (cont.)

	Score			
	1	*0*	x^2	*Significance Level*
%	73.4%	52.3%	38.299	0.001
Success	N = 617	N = 285		

Item E–Parole Revoked

Never had parole revoked = 1
Otherwise = 0

	Score			
	1	*0*	x^2	*Significance Level*
%	70.0%	54.3%	15.975	0.001
Success	N = 714	N = 188		

Item F–Drug History

No history of opiate or barbiturate usage = 1
Otherwise = 0

	Score			
	1	*0*	x^2	*Significance Level*
%	72.8%	64.2%	5.886	0.001
Success	N = 265	N = 637		

Item G–Grade Claimed

Has completed 12th grade or received GED = 1
Otherwise = 0

	Score			
	1	*0*	x^2	*Significance Level*
%	72.2%	60.9%	12.324	0.001
Success	N = 467	N = 435		

Item H–Employment

Verified employment (or full-time school attendance) for a total of at least 6 months during last 2 years in the community = 1
Otherwise = 0

	Score			
	1	*0*	x^2	*Significance Level*
%	82.5%	62.9%	23.720	0.001
Success	N = 177	N = 725		

Item I–Living Arrangement

Release plan to live with spouse and/or children = 1
Otherwise = 0

Table 3-2
Salient Factor Score/Outcome Distribution

	Score												R	χ^2	Sig Level	
	0	1	2	3	4	5	6	7	8	9	10	11				
% Favorable Outcome	—	44.1%	40.0%	57.5%	60.3%	61.5%	72.0%	83.1%	79.3%	93.0%	90.6%	100.0%	.318	97.506	0.001	N = 902
Construction Sample	N = 0	N = 34	N = 85	N = 134	N = 146	N = 122	N = 107	N = 77	N = 82	N = 53	N = 43	N = 19				
% Favorable Outcome	25.0%	53.2%	50.0%	61.0%	66.3%	70.7%	76.3%	78.0%	84.0%	83.7%	94.7%	100.0%	.277	126.904	0.001	N = 1,581
Combined Validation Sample	N = 4	N = 62	N = 158	N = 200	N = 246	N = 225	N = 169	N = 159	N = 131	N = 92	N = 94	N = 41				

Table 3-3
Salient Factor Collapsed Score/Outcome Distribution

	Poor (0-3)	Fair (4-5)	Good (6-8)	Very Good (9-11)	MCR	
% Favorable Outcome	49.8%	60.8%	77.4%	93.0%	0.36	
Construction Sample	N = 253	N = 268	N = 266	N = 115		N = 902
% Favorable Outcome	55.4%	68.4%	79.1%	91.2%	0.32	
Validation Sample	N = 424	N = 471	N = 459	N = 227		N = 1,581

0 to 11 point scale was collapsed to form a four-category scale. These four risk categories are combined with a six-category offense scale to form explicit parole selection policy guidelines—a four by six (risk by severity) matrix that displays the customary range of time to be served before release for each matrix cell.[58] Also included is a provision for clinical override of the salient factor score. That is, if the examiner panel feels that the salient factor score is substantially inaccurate, it may substitute its clinical judgment, provided it gives a written explanation and justification.

Moreover, the definitions of two items were modified slightly by the board for operational usage. Item E (parole revocation) as originally coded did not include a new commitment unless it resulted in formal revocation. However, it is known that parole violation warrants are often withdrawn if a parolee receives a substantial sentence on a new charge. Consequently, a definition of "parole revoked or new commitment while on parole" was deemed more appropriate. In item F (drug use) subjects with previous opiate or barbiturate usage did substantially poorer than persons with no drug use (54.5 percent versus 70.2 percent favorable outcome rate). Users of hallucinogens or stimulants (including cocaine) also did somewhat poorer than nondrug users (63.6 percent versus 70.2 percent favorable outcome rate). A definition of heroin, cocaine, or barbiturate dependence (in contrast to simple use) was adopted as a negative indicant.

This salient factor score has been in use as an aid in federal parole selection decisions throughout the United States since November 1, 1973, when it replaced an earlier version. Board members and hearing examiners have made over 3,000 decisions using this instrument to date and appear well satisfied with its performance. Operationally, the salient factor score requires no special skills to compute and can be completed in a short time; thus, it does not impose an undue administrative burden. A sample salient factor score sheet is shown in figure 3-1.

Discussion

The validity of the salient factor score compares well with that of actuarial devices developed previously. In a California study using a similar criterion and follow-up period, Gottfredson reported a validation sample point biserial correlation of 0.26 between score and outcome and a mean cost rating of 0.29 for an instrument using multiple regression.[59] This is slightly less than the point biserial correlation of 0.28 and mean cost rating of 0.32 found for the combined validation sample in this study. Studies by Ohlin, Glaser, Gottfredson and Beverly, and Gottfredson and Ballard[60] produced similar results. Considering these results, as well as the demonstrated effectiveness of actuarial (as opposed to clinical) measures,[61] the predictive power of this measure was deemed sufficient to recommend implementation as a risk assessment aid in actual case decision making.

Case   Name   Register Number

Item A   ☐
    No prior convictions (adult or juvenile) = 2
    One or two prior convictions = 1
    Three or more prior convictions = 0

Item B   ☐
    No prior incarcerations (adult or juvenile) = 2
    One or two prior incarcerations = 1
    Three or more prior incarcerations = 0

Item C   ☐
    Age at first commitment (adult or juvenile):
      18 years or older = 1
    Otherwise = 0

Item D   ☐
    Commitment offense did not involve auto theft = 1
    Otherwise = 0

Item E   ☐
    Never had parole revoked or been committed
      for a new offense while on parole = 1
    Otherwise = 0

Item F   ☐
    No history of heroin, cocaine, or barbiturate
      dependence = 1
    Otherwise = 0

Item G   ☐
    Has completed 12th grade or received GED = 1
    Otherwise = 0

Item H   ☐
    Verified employment (or full-time school attendance)
      for a total of at least six months during the last two
      years in the community = 1
    Otherwise = 0

Item I   ☐
    Release plan to live with spouse and/or children = 1
    Otherwise = 0

Total Score   ☐

Figure 3-1. Salient Factor Score Sheet
(effective 10/1/73)

Several limitations common to all such prediction devices are to be noted. Actuarial devices make predictive statements about outcome for groups and not for individuals. That is, an actuarial device should be able to tell quite accurately that two-thirds of all cases in a particular risk category will fail, but it will not make statements about which ones will fail. When a particular inmate comes up for parole, the decision maker still will not know whether he will succeed or fail on parole. All that he will know is the percentage of inmates with similar characteristics who may be expected to succeed or fail on parole. In this regard, using an actuarial parole aid is a little like using a weather report that says there will be a 60 percent chance of rain. What the weather report actually means is that on similar days it rained 60 percent of the time. It does not tell whether or not it will actually rain today. Nevertheless, such information can be useful in deciding whether or not to carry an umbrella. A parole board making many hundreds or thousands of decisions each year will make a certain number of errors in relation to assessment of risk. On a macroscopic level, the fairest policy is the one that makes the fewest errors overall. Thus, while utilization of a predictive device cannot prevent error in any particular case, utilization as opposed to nonutilization should reduce the overall number of errors made.

A second limitation is that actuarial devices may overlook other elements such as attitude or prison adjustment that may be relevant to parole success. As Gottfredson has noted, actuarial devices can be invaluable tools if properly constructed, but by their very nature they are limited in scope.[62] That is, there may be important elements in certain cases not covered by the actuarial device that the decision maker must consider. This was the reason for the provision of "clinical override" built into the guidelines. With this provision for clinical override, the decision maker retains his discretion for those cases that do not "fit the pattern."

A third limitation is that actuarial devices are based primarily on information found in the inmates' institutional files. These files often have been found to contain inaccurate or even contradictory information.[63] However, this problem similarly hinders clinical judgments. As Wilkins has noted, improvement in accurate record keeping and more concise reporting will likely precede any substantial improvement in predictive power.[64]

Suggestions for Further Research

Overall, the salient factor score appears to predict well enough to justify implementation and has proved administratively feasible in operation. Nevertheless, there may be more homogeneous subgroups within the total sample (for example, youth cases, NARA cases, females) for which separate salient factor scores might be developed as samples of sufficient size are generated, thus increasing overall predictive power. At present, the small sample sizes available for these subgroups are not adequate for this task.

Moreover, any actuarial device must be periodically tested to determine whether or not it retains validity for subsequent samples. To the extent that the population concerned changes over time and place, an actuarial device may become less useful. This means that a continuing program of research is necessary to monitor, revise, and update the actuarial device as conditions require.

Salient Factor Score Validation[a]

The actuarial device (salient factor score) presently used by the United States Board of Parole as a decision-making aid in assessing parole prognosis was adopted in October 1973. Containing nine items scoring to eleven points, this device was developed from a sample of federal prisoners released in 1970. For research purposes, this sample was divided into construction ($N = 902$) and validation ($N = 1,581$) subsamples. Construction and initial validation of this device were described in the preceding section.

However, the purpose of any actuarial parole selection aid is to predict to prospective samples; thus, periodic validation is required. Recently, coding has been completed on a 1972 release cohort sample ($N = 1,011$) selected in the same manner as the 1970 sample. That is, all cases released to the community during the first six months of 1972 (by parole, mandatory release, or expiration of sentence) whose prison identification numbers ended in selected digits were included.[65] As prison identification numbers are assigned sequentially, this is assumed to be the equivalent of random selection. Two-year follow-up from date of release for each case was obtained through the cooperation of the Federal Bureau of Investigation. Initially, a deck of computer cards containing identifying information for all sample cases was sent to the FBI National Crime Information Center (NCIC), which provided a "rap sheet" printout for all cases located in their computerized criminal history (CCH) system. Cases not located (matched) via this method had identifying information sent to the FBI Identification Division for manual pulling and forwarding of "rap sheet" copies.[66] This represented a change from the procedure used with the 1970 cohort follow-up. For the 1970 cohort, parole folders of all sample cases under parole or mandatory release supervision for all or part of the follow-up period were manually pulled for coding and only those cases in which additional information was required (no indication of unfavorable outcome—subject under supervision for less than two years)[67] were sent for FBI follow-up information. At that time, the FBI's computerized criminal history system was in an embryonic stage and this method was required to minimize the demand on FBI clerical staff time.

One problem with use of FBI "rap sheets" as a data source is that there is not always adequate dispositional information.[68] Thus, as with the 1970 sample, a letter was sent to the arresting agency (and/or court) for each case in which an arrest without disposition was noted that might have affected case

[a]Adapted from P.B. Hoffman and J.L. Beck, Report 8, United States Board of Parole Research Unit, July 1975; also published as "Salient Factor Score Validation: A 1972 Release Cohort," *Journal of Criminal Justice*, vol. 4, no. 4, Spring 1976. Reprinted with permission.

outcome classification.[69] All cases for which the status was unresolved as of July 25, 1975 ($N = 43$) were classified—for purposes of this report—as having favorable outcome. Definitions of favorable/unfavorable outcome for the 1970 and 1972 release cohorts are shown in table 3-4. The differences between the definitions is minimal and for purposes of the following comparison may be safely ignored.[70]

Findings and Discussion

Table 3-5 enables comparison between the 1970 and 1972 samples. The percentage of cases with favorable outcome for each salient factor score category is displayed for each of the three samples: the 1970 construction sample (sample A); the 1970 validation sample (sample B); and the 1972 validation sample (sample C). It may be seen that the measure of predictive power calculated for the device (point biserial r) remained relatively stable over the three samples ($r_A = 0.318$, $r_B = 0.277$, $r_C = 0.320$). Thus, it appears that the salient factor score has retained predictive power for the 1972 release sample.

Table 3-4
Outcome Classification

	1970 Sample	*1972 Sample*
Favorable Outcome	No new convictions resulting in a sentence of sixty days or more; No absconder warrants outstanding; No return to prison for parole/mandatory release violation; and No death during commission of a criminal act.	No new commitment of sixty days or more; No absconder warrant outstanding; No return to prison for parole/mandatory release violation; and No death during commission of a criminal act.
Unfavorable Outcome	New conviction resulting in a sentence of sixty days or more[a] or Absconder warrant outstanding or Return to prison for parole/mandatory release violation or Death during commission of a criminal act.	New commitment of sixty days or more or Absconder warrant outstanding or Return to prison for parole/mandatory release violation or Death during commission of a criminal act.

[a]Including sentences to probation for sixty days or more, and sentences to confinement of sixty days or more which were suspended.

Table 3-5

Percentage Favorable Outcome by Score—Comparison of the 1972 and 1970 Samples

Sample A: 1970 Construction

Score	11	10	9	8	7	6	5	4	3	2	1	0	All Scores	Rpbis
Percentage Favorable Outcome	100	91	93	79	83	72	62	60	58	40	44	–	67	0.318
N	19	43	53	82	77	107	122	146	134	85	34	0	902	

Sample B: 1970 Validation

Score	11	10	9	8	7	6	5	4	3	2	1	0	All Scores	Rpbis
Percentage Favorable Outcome	100	95	84	84	78	76	71	66	61	50	53	25	71	0.277
N	41	94	92	131	159	169	225	246	200	158	62	4	1581	

Sample C: 1972 Validation

Score	11	10	9	8	7	6	5	4	3	2	1	0	All Scores	Rpbis
Percentage Favorable Outcome	100	92	96	88	87	77	72	67	61	61	39	20	74	0.320
N	24	49	77	101	83	105	149	148	139	90	41	5	1011	

Data collected for the 1972 sample also provide an opportunity to examine the utilization of different criterion measures. Given the burden of proof required to obtain a criminal conviction and the effect of plea bargaining on sentencing, it could be argued that utilization of new arrest(s) as a criterion measure of unfavorable outcome would be more reflective of underlying criminal behavior than use of either new conviction or commitment. Thus, three criterion measures were selected for comparison. Criterion measure X refers to the criterion measure for the 1972 release sample noted in table 3-4. Criterion measure Y counts, in addition, any conviction—regardless of the sentence imposed—as indicative of unfavorable outcome. Criterion measure Z counts, in addition, any arrest—regardless of disposition—as indicative of unfavorable outcome (see table 3-6).[71] Criterion measure X contains the most liberal definition of favorable outcome, criterion measure Y is less liberal, and criterion measure Z is the least liberal.

Figure 3-2 displays the percentage of cases with favorable outcome in each salient factor score category for the 1972 sample using these criterion measures.

Table 3-6
Outcome Classification–Comparative Criterion Measures

	Criterion Measure Y	*Criterion Measure Z*
Favorable Outcome	No new conviction (other than for a petty offense);[a] No return to prison for parole/mandatory release violation; No death during commission of a criminal act.	No new arrest for criminal offense (other than a petty offense);[a] No return to prison for parole/mandatory release violation; No death during commission of a criminal act.
Unfavorable Outcome	New conviction (other than for a petty offense or Return to prison for parole/mandatory release violation or Outstanding absconder warrant or Death during commission of a criminal act.	New arrest for criminal offense (other than a petty offense) or Return to prison for parole/mandatory release violation or Outstanding absconder warrant or Death during commission of a criminal act.

[a]The computerized criminal history (CCH) system excludes arrest(s) and conviction(s) for juvenile offenders as defined by state law (unless the juvenile is tried in court as an adult) and for petty offenses such as drunkenness, gambling, and vagrancy. Arrest and convictions for petty offenses were contained on the rap sheets obtained from Identification Division, but were specifically excluded from consideration during coding.

The best fit (least squares) line for criterion measure X is the dashed line. The dotted line refers to criterion measure Y, while the solid line refers to criterion measure Z. As may be seen, the slope of the solid line for the arrest criterion (criterion measure Z) appears somewhat steeper than for either of the other criteria.[72] The point biserial correlation coefficient is also slightly higher for the arrest criterion ($r = 0.342$ for criterion measure Z, 0.330 for criterion measure Y, and 0.320 for criterion measure X). This would seem to indicate that the salient factor score has slightly greater power of discrimination in reference to the new arrest criterion than in reference to either the new conviction or new commitment criterion. Whether this is because the arrest criterion is more reflective of the actual incidence of criminal activity among the subjects of study, or whether it means that the salient factors merely do a better job of predicting police behavior (by identifying those the police are most likely to suspect) remains, of course, open to question. In terms of the rank order of outcome rate by score, the choice of criterion measure would appear to make little difference. For those who wish to make inferences about the actual incidence of criminal behavior

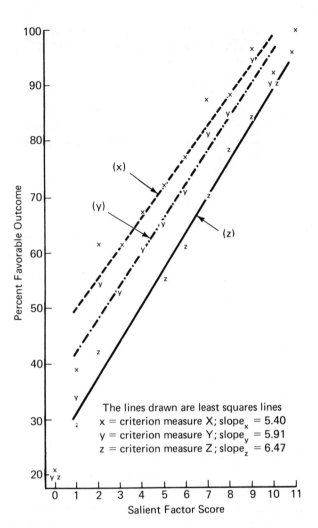

Figure 3-2. Percentage Favorable Outcome by Score: Three Criterion Measures

among the score groups, however, it is obvious that the choice of criterion will have considerably more impact,[73] particularly at the lower end of the scale.

Notes

1. For a more detailed description of case selection procedures, see S.M. Singer and D.M. Gottfredson, *Development of a Data Base for Parole Decision-*

Making, Parole Decision-Making Project, Report 1 (Davis, Calif.: National Council on Crime and Delinquency Research Center, June 1973).

2. For example, a 50 percent sample might be drawn by selecting all cases with register numbers ending in all even or all odd digits. Federal prison register numbers contain eight digits; however, the last three digits are not included in this selection procedure as they refer to the institution number.

3. D.M. Gottfredson and S.M. Singer, *Parole Decision-Making Coding Manual*, Parole Decision-Making Project, Report 2 (Davis, Calif.: National Council on Crime and Delinquency Research Center, June 1973).

4. For cases with arrests but no dispositions during the two-year follow-up period, the arresting agency was contacted to obtain the missing dispositions. If a disposition was not obtained by November 1973, the case was coded as having a favorable outcome.

5. *Uniform Parole Reporting Coding Manual* (Davis, Calif.: Uniform Parole Reports of the National Parole Institutes, National Council on Crime and Delinquency, July 1, 1966).

6. It must be noted, however, that this criterion does not entirely remove the problem concerning the classification of persons returned to prison for technical parole violations (violations not resulting from conviction for a new offense). Since only persons released to parole (or mandatory release) supervision are liable for return to prison for technical violations, the classification of such cases as having unfavorable outcome means that those persons released under supervision are subject to greater risk of being included in the unfavorable outcome category than those released without supervision. On the other hand, if technical violators were classified as having favorable outcomes, parolees would be subject to less risk of being classified as having unfavorable outcome than unsupervised releasees. In the opinion of the researchers, the first alternative appeared as the most desirable for the purpose at hand.

7. Frances H. Simon, *Prediction Methods in Criminology* (London: Her Majesty's Stationery Office, 1971).

8. E.W. Burgess, in A.A. Bruce, E.W. Burgess, and A.J. Harno, "The Working of the Indeterminate Sentence Law in the Parole System in Illinois," (Springfield, Ill.: Illinois Parole Board, 1928).

9. W. Wilbanks and M. Hindelang, "The Comparative Efficiency of Three Predictive Methods," Appendix B in D.M. Gottfredson, L.T. Wilkins, and P.B. Hoffman, *Summarizing Experience for Parole Decision-Making*, Parole Decision-Making Project, Report 5 (Davis, Calif.: National Council on Crime and Delinquency Research Center, 1973).

10. Shrinkage refers to a loss in predictive power as evidenced by a lower correlation coefficient.

11. H. Mannheim and L.T. Wilkins, *Prediction Methods in Relation to Borstal Training* (London: Her Majesty's Stationery Office, 1955); Simon, *Prediction Methods*, chap. 3, pp. 30-57.

12. F.B. Warner, "Factors Determining Parole from the Massachusetts Reformatory," *Journal of Criminal Law and Criminology* 14 (1923):172-207.

13. H. Hart, "Predicting Parole Success," *General Criminal Law and Criminology* 14 (1923):405-413.

14. Burgess, "Working of the Indeterminate Sentence Law "

15. S. Glueck and Eleanor T. Glueck, *Five Hundred Criminal Careers* (New York: Alfred A. Knopf, 1930); *Five Hundred Delinquent Women* (New York: Alfred A. Knopf, 1934); *One-Thousand Juvenile Delinquents* (Cambridge: Harvard University Press, 1934); *Later Criminal Careers* (New York: Commonwealth Fund, 1937); *Juvenile Delinquents Grown Up* (New York: Commonwealth Fund, 1940); *Criminal Careers in Retrospect* (New York: Commonwealth Fund, 1943); *After-Conduct of Discharged Offenders* (New York: MacMillan, 1945); *Unraveling Juvenile Delinquency* (New York: Commonwealth Fund, 1950).

16. G.B. Vold, *Prediction Methods and Parole* (Hanover, N.H.: Sociological Press, 1931).

17. E.D. Monachesi, *Prediction Factors in Probation* (Hanover, N.Y.: Sociological Press, 1932).

18. C. Tibbits, "Success and Failure in Parole Can Be Predicted," *Journal of Criminal Law, Criminology and Police Science* 22 (1931):11-50.

19. W.W. Argow, "A Criminal-Liability Index for Predicting Possibility of Rehabilitation," *Journal of Criminal Law, Criminology and Police Science* 26(4) (1935-36):561-577.

20. *Attorney General's Survey of Release Procedures*, 4: *Parole* (Washington, D.C.: Department of Justice, 1939).

21. L.E. Ohlin, *Selection for Parole, A Manual of Parole Prediction* (New York: Russell Sage Foundation, 1951).

22. M.G. Caldwell, "Preview of a New Type of Probation Study Made in Alabama," *Federal Probation* 15 (June 1951):3-15.

23. A.J. Reiss, "The Accuracy, Efficiency, and Validity of a Prediction Instrument," *American Journal of Sociology* 61 (May 1951):552-561.

24. R. Schiedt, *Ein Beitrag zum Problem der Rukfallsprognose* (Munich, 1936).

25. H. Trunk, *Soziale Prognosen an Strafgefangenen* 28 Monatsschrift fur Kriminalbiologie und Strafeschtsreform, 1937.

26. Gerecke, "Zur Frage der Rückfallsprognose," *Monatsschrift für Kriminalbiologie und Strafrechtsreform*, 30 (1939):35-38.

27. W. Meywerk, "Beitrag zur Bestimmung der sozialen Prognose an Ruckfallsverbrechern," 29 *Monatsschrift*, 1938.

28. E.F. Kohnle, *Die Kriminalitat entlassener Fursorgezoglinge un die Moglichkeit einer Erfolgsprognose* (Leipzig: Kriminalistische Abahandlungen, no. 33, 1938).

29. E. Frey, *Der fruhkriminelle Ruckfallsverbrecher. Criminulite precoce et*

recividisme, Schweizerische Criminalistische Stud., 4 (Basel: Verlag fur Recht und Gesellschaft, 1951).

30. H. Mannheim, *Juvenile Delinquency in an English Middle-Town*, International Library of Sociology and Social Reconstruction (London: Routledge & Kegan Paul, 1948).

31. R.E. Dunham, "Factors Related to Recidivism in Adults," *Journal of Social Psychology* 39 (1954):77-91.

32. D. Glaser, "A Reconsideration of Some Parole Prediction Factors," *American Sociological Review* 19 (1954):335-341.

33. A.J. Reiss, "The Accuracy, Efficiency and Reliability of a Prediction Instrument," diss., University of Chicago, 1949.

34. B.C. Kirby, "Parole Prediction Using Multiple Correlation," *American Journal of Sociology* 59 (1953-54):539-550.

35. Mannheim and Wilkins, *Prediction Methods.*

36. H.P. Bechtoldt, "Selection," in S.S. Stevens, *Handbook of Experimental Psychology* (New York: Wiley, 1951), pp. 1237-1266.

37. The relationship, in the case cited, between the discriminate function and multiple regression methods, is demonstrated in O.R. Porebski "On the Interrelated Nature of the Multivariate Statistics Used in Discriminatory Analysis," *British Journal of Mathematical and Statistical Psychology* 19(2) (November 1966):197-214, p. 202.

38. D. Glaser, "Prediction Tables as Accounting Devices for Judges and Parole Boards," *Crime and Delinquency* 8(3) (1962):239-258.

39. P. MacNaughton-Smith, *Some Statistical and Other Numerical Techniques for Classifying Individuals* (London: Her Majesty's Stationery Office, 1965).

40. L.T. Wilkins and P. MacNaughton-Smith, "New Prediction and Classification Methods in Criminology," *Journal of Research in Crime and Delinquency* 1 (1954):19-32.

41. T. Grygier, *Treatment Variables in Nonlinear Predictions*, paper presented to the joint annual meeting of the American Society of Criminology and the American Association for the Advancement of Science, in Montreal, December 1964.

42. K.B. Ballard, Jr., and D.M. Gottfredson, *Predictive Attribute Analysis and the Prediction of Parole Performance* (Vacaville, Calif.: Institute for the Study of Crime and Delinquency, December 1963).

43. D. Glaser, *The Effectiveness of a Prison and Parole System* (New York: Bobbs-Merrill, 1964). See especially chapters 2, 3, 4, and 13, which deal generally with the prediction problem and specifically with federal offenders and the United States Board of Parole.

44. J.W. Mannering and D.V. Babst, *Wisconsin Base Expectancies for Adult Male Parolees*, Progress Report No. 4, Wisconsin State Department of Public Welfare, Bureau of Research in Division of Corrections, April 1963.

45. D.V. Babst, J.A. Inciardi, and Dorothy R. Jaman, "The Uses of Configural Analysis in Parole Prediction Research," *Canadian Journal of Criminology and Corrections* 13(3) (1971):200-208.

46. D.M. Gottfredson et al., *Wisconsin Base Expectancies for Reformatories and Prisons* (Vacaville, Calif.: Institute for the Study of Crime and Delinquency, June 1965).

47. D.M. Gottfredson and K.B. Ballard, Jr., *Association Analysis, Predictive Attribute Analysis, and Parole Behavior*, paper presented at the Western Psychological Association meetings, Portland, Oregon, April 1964.

48. W.T. Williams and J.M. Lambert, "Multivariate Methods in Plant Ecology: Parts I, II and III," *Journal of Ecology* 47 (1959):83-101; 48 (1960):680-710; 49 (1961):717-729.

49. L.T. Wilkins and P. MacNaughton-Smith, "New Prediction and Classification Methods in Criminology," *Journal of Research in Crime and Delinquency* 1 (1954):19-32; and L.T. Wilkins, "What is Prediction and is it Necessary in Evaluating Treatment?" in *Research and Potential Application of Research in Probation, Parole, and Delinquency Prediction* (New York: Citizens' Committee for Children of New York, Research Center, New York School of Social Work, Columbia University, July 1961).

50. D.M. Gottfredson, K.B. Ballard, Jr., and L. Lane, *Association Analysis in a Prison Sample and Prediction of Parole Performance* (Vacaville, Calif.: Institute for the Study of Crime and Delinquency, November 1963).

51. D.M. Gottfredson, and K.B. Ballard, Jr., *Offender Classification in Parole Prediction* (Vacaville, Calif.: Institute for the Study of Crime and Delinquency, December 1966).

52. See, for example, D.M. Gottfredson and R.F. Beverly, "Development and Operational Use of Prediction Methods in Correctional Work," *Proceedings of the Social Statistics Section* (Washington, D.C.: American Statistical Association, 1962); D.M. Gottfredson and K.B. Ballard, Jr., *The Validity of Two Parole Prediction Scales: An Eight-Year Follow-Up Study* (Vacaville, Calif.: Institute for the Study of Crime and Delinquency, 1965), Department of Youth Authority, *The Status of Current Research* (Sacramento: State of California, 1968), pp. 47-52; R.F. Beverly, *A Comparative Analysis of Base Expectancy Tables for Selected Subpopulations of California Youth Authority Wards* (Sacramento: Department of Youth Authority, State of California, 1968); H.G. Gough, E.A. Wenk, and V.P. Rozynko, "Parole Outcome as Predicted from the CPI, the MMPI, and A Base Expectancy Table," *Journal of Abnormal Psychology* 70(6) (December 1965):432-441.

53. Mannheim and Wilkins, *Prediction Methods.*

54. D.M. Gottfredson, "Assessment and Prediction Methods in Crime and Delinquency," *Task Force Report: Juvenile Delinquency and Youth Crime*, The President's Commission on Law Enforcement and Administration of Justice (Washington, D.C.: Government Printing Office, 1967).

55. Simon, *Prediction Methods.*

56. Gottfredson and Singer, *Development of Data Base and Parole Decision-Making.*

57. J. Berkson, "Cost Utility as a Measure of Efficiency of a Test," *Journal of the American Statistical Association* 42 (1947):246-255; see also, J.A. Inciardi, D.V. Babst, and M. Koval, "Computing Mean Cost Ratings (MCR)," *Journal of Research in Crime and Delinquency* 10 (1973):22-28.

58. See chapter 2.

59. D.M. Gottfredson, "Efficiency of Two Methods of Prediction of Parole Success," paper presented at the Western Psychological Association Meeting, April 1960, San Jose, California.

60. Ohlin, *Selection for Parole*; Glaser, "Reconsideration of Prediction Factors"; Gottfredson and Beverly, "Development of Prediction Methods"; Gottfredson and Ballard, *Validity of Prediction Scales.*

61. Gottfredson, "Assessment in Crime and Delinquency."

62. Ibid.

63. Gottfredson and Singer, *Parole Decision-Making.*

64. See L.T. Wilkins, *The Problem of Overlap in Experience Table Construction*, Parole Decision-Making Project, Report 3 (Davis, Calif.: National Council on Crime and Delinquency Research Center, 1973).

65. Short-term cases (sentence of one year and one day or less) and cases released to detainer or deportation warrants were excluded. Thirty-two other cases selected for this sample could not be located or contained insufficient file material and, thus, were also excluded.

66. Identification Division "rap sheets" and CCH printouts contain the same material with the exception that certain petty offenses (e.g., drunkenness, gambling, vagrancy) are specifically excluded from the CCH system (National Crime Information Center, 1974). To ensure comparability, CCH coding rules were followed to exclude such offenses from consideration in those cases in which the identification "rap sheets" provided the data base.

67. Plus all cases released by expiration of sentence (without release supervision).

68. For example, in 157 cases an arrest without disposition which might have affected the outcome code was noted. There were, in addition, a significant number of arrests without dispositions which did not affect the outcome code.

69. The first letters were mailed March 6, 1975.

70. There were twenty-six cases (approximately 3 percent of the total sample) receiving suspended sentences or probation, some of whom may have been classified as having favorable outcome using the 1972 criterion and unfavorable outcome using the 1970 criterion.

71. As mentioned in note 66, arrests and convictions for certain petty offenses have been excluded from consideration.

72. The differences in slopes between criterion measure X, criterion

measure Y, and criterion measure Z are statistically significant at the 0.001 level (X vs. Y: $t = 5.100$, $df = 2018$; Y vs. Z: $t = 5.333$, $df = 2018$; X vs. Z: $t = 10.190$, $df = 2018$) (McNemar, 1962: 143).

73. The overall favorable outcome rate is 74 percent for criterion measure X, 68.4 percent for criterion measure Y, and 59.5 percent for criterion measure Z.

The Sanctioning Dimension

Recent explorations of parole decision making by the United States Board of Parole, described in chapter 2, have revealed that these decisions generally are based upon three major considerations: seriousness of offense, parole prognosis, and institutional performance. The factor of offense severity especially appears to be given substantial weight in determining the amount of time to be served before release. In the interest of providing a rational and consistent paroling policy, explicit decision guidelines (which display the customary range of time to be served before release for combinations of severity, risk, and institutional performance) were developed and are currently being used by the board as a tool in actual case decision making.

Even with explicit guidelines relating time to be served to these major considerations, decision inequity or disparity still may present a problem, especially in relation to the factor of offense severity. That is, if similar offense behaviors are given different severity ratings by different decision makers, different (disparate) decisions are likely to result. This chapter reports the results of two exercises conducted with decision makers of the United States Board of Parole in an effort to develop a method for producing more consistent offense severity judgments and, thus, more equitable decisions.

Method

The subjects for this study were all eight hearing examiners and all eight board members of the United States Board of Parole. They were asked to complete exercises which involved ranking a number of offense descriptions in accordance with their judgments as to the severity of the offense behavior involved. These descriptions, derived from experience in coding a large sample of federal offender files during the Parole Decision-making project, were designed to reflect offense behaviors (rather than purely legal categories) commonly seen by the parole board.

Two separate exercises were conducted during a two-month period (February and March 1973). Each involved sorting a deck of 3-by-5 cards (each containing an offense description) into a number of severity classifications.

Adapted from P.B. Hoffman, J.L. Beck, and L.K. DeGostin, *The Practical Application of a Severity Scale*, Parole Decision-Making Project, Report 13 (Davis, Calif.: National Council on Crime and Delinquency Research Center, June 1973) pp. 1-31.

Descriptions of offense behaviors were sorted on a scale from least to most serious using a seven- (exercise 1) and then a six- (exercise 2) category scale.

Originally, there were 224 offense descriptions to be ranked. As this number appeared unwieldy, it was reduced after a pretest to sixty-five offense descriptions. These were generally short statements explaining the offense behavior (for example, armed robbery, embezzlement less than $20,000, possession of heavy narcotics by addict less than $500), one per card.

It is to be noted that, in actual practice, the determination of the seriousness of an offense presents several problems. It is often difficult or impossible to obtain an accurate picture of the actual behavior involved in the offense. The offender's account may be drastically different from the official version reported in the presentence investigation. Moreover, the legal offense of commitment often cannot be considered an accurate behavioral description owing to the procedures of plea bargaining. Furthermore, there may be many shades of variations of behavior lumped into the same legal category without regard for what might be considered to be aggravating or mitigating circumstances. Similarly, the length of the maximum sentence cannot be relied upon as a good indicant of the offense severity owing to the considerable variations (disparity) in sentencing among judges. Nevertheless, in day-to-day decision making, examiners and board members are faced with making these determinations as best they can.

Exercise 1

Exercise 1 was designed to examine the agreement among examiners and board members in rating the set of offense descriptions and to provide a feedback device to display the results produced.

In this exercise, subjects were asked to sort the deck of offense behavior cards into seven piles numbered 1 to 7 (with pile 1 labeled "least serious" and pile 7 labeled "most serious"). This provided a seven-point severity scale. Exercise 1 was completed by each hearing examiner twice. The elapsed time between trials was at least three days and no more than three weeks. In addition, each board member completed this exercise once.

Each subject completed the exercise individually and was given the following instructions orally:

This deck of cards contains a number of different offense behaviors, one per card. You may briefly look through the cards to see the type of offense behaviors listed. Please place each of the cards into one of the seven piles (numbered 1 to 7) in front of you according to your judgment as to the severity of the offense behavior listed. If you consider the offense description to be too vague or too broad, imagine the most typical offense behavior with that description. As you will note, pile number seven is labeled "most serious" while pile number one is labeled "least serious." Please do not deliberate for more than a few minutes on each card and do not rearrange a card once you have sorted it.

The cards were thoroughly shuffled before each trial. However, the offense description considered the most serious (planned homicide) was placed at the top of the deck each time, enabling the person administering the exercise to watch for any confusion as to the direction of the scale.

After the cards were sorted, the number of the pile chosen was marked on the back of each card. Subjects were allowed to watch this procedure and to compare their ratings with those of the persons preceding them (and, for the hearing examiners, to compare their second trial responses with those of their first trial). This immediate feedback, although limited, added interest to the proceeding and appeared to be of substantial help in obtaining willing (as opposed to passive) cooperation in the exercise. Although it was specifically pointed out to both examiners and members that their responses would not be identified by name, this did not appear to be of concern to either group and, subsequently, comparisons of responses between and among individuals were made freely.

Findings

Table 4-1 shows the average rating for the two trials given to each offense description by each examiner (and the examiner group combined). The offense descriptions are listed in order of average severity rating (for the examiner group combined) from least to most serious.

It may be seen that there was fairly high agreement among the examiners' ratings. A measure of reliability[1] (*r*) was calculated and showed a coefficient of 0.97. Ratings which deviated by more than one full point from the average (mean) for the group are marked (higher ratings are bracketed; lower ratings are italicized). It is noted that 85 percent of all ratings were within one point of the group mean. The reliability of ratings between the first and second trials was also high. A correlation (Pearson's *r*) between ratings on the first and second trials for the entire examiner group was calculated and showed a coefficient of 0.84.

After completion of this exercise, individual feedback was provided to each participant. Table 4-1 was distributed to each examiner and a card identifying the examiner by letter (A to H) was attached. In this way, examiners could examine their consistency as a group concerning the offense descriptions, as well as see how their individual ratings varied from the group average. As noted, individual scores which differed by more than one point from the group average were italicized (if below the average) or bracketed (if above the average). In addition, these results were discussed by the research staff and examiners on an informal basis both individually and at the examiners' monthly meeting in

Table 4-1
Examiners' Severity Ratings (Two Trials)

Offense	A	B	C	D	E	F	G	H	Group Average
	Average Rating by Examiner								
Prostitution	1.5	1.0	1.0	1.0	1.5	1.0	[2.5]	1.0	*1.3*
Liquor law	1.5	1.5	1.0	1.0	1.5	1.0	[2.5]	1.0	*1.4*
Immigration laws	1.0	1.5	1.0	2.0	1.0	1.0	[3.0]	1.5	*1.5*
Walkaway	2.0	2.0	1.0	1.0	1.0	1.0	2.0	2.0	*1.5*
Checks, insufficient funds	1.5	1.0	1.5	2.0	2.5	1.0	2.0	[3.0]	*1.8*
Selective Service	2.0	1.5	1.5	2.0	1.5	1.0	[4.0]	1.0	*1.8*
Possession of marijuana under $500	1.5	1.5	*1.0*	2.0	2.5	2.0	3.0	3.0	*2.1*
Other theft under $999	2.5	2.0	*1.0*	2.5	2.5	2.5	2.5	3.0	*2.3*
Income tax evasion	2.0	2.5	*1.0*	2.0	3.0	2.0	[5.0]	3.5	*2.6*
Possession of other than marijuana or heroin under $500	2.0	2.0	*1.5*	2.0	3.5	2.5	3.5	[4.0]	*2.6*
Receiving stolen property under $999	2.5	2.5	*1.0*	3.0	3.0	3.0	3.0	3.0	*2.6*
Possession of other than marijuana or heroin $500-$4,999	2.0	3.0	2.0	2.5	3.0	2.5	3.5	3.5	*2.8*
Sale of marijuana under $500	2.0	2.5	*1.0*	3.0	3.0	2.5	3.5	[4.5]	*2.8*
Theft of vehicle for own use	2.5	3.5	*1.5*	2.0	2.0	[4.0]	3.0	3.5	*2.8*
Possession of marijuana $500-$4,999	2.5	3.0	*1.0*	2.5	3.0	3.0	3.5	[4.0]	*2.8*
Sale of other than marijuana or heroin under $500	2.0	2.0	*1.5*	2.5	[4.5]	2.5	3.5	[4.0]	*2.8*

Table 4-1 (cont.)

Offense	Average Rating by Examiner								Group Average
	A	B	C	D	E	F	G	H	
National Firearms Act	3.0	3.5	2.5	3.0	3.0	3.0	3.0	2.0	2.9
Larceny, confidence games	[4.0]	[4.5]	1.0	3.0	2.5	2.5	3.0	3.0	2.9
Postal theft	3.0	2.5	2.0	3.0	3.0	3.0	3.0	[4.0]	2.9
Interstate theft under $999	3.0	3.5	1.5	2.5	3.0	3.5	3.0	4.0	3.0
Sale of marijuana $500-$4,999	2.5	3.5	1.0	3.0	3.5	3.0	3.5	4.0	3.0
Escape	3.5	4.5	3.5	2.0	4.0	3.0	2.5	2.5	3.2
Burglary other than dwelling	4.0	4.0	3.0	3.5	3.0	2.5	3.0	4.0	3.4
Counterfeiting under $999	3.0	3.5	3.0	3.5	3.0	3.5	3.0	[5.0]	3.4
Other theft $1,000-$20,000	3.5	3.5	2.0	3.0	4.0	3.5	4.0	4.0	3.4
Receiving stolen property $1,000-$20,000	3.0	[4.5]	2.0	3.5	3.5	3.0	4.0	4.0	3.4
Embezzlement, $20,000 or less	3.5	3.5	2.0	3.5	3.5	3.0	[5.0]	4.0	3.5
Forgery, fraud, larceny, by check or credit card	4.5	4.5	2.5	3.0	3.0	3.0	4.0	3.5	3.5
Possession of marijuana $5,000 or over	3.5	3.5	1.5	3.5	4.5	3.5	3.5	4.5	3.5
Statutory sex offenses	3.0	3.0	1.0	3.0	3.0	[5.0]	[5.5]	4.5	3.5
Possession other than marijuana or heroin $5,000 or over	3.5	4.0	2.0	3.0	4.0	3.0	4.5	4.5	3.6

Table 4-1 (cont.)

Offense	Average Rating by Examiner								Group Average
	A	B	C	D	E	F	G	H	
Sell marijuana $5,000 or over	2.5	[5.0]	2.0	3.5	4.0	3.5	4.0	4.0	3.6
Theft of vehicle for resale	3.5	4.0	3.5	3.0	3.0	4.5	3.5	3.5	3.6
Interstate theft $1,000-$20,000	4.5	4.0	2.0	3.0	3.5	3.5	4.0	4.5	3.6
Possession of heroin under $500	3.5	4.5	2.5	3.5	3.5	3.5	4.0	[5.0]	3.8
Possession of heroin $500-$4,999	3.0	4.5	2.5	4.0	3.5	3.5	[5.0]	[5.0]	3.9
Sale of heroin under $500 to support own use	3.0	4.0	2.5	4.0	4.0	4.0	4.0	[5.5]	3.9
Sale of other than marijuana or heroin $500-$4,999	4.0	4.5	2.5	3.5	4.0	3.5	[5.0]	4.0	3.9
Assault–no weapon, no serious injury	2.5	3.5	4.5	3.0	4.5	4.0	[6.0]	3.5	3.9
Sale other than marijuana or heroin $5,000 or over	3.5	4.0	3.0	4.5	4.0	3.0	[5.0]	4.5	3.9
Burglary of a dwelling	5.0	[5.5]	3.0	5.0	3.0	3.0	3.0	4.5	4.0
Sale of heroin under $500 for profit	3.0	4.0	2.5	4.5	4.0	4.0	4.5	[5.5]	4.0
Sale of heroin $500-$4,999 to support own use	3.5	4.5	2.5	4.0	3.5	4.0	4.5	[5.5]	4.0
Counterfeiting $1,000-$20,000	4.0	4.0	4.0	4.5	3.5	4.0	4.0	5.0	4.1

Table 4-1 (cont.)

Offense	A	B	C	D	E	F	G	H	Group Average
Other theft over $20,000	4.5	4.5	3.5	4.5	4.5	3.5	4.0	4.5	4.2
Embezzlement over $20,000	4.5	4.5	3.0	4.0	4.5	4.0	5.0	4.5	4.2
Interstate theft over $20,000	4.0	5.0	3.0	4.5	5.0	4.0	3.5	5.0	4.2
Receiving stolen property over $20,000	4.5	4.5	3.5	4.5	4.5	4.5	4.0	4.5	4.3
Possession of heroin $5,000 or over	4.5	4.5	2.5	4.0	5.0	4.0	[5.5]	5.0	4.4
Sell heroin $5,000 or over to support own use	4.0	4.0	3.0	4.5	4.5	4.5	5.0	[5.5]	4.4
Assault with weapon, no serious injury	4.0	3.5	5.0	3.5	5.0	4.5	[6.5]	4.0	4.5
Sell heroin $500-$4,999 for profit	4.5	4.5	3.0	5.0	4.0	4.5	5.0	5.5	4.5
Counterfeiting over $20,000	4.5	5.0	4.5	5.0	4.0	5.0	4.5	5.0	4.7
Unarmed robbery	4.0	5.5	4.0	4.0	5.0	5.0	[6.0]	5.0	4.8
Extortion	4.5	5.5	5.5	6.0	4.0	3.5	6.0	5.5	5.1
Sell heroin $5,000 or over for profit	5.0	5.0	3.5	5.5	5.5	5.0	5.0	6.0	5.1
Assault, serious injury	5.5	4.0	5.5	4.5	6.0	6.0	[7.0]	5.5	5.5
Assault, weapon and serious injury	5.0	5.0	5.5	5.5	6.0	6.5	[7.0]	5.5	5.6

Column header: *Average Rating by Examiner*

Table 4-1 (cont.)

Offense	*Average Rating by Examiner*								Group Average
	A	B	C	D	E	F	G	H	
Armed robbery	6.0	6.0	5.0	5.0	6.0	6.0	[7.0]	6.0	*5.9*
Unplanned homicide	5.5	*4.5*	6.5	5.5	7.0	6.0	7.0	6.0	*6.0*
Kidnapping other than for ransom	*5.0*	6.0	5.5	6.0	7.0	6.0	7.0	6.5	*6.1*
Forcible rape and other forcible sex offenses	6.0	6.0	6.0	6.0	6.0	7.0	7.0	6.5	*6.3*
Homicide during commission of a felony	6.0	6.5	7.0	6.5	7.0	7.0	7.0	7.0	*6.8*
Kidnapping for ransom	6.5	7.0	6.0	7.0	7.0	7.0	7.0	6.5	*6.8*
Planned homicide	7.0	7.0	7.0	7.0	7.0	7.0	7.0	7.0	*7.0*

February 1973. Responses were compared freely at this meeting, and a lively discussion concerning the appropriate ratings for the various offense descriptions ensued with an acknowledged concern for the development of a consistent policy as a prominent theme.

Agreement among the board members was also quite high ($r = 0.95$); 83 percent of their ratings were within one point of their group mean.

Individual feedback concerning their ratings in this exercise was given to the board members. As with the examiner group, a table showing the board members' ratings was distributed with a card identifying the member by letter attached. Responses differing from the average by more than one point were marked; however, extensive discussion concerning this feedback was not encouraged at this time. Rather, this exercise was described as a preliminary stage to acquaint the board members with the scale concept, as an improved variation of the exercise (to be described) had been developed and was ready for testing.

Exercise 2

In this exercise, members were asked to sort a modified deck containing fifty-one cards[2] into six piles labeled "low severity," "low/moderate severity," "moderate severity," "high severity," "very high severity," and "greatest severity" offenses, producing a six-point severity scale.[3]

In contrast to exercise 1, in which first impressions were desired and respondents were discouraged from deliberating more than a minute or so on each card, in exercise 2 the members were encouraged to deliberate on each choice carefully. Generally, each board member kept the deck of cards for a full day. Also, in contrast to exercise 1, the board members were asked to place the cards into the six piles as if playing solitaire; that is, the cards were to be arranged so that all could be seen simultaneously. Furthermore, they were encouraged to recheck their choices and make as many changes as desired. Thus, while exercise 1 was designed to produce a feedback measure that would be administered quickly and efficiently, exercise 2 was designed to assist in the formulation of a carefully thought out prospective policy. As each member returned the cards in six piles, a sheet was prepared which listed the offense descriptions placed in each of the six severity categories.

Guideline Modification—A Practical Application

At the March 1973 business meeting of the board, the first six-month pilot project guideline modification consideration was scheduled. Part of this consideration involved the refinement of the guideline severity scale. Each member was given a copy of his own rating sheet as well as the pooled ratings for the group. Table 4-2 illustrates the pooled rating sheet. The members then discussed and voted as to the appropriate severity level for each of the offense descriptions to be used (for the next six-month period) in the decision guidelines.

Several related offense descriptions (for example, "possession of marijuana over $5,000" and "possession of marijuana $500-$5,000") were combined as the board members had placed them at the same level. Moreover, two offense descriptions were added upon the suggestion and vote of the board members. These were: "counterfeiter" and "possession of heavy narcotics by addict—$500 or more." The results of this policy determination are shown in table 4-3 and may be compared both with the original guidelines and with a more recent modification, which appear in chapter 2.

Conclusions

It is likely that the perceived seriousness of the offense behavior for which an offender has been committed will continue to be one of the major factors considered in parole selection decision making. The exercises conducted in this study were utilized by the United States Board of Parole in developing an explicit prospective policy regarding this factor. This usage represents a practical attempt by an operating criminal justice agency to develop a tool to aid in making more consistent severity judgments and, thus, more equitable decisions.

Table 4-2

Pooled Rating Sheet Examples: Guideline (Severity Rating) Consideration, Board Meeting, March 1973

Offense	Low	Low Moderate	Moderate	High	Very High	Greatest
Immigration Law Violations	* xxxx xxx	x				
Walkaway	* xxxxxx	xx				
Minor theft (includes larceny and simple possession of stolen property, less than $1,000)	* xx xxxx	xx *				
Alcohol Law Violations	x	xxxx xxx *				
Selective Service	xx	xxxx	xx			
Mann Act (no force—commercial purposes)	xx	* xxxx *	x	x		
Theft from Mail		xxxx	xx	xx		
Forgery/fraud (less than $1,000)		* xxxxx	xxx			
Possession of Marijuana (less than $500)	x	* xxxxx	xx			
Passing/possession of counterfeit currency (less than $1,000)		* xxxx	xxxx			
Simple theft of motor vehicle (not multiple or for resale)	x	xxx	* xxxx			
Theft/forgery/fraud $1,000-$20,000			* xxxxx	xxx		
Possession of marijuana $500-5,000		xxx	* xxxxx			
Possession of marijuana $5,000 or over			* xxxxx	xxx		

Notes: Each "x" indicates one vote.
Asterisk indicates final outcome of Board vote.

Table 4-3
A Prospective Policy Regarding Offense Severity
(Board Meeting, March 1973)

Category A: Low Severity Offenses

Immigration law violations; walkaway; minor theft (includes larceny and simple possession of stolen property less than $1,000).

Category B: Low/Moderate Severity Offenses

Alcohol law violations; Selective Service; Mann Act (no force–commercial purposes); theft from mail; forgery/fraud (less than $1,000); possession of marijuana (less than $500); passing/possession of counterfeit currency (less than $1,000).

Category C: Moderate Severity Offenses

Simple theft of motor vehicle (not multiple theft or for resale); theft, forgery/fraud ($1,000-$20,000); possession of marijuana ($500 or over); possession of other "soft drugs" (less than $5,000); sale of marijuana (less than $5,000); sale of other "soft drugs" (less than $500); possession of "heavy narcotics" (by addict–less than $500); receiving stolen property with intent to resell (less than $20,000); embezzlement (less than $20,000); passing/possession of counterfeit currency ($1,000-$20,000); interstate transportation of stolen/forged securities (less than $20,000).

Category D: High Severity Offenses

Theft, forgery/fraud (over $20,000); sale of marijuana ($5,000 or more); sale of other "soft drugs" ($500-$5,000); possession of other "soft drugs" (more than $5,000); sale of "heavy narcotics" to support own habit; receiving stolen property ($20,000 or over); embezzlement ($20,000-$100,000); passing/possession of counterfeit currency (more than $20,000); counterfeiter; interstate transportation of stolen/forged securities ($20,000 or more); possession of "heavy narcotics" (by addict–$500 or more); sexual act (fear–no injury); burglary (bank or post office); robbery (no weapon or injury); organized vehicle theft.

Category E: Very High Severity Offenses

Extortion; assault (serious injury); Mann Act (force; armed robbery; sexual act (force –injury); sale of "soft drugs" (other than marijuana–more than $5,000); possession of "heavy narcotics" (nonaddict); sale of "heavy narcotics" for profit.

Category F: Greatest Severity Offenses

Aggravated armed robbery (or other felony)–weapon fired or serious injury during offense; kidnapping; willful homicide.

Furthermore, the applicability of these or similar methods for use in other criminal justice decisions (for example, sentencing or prosecution priority) appears straightforward.

It is to be stressed that the use of this rating scale in actual case decision making is not intended to make the offense severity decision automatic. The factors surrounding each individual's offense still must be considered in each decision, and the use of this scale does not, in any way, reduce the opportunity for that. It merely displays board policy for the more frequent offense types and, indeed, may thereby allow the decision makers more time to focus on those cases with special mitigating or aggravating factors. For example, cases in which the offense behavior actually involves a series of separate offenses may be treated as exceptions. Moreover, the rating scale does not attempt to include all offense behaviors. Those that are not listed may be judged properly by comparison with similar offenses that are listed.

Like any other policy, monitoring and the provision for periodic revision are necessary to prevent rigidity. For example, the public attitude toward a particular offense (possession of marijuana) may change over time. Since the board is mandated to act as an agent of society, a corresponding change in board policy may be deemed desirable. As part of explicit guideline usage, the board has provided that at least once every six months formal consideration be given to guideline modification, including reevaluation of the offense severity rating scale.

Notes

1. A.L. Edwards, *Statistical Methods for the Behavioral Sciences* (New York: Holt, Rinehart, and Winston, 1956), pp. 412-413.

2. These modifications resulted from discussions with examiners and board members during exercise 1 concerning the specificity of certain offense definitions or their frequency of occurrence.

3. This conformed with the six-point severity scale, formed by combining offense behaviors with similar times served into six categories, which was used in the original pilot project guidelines.

5

Information in Decision Making: The Prediction Problem

Present Position

The problem of estimating the probability of recidivism of offenders by the use of data available at different points throughout the criminal justice process has been referred to many times in this book and elsewhere. It has been noted that simple methods of weighting information may be more useful than more complex methods, when the tables so calculated have been applied to samples drawn later than those upon which the initial information was based.

It has also been shown that information recorded about offenders is not without error.[1] There is a possibility that errors in the data-base (upon which the prediction tables have been calculated) may be an explanation of the failure of the more complex methods to show superior results. This has been explored to some degree, and the results to date give support to this possibility.

It is clear, also, that those of us who have concerned ourselves with the building of prediction tables have not been as flexible in our thinking as we might. We have tended to use those few methods that we thought were best (being perhaps a little too easily convinced by theory), and we have not explored the several hundreds of possible combinations and permutations of methods that may be developed from the known mathematical models. While we should, perhaps, take the blame for being persuaded to look only at a few methods (and usually those which had been tried before in the field!), we must plead that money for merely playing with different forms of equations has not been forthcoming in criminal justice research.

Do We Need Efficient Prediction Tables?

To ask whether efficient prediction tables are needed may seem like the beginning of a heresy, or perhaps a capitulation to those who have always claimed that decision makers did not need any assistance of this kind. Heresy it may be, but capitulation it is not. If prediction tables are to be superseded, then they must be replaced by something that does the job better. The problem, of course, is in defining the terms *the job* and *better*.

Perhaps we should first clear up a few points of terminology. Without a

Adapted from L.T. Wilkins, *Inefficient Statistics*, Parole Decision-Making Project, Report 6 (Davis, Calif.: National Council on Crime and Delinquency Research Center, June 1973).

doubt, regression equations and related techniques will always be required for appropriate purposes in research designs. When we have mentioned prediction tables, however, we have in mind more than the research operations with various forms of equations. Rather, we have in mind the provision of tables that may be referred to by decision makers. That is, the use of the provided estimates (of whatever form) is not seen as confined to the making of inferences in terms of research results, but extends to the use in some decisions by persons other than the research workers themselves. Statistical methods are generally assessed in terms of the appropriateness to the research questions. When we consider a more general purpose instrument, in the form of a prediction table, a different question of utility arises. The provision of different kinds of instruments can be assessed only in terms of the user requirements, and the users of the prediction tables are not primarily research workers. If different users are using an instrument, then, presumably, it will have differing functions. If designers of prediction tables have shown some rigidity in their thinking about data and the means for adding them together, perhaps this rigidity has also infected their thinking about the kinds of instruments that other kinds of users should find useful. We should examine our methodologies—which have been expanded very considerably in recent years—to see what we have in our tool kit that might be appropriately developed to provide instruments of value to decision makers in the criminal justice process. It has been said that if a man can make a better mousetrap than anyone else, a path will be beaten to his door. But perhaps the purpose that "mousetraps" are supposed to serve is better met by a quite different approach—not a trap at all! There is an implicit suggestion in this old proverb that improvements are better than innovations! Perhaps we should not devote too much attention to "making better mousetraps"!

Whether we look for the construction of instruments that will satisfy different needs, or look for different ways of providing for the needs we believe (or believed) were met by the provisions of prediction tables, it is still important to know where we stand about the problems of prediction. At the moment, we do not have very firm ground upon which to stand; and we need firm ground from which to make any leap forward. So, before departing from the general area of prediction tables, let us consider the present state of the art or science.

Untried Methods

Sequential methods have not been used in criminal prediction. This means that a large area of mathematical model building is still unexplored, even though it seems highly attractive as a means for increasing the utility and precision of prediction equations. There is, of course, still considerable hope that sequential methods might be developed. Perhaps as an interim measure, we should now also examine a related area, which also has not been explored in the criminal justice field, namely, the use of "dynamic coding." Although this method may have considerable promise, the difficulty has been that the kinds of projects that are concerned with the exploration of models do not commend themselves to fund granting agencies who find the level of abstraction too high and do not define this work as within their area of support.

Possible Improvements in Prediction Table Building

In the usual coding of data for input to multiple regression analysis, we have sought quick and simple methods. The main reason for this strategy has been its relative economy in terms of computer programming time and the emphasis on quick, practical results, rather than development of mathematical models in their own right. The basic data have been taken in almost their original form and coded into categories. The processed data have resembled closely the case files and the way in which information has been considered by clinical decision makers. Indeed, much of our thinking about what now appear to be statistical problems has been conditioned by the clinical viewpoint. We have fallen into the cognitive bind in which others in the field have already become confined. It would have been possible from the start to take the statistical viewpoint and to reject any clinical reference bias. It may be that more power could have been achieved from the equations if this kind of approach had been taken. This must now be examined. Further, there is no need to stay with either approach; we can work for a while, with certain data, as though the clinical viewpoint did not ex.st, and later (with other data) we can take up again the clinical reference. The utility of any model is in terms of how well it works; it is not dependent upon the theory upon which it is based. Indeed, theory has a way of following successful demonstration as well as sometimes leading it!

Dynamic Coding

In coding data about offenders, we have usually noted such things as whether they had previously served time on probation or in a local jail. However, we have not coded the sequence of these events. Is a period in jail that follows a period on probation the same thing as a period on probation that follows a period in jail? Our methods of data handling have usually assumed that this is so. This is, of course, only one example of a sequence that is ignored in the usual forms of coding of data about offenders. If the data are not coded, the information is not included in the building of prediction equations. In addition to the sequence of treatment factors, it may be thought that the sequence of offenses is important. Is a person who reveals a "rake's progress" not different in some way from a person who seems to commit different types of crimes almost at random? There seems to be some probability of our picking up some previously unexplained variance by looking at the time factor and incorporating some aspects of sequence into the code for the information. Now, clearly, if we utilize sequence in respect of all items where sequence could be used, we are expending "degrees of freedom" at a fast rate. However, the few studies that have looked at this kind of issue have found that there are "lines of aggregation" in terms of sequence.

Dynamic coding of data from the past is of similar form to the use of sequential factors. However, it is possible to look at sequences in a somewhat different way. It is possible to take the individual as his own control and to consider factors about him as variants of his prior behavior rather than, or in addition to, variants of behavior on the part of persons in general. Instead of the norm being that of the sample of offenders, the norm in this model is that of the individual person who deviates from his own norm from time to time and in different ways. This is usually termed *ipsative* scoring. Again, this kind of use of data has not been explored. We will look further into this method later.

Multiple Coding and Free Scales

If we free ourselves from the clinical reference and the ways in which such a reference set relates to the ways in which we perceive classifications, we can substitute for clinical kinds of categories those determined by other assumptions. There is no reason to expect (unless we are tied to some theoretical framework) that the scales of variables will be monotonic. There is no essential ordering of the classifications except in terms of some theory. We loosely use the term *higher level occupations* for those that are highly regarded or are paid more or paid less frequently; but these are not necessarily the same kinds of scales, nor are the values necessarily positively correlated. If we were to classify occupations in terms of the concept of psychological stress, we would have a very different ordering from that which we might obtain if we had some other concept as our reference. Thus, the ordering of the input variables is usually determined in terms of some theory or perceptual set. There has been a tendency in the classification of input data for prediction tables to use those sets that are commonly found in the field of criminal justice, namely the sociological or psychological reference set. If the purpose of the building of prediction tables were to test psychological or sociological theory, this might be appropriate. But we are not proposing to test existing theory. We are using methods in relation to a decision framework where the criterion is *not how right or wrong some particular theorist was, but how well the particular method of handling the data carries out some function.* We can specify this function in terms of the behavior of offenders and of decision makers in the criminal justice process. Our reference can be independent of constraints suggested by any theory of crime.

Constraints of some kind must, of course, be accepted; indeed, their nature in any model is a matter for research design, as in any other aspect of research methodology. But we may develop models that fit different forms of constraints and test each in turn against experience and observations of behavior. The reference used in such models may be that of statistical probability and decision theory. If this is accepted, we see that we can regard all variables for our purposes (including those which relate to measurements such as intelligence or other scales) as free from constraints as to the intervals or even the direction of the initially proposed scales. We may then examine the relations between various cuts in the continua with a view to estimation of the odds for such division being associated with recidivism or as relating to any other category that we wish to predict.

Stable Predictors

There is no particular reason to expect that items of information that accord with theory will be more stable over time or over groups in their association with criteria of interest to us than items for which there is no plausible theory. What constitutes plausible theory at this time is wholly or mainly derived from observations of the past. Many of the observations were based on biased samples, with observers influenced to look for factors that fitted their prior theoretical reference set.

If items of information are to be used in prediction equations, they should tend to be stable over time as well as resistant to variation due to coding errors or errors of observation and recording. It has generally been assumed that if the samples of individuals were drawn according to sound statistical procedures, the variance of the factors measured would fit statistical theory—the normal curve (Gaussian), the binomial distribution, the Poisson distribution, and the like could be assumed to apply. However, such assumptions may be expected to hold only where the population sampled is homogeneous with respect to time (or place). It is not reasonable to assume that incarcerated populations are so stable or homogeneous. It is known that prediction tables worked out for one sample do not work on other samples of different populations of offenders. Often there is no expectation that tables should work for different populations. However, we do expect the same prediction equations to hold for similar populations over time. While there are certain uses to which prediction tables can be put, even where they relate only to construction samples, it is usually assumed that what was good in the construction sample will be good in the validation and other samples (neither the construction nor validation sample). Some criminologists have defined what they mean by a cause as that which remains a predictor at different periods of time and at different geographical locations. Ignoring such philosophical irrelevance, we can agree that items of information that continue to be predictive despite location and time differences are, in many ways, to be preferred to those that do not display this invariance. It has usually been assumed that statistical tests of significance provided a means for the sorting out of items which should withstand changes from those that might be more liable to vary. Thus, prediction tables have, conventionally, been built from items of information that have a high chi-square, high correlation, or other such measure.

It is probable that items of information which, in one sample, show correlations with a criterion such that there is only a small probability that this was due to chance, should, in other independent samples, reveal a similarly significant correlation. It is probable, however, that some of the variance between samples may be underestimated by the use of within sample variance. Estimates of variance are dependent upon the extent to which the data are normally distributed. It may be possible to obtain better measures for the probability of correlations to remain stable by use of "Monte Carlo" methods. In any event, such methods would be worth exploration.

Evolutionary Processes

The coding of the sequence of events in the case history, in addition to the nature of those events, we have termed *dynamic coding*. We wish to reserve the word *sequential* for a different kind of operation. Our methods, so far as we are aware, and all other methods used in the criminal justice area, relate each individual to a general norm. We classify each individual in terms of the information we have about him and the general pattern of that information in the population of offenders studied. It is possible to describe as many norms as we may wish, and to describe individuals in terms of their conformity with, or departure from, these norms. It is, of course, expected that within different samples, there will be different norms. It is partly for this reason that we do not expect prediction tables constructed for one population (base for norms) to apply to another population (probably different norms).

It is possible to describe a person's body temperature in terms of some measure of magnitude of departure from 98.6 degrees (the general population norm being taken as an arbitrary zero). It is also possible to describe a person's body temperature, as now measured, as a departure of a certain magnitude from the reading when his temperature was *last* taken. Any arbitrary point of origin could be selected as the reference—as when a person is received into the reception center at the first medical examination. But one reading, taken at initial examination, does not usually provide any better basis for making statements about the individual's characteristics than the readings taken at any other time. If we are to use the *individual's* norm as the control (arbitrary zero) for our measurements, we need some "sample" of such readings. In a very interesting paper several years ago, G.P. Box suggested a statistical model and method which he termed "evolutionary processes."[2] The method we now propose in relation to methods for prediction is essentially similar to this, except in regard to the nature of the construction of the data and the inferences to be drawn. Box noted that "nature," in order to "decide" how to evolve, had to make use of information, and that this information was obtained in the very process of evolution itself. He applied his model to the chemical industry. Information about the output of the product was obtained in the course of production of the product, and this information provided the basis for determining whether changes should be made in such variables as time or temperature. Certain values for such variables as time and temperature were held constant for a sufficient time to generate information about output, then another set of values was chosen and similarly held constant while information was generated. The whole system was thus "hunting"[3] for an optimal output. With each iteration of the process, under stable conditions, it was closing in on the optimum value for all the variables in terms of the output. In our case, the method would draw some analogy between personal development and evolutionary processes models. What happens when an individual departs from his norm for a particular variable or in any particular direction? If we can establish norms for individual persons, we can discuss departures from these norms by persons. Thus, we might take sufficient measures of a person's body temperature to establish that his norm was, say, 98.3 degrees (there are apparently such persons who are quite healthy). A temperature of 98.6 degrees would represent for such a person a departure in an upward direction, although presumably of insignificant magnitude. In a similar way, if it were possible to obtain the basic information: the changes in an offender's career; his reactions to treatment; and many other kinds of data could be analyzed in this form. The availability of computers makes it possible to contemplate the development of such methods. It means, of course, that almost as much computational effort will have to be put into one individual case as is currently put into a whole sample.

A new approach to kinds of data which may be useful is also called for. We are now interested in finding stable correlates, and hence we look for measures that are also stable. At present, we prefer to measure whatever we measure only once and to hope that that measure is not only correct at that time, but that it is sufficiently correct for the person for almost all time. If the sequential methods are to be put to best use, we shall have to look specifically for behaviors, measures, or symptoms that we expect to change, preferably frequently. If we can relate the changes to theories, which in turn relate to decision making, this will also suggest interesting developments.

If one of the factors in which penal treatment has an investment can be termed *the adjustment* of the offender, then it might be expected that changes that indicate a trend toward adjustment would be noticeable, and hence recordable and measurable. The sequential method would be appropriate as a method for interpreting these kinds of data. Whether sequential measures would best be keyed into prediction remains doubtful. A decision base seems preferable and that entails more than predictive statements. The question is not one of the use of prediction methods, but rather is related to the nature of decisions and the value of kinds of data to decision makers who are concerned with various kinds of tasks. There are kinds of decisions that are made frequently, and each decision maker makes many. There are kinds of decisions that are made rarely by any one decision maker, but frequently by people generally. And there are decisions that very few people ever have to make. The decision regarding what to order from the lunch menu, the decision to get married, and the decision of a king to go to war would typify each of these three broad classes. Most management decisions concern events that fall into the first class. This is the class within which the decisions of parole board members fall. Each case is unique, but each has considerable similarities with others, and many decisions are made by board members. It would generally seem to be absurd to discuss the parole board's decision regarding the time to hold an offender in the same terms as though it were the decision to get married or to declare war! How much and what type of information is useful for board members to have in making decisions about offenders? That is the central issue, and cannot be answered in ideal, but only in operationally relevant, terms.

Let us consider the present "state of the art" of prediction; examine what improvements seem likely to be achieved if they are sought; and test each case against the hard test of utility in respect to parole decisions.

Better or Different?

A well-known mousetrap manufacturer may be expected, when challenged regarding the efficiency of his product, to claim that he could make a "new, improved" mousetrap. It is hardly to be expected that he would recommend that the inquirer go to a dispenser of poisons. The authors of this and related reports are usually regarded as "mousetrap makers" (prediction/base expectancy/prior probabilities and variants thereof). We are inclined, therefore, to think that we could make better prediction tables. We have set down, thus far, some possible means which might work out toward this end, namely:

1. Dynamic coding of information: using sequence of events to a greater degree than has been done to date;
2. Use of probits or logits and other related measures to assess individual items of information and their contribution to any summed information;
3. A search for stable predictors, perhaps by the use of Monte Carlo methods, rather than a reliance on coefficients of variation and measures of significance as found in construction samples or in subdivisions of a sample (split-half);

4. Sequential, ipsative measures of change could be explored and a different form of instrument developed.

But do we need a better mousetrap? Or do we need a modified mousetrap? Have we thought of the best ways in which to deploy the prediction methods we already have? Should we consider predicting other factors or estimating other kinds of criteria? Is the major problem *how* to predict, or *what* to predict? Perhaps we could profitably devote some attention to rethinking what it is we should be predicting, if, indeed, we should be predicting at all. We may make up equations that are more resistant to poor quality data by working with "noise";[4] we may produce equations that account for larger proportions of the variance in outcome, and so on; but are these the things that are most needed?

Different Kinds of Prediction?

It is not possible to say by how much prediction could be improved if and when it becomes possible to examine the various suggestions made in the preceding paragraphs. It is reasonably certain that a fair degree of improvement could be expected. However, such improvements would require a sound data base. Let us assume that the data base can be repaired and that, given the necessary investments, much more powerful prediction statements could be made. Would it be desirable to give such investment? Should the work concentrate on those forms of predictive statements that have been made (however poorly) in the past? Let us consider two variations of the present theme and ask about their possible utility in parole decision making.

Conditional Probability Statements

Instead of providing a general statement of the probability for an individual to be reconvicted (or other criteria), it would be possible (given adequate base data) to make estimates in conditional terms, such as the following examples:

Pr/a = if offender is released and goes to his old address, his chance of reconviction is $x\%$.

Pr/m = if offender is released and goes into the armed forces, his chance of reconviction is $y\%$.

And so on for $Pr/\ldots$ (the probability of r given a variety of other factors as assumed).

It is unlikely that there will be sufficient data for many such statements to be made; however, it should be possible to consider some factors. Of course, there must be experience of the particular conditions (a) . . . (m); theoretical estimates relating to hypothetical considerations are outside the scope of this kind of analysis.

Predicting the "Predictors"

In addition to estimates of conditional probability and to some extent related to this method, it would be possible to consider the calculation of predictors for those factors that themselves predict reconvictions. How many such predictions might be of utility cannot at this time be estimated. The factor predicted would, presumably, best be an item about which some action could be taken and which was reasonably strongly associated with criminal activity. Thus, for example, if we know that drunkenness is a predictor of reconviction we could examine the data to ascertain whether, and if so to what degree, drunkenness was predictable in terms of other factors, and how much of the variation was unique to this item of information.

It is obvious that at this point, if not well before, we have moved from an area of concern for the provision of instruments that can be used by decision makers in individual cases in the course of their own decisions to research analysis to answer specific questions. It is equally obvious that multiple regression, discriminant function analysis, numerical taxonomies, partial differential equations, and many more related and unrelated methods can be used to investigate a large number of issues. However, as already stressed, investigation of issues is not the same as the *provision of instruments* to be used in decision processes. The work of administering a parole system is not the same as that of research into parole or other aspects of criminal behavior. Research workers have tended to assume that those results which they found interesting and useful for purposes of research should also be found interesting and useful by others whose main concerns were with different aspects of social control. Early prediction workers may have assumed that the probability of reconviction was the only rational element to be considered in the parole decision. They could not understand why parole boards did not make use of the instruments they had provided. It is easy to fall into the trap (mousetrap?) of thinking that the provision of other forms and more powerful versions of prediction methods will provide the answers. It is necessary, however, to devise a strategy of operations that divides the research effort from the operational effort in such a form that the two components can complement each other. It may be important for research to be devoted to the construction of instruments that are not themselves used for research but are designed specifically for providing assistance to operational decision makers. It may also be important for research to concentrate on specific problems. It is certainly inappropriate to assume that both kinds of tasks can be achieved by the same means.

Design and Use of Instruments versus
Research Investigations?

There are interesting examples in the physical sciences of the relationship between the development of instruments (enabling and facilitating measurement) and discoveries. Any analogous relationship which may be postulated to apply in the social sciences is of doubtful validity. The measurement of intelligence is the measurement of that which intelligence tests measure, and what they measure is not independent of the methods of construction and analysis. In some psychophysical methods, the relationship is close and the analogies hold reasonably well, but as we move toward the sociopsychological, the analogies with the measurement by instruments become extremely strained. In particular, attitude measurement is often no more than the construction of an intervening variable of undemonstrated utility. The research worker may construct means for measurement or devise other forms of comparison in order to consider the reasonableness of his inferences. The public decision maker is not so much concerned with inferences from his observations as he is with how others will see his decision—will they (his public critics) regard them as reasonable, fair, expedient, or unfair? In a word, the assessment of a public decision maker is in terms of a value system, not necessarily a rational system. Whether the latter is also moral is not a question that scientific methods can arbitrate.

If this line of reasoning is sound, then there is clearly a difference between instruments, which satisfy a scientific purpose (whatever that may be), and an instrument that will prove useful to public decision makers who are proposing to use it to facilitate individual decisions. It appears that the provision of a prediction device, by itself, is not sufficient to qualify as useful in the latter category. Simply improving the instrument will not change this circumstance. The point is that the parole decision is a complex one. The prediction table provides a one-dimensional assessment—that is what it is designed to do. The parole board decision maker is required by society to provide a best decision in terms of a balancing of several important considerations and to resolve these several dimensions into a one-dimensional answer. The one-dimensional answer is, of course, to be in terms of whether and when to release an offender from incarceration—the dimension is that of time. The one-dimensional estimate of probability is not sufficient in itself to transform into the one-dimensional (answer), time. How do we know this? There is no proof; indeed, we could take up a moral position which declared that probability should be the only factor to be transformed into time in the parole decision case. This is, of course, a claim to a value, and the question at issue is who has the right or duty to declare such values.

Scientists cannot avoid taking a moral position. Nonetheless, it is possible to utilize our methodologies to insulate, to some degree, our observations and inferences from interaction between our values and our reasoning. Such insulation is, of course, never complete; social science research will usually reveal some value positions—the stronger where the methodology is weaker![5] If we are looking for expressions of values in regard to parole decisions, we can look to parole boards. It is clear that they have not made the transformation from probability into time; this is another way of saying, as we did many pages earlier, that parole boards have not used prediction tables! They may well have been right in this! Moreover, the failure to use such tables has not, it seems, been due only to their lack of power, since they have been shown to be more powerful than other means for estimations of probability.[6] In the United States Parole Board study, the very close cooperation between the research workers (methodologists) and the parole board (public policy interpreters) has enabled communication in considerable depth. Each viewpoint has been examined by the other and attempted to translate what was seen into its own language. We have learned that the probability of reconviction is certainly one of the items of information or belief that is taken into account in determining the time an offender is to be held; but it is not the only factor.

Of Models and Simulation

It is not necessary to reject the idea of prediction of reconviction (or other criteria); it is necessary to go beyond this concept and to furnish parole boards with more complex models of the decision process. (It does not follow that a model that takes into account more of the complexities of a situation is itself more complex to use!) Improved, expanded, and refined prediction methods will be one component of these models, but other components will also be necessary. One of these other components is the assessment of the seriousness of the offense for which the offender is serving his time in prison. Another consideration of parole board members is the behavior of the offender in the institution, perhaps with somewhat more emphasis on recent violations of prison rules. Thus, we can now assemble three items of information or estimates: (1) seriousness of offense; (2) probability of reconviction; (3) institutional adjustment, which can be related to time to be served. Another factor may be the probable seriousness of any recidivism. In some way, this may be seen as (although difficult to visualize as), a four-dimensional model of the decision process. It has been shown that a model of this kind may fit the present decision processes fairly closely. Perhaps further sophistication of models could increase the closeness of the fit of the model to the decision process.

It may be thought that this procedure of research is merely trying to find ways of replacing the human decision maker by a formula, which is only partly true. The objective is to remove from the decision maker some elements of his decision processes in order to permit his concentration upon other elements of the decision. Some elements of the decision can be simulated, and we can consider in what ways the simulation might be varied to accommodate more preferred values. If a decision maker were prepared to specify the function $P \propto T$ (probability proportional to time), he could be replaced by a prediction table. Thus, the decision as to whether a decision maker can or cannot be replaced by an equation is his decision, or more precisely, is determined by the nature and quality of his decisions. A rational decision maker would presumably desire that as much of his decision making as possible be taken over by mechanical means, since then he could develop more of his ability as a human person of greater complexity than the machine.

If, then, easy-to-operate complex models of decision processes can be developed, the decision maker could first examine the decision suggested by the model. If he had reason to adjust the model in terms of its parameters, his modification could be an improved decision. If, however, the decision maker believes that his subjective estimate of the probability of reconviction is more accurate than the objectively ascertained estimate of that probability, he is quite likely to be incorrect. If the human decision maker disagrees with the implied values of the model, then he may well be correct. It will be necessary to sort out what types of work are best done by models and which activities must be the focus of human value assessments and human imagination and daring. At present we must (as it were) tell the computer the values, and we do not design computers to be either imaginative or daring! In even the ideal case, policy and ethics are human inputs, but they may be more effectively applied to suggesting changes in scales than in attempts to fit in an individual case. Thus, if a model shows that seriousness, probability of reconviction, and institutional misconduct are treated equally in a representational map of decisions, the human decision makers may suggest that this implied policy is incorrect; that, say, institutional conduct should receive less consideration than the other two variables. Such decisions are related to values, are essentially human ones, and can more effectively be put into operation by the use of models than by attempts to deal with individual cases.

Moreover, we have noted that models are not restricted to general norms. The sequential methods open up a different kind of approach. The generalized norm models provide a different kind of map from those provided by ipsative scoring. The individual varies from time to time about his own norm, which varies from the general norm of the population. There are, as it were, two sources of variance—within individual and between individuals. The variance between individuals has conventionally been regarded as error. Perhaps an analogy for the kind of approach we now consider to be most worth developing in future research may be given. Maps of a given area often have insets of more detailed maps of particularly significant areas, such as the centers of cities. The detail is not required in the surrounding rural areas (except for a small and specialized group of users), and the provision of such detail would inhibit the utility of the map for the general user. If all maps were of one-inch-to-the-mile detail, we should almost certainly have many more motorists lost! Perhaps there is a case for considering certain periods in an offender's career as requiring a close-up of the trajectory at that point. Or, to stay with the previously used analogy, the larger-scale maps may require insets for specific locations.

The significance of these considerations is that the provision of instruments for use by the decision-making body (in this case, the United States Board of Parole) is seen as involving a different set of research operations from those necessary in general research in relation to parole and the criminological field of inquiry. The provision of instruments to facilitate decisions must be able to reflect complex processes and to make clear the underlying value postulates upon which the models rely so that board decisions may be related to such policy or value considerations. Fact-finding and other research operations should continue and feed into the model building so that the instruments that are provided are soundly based. The provision of prediction instruments as single dimension estimates of probability of reconviction is not the goal of "computer-assisted decision making"; rather, it is a section of work which is necessary in order to build models that are more closely related to the complex goals of parole and, of course, as a basic tool in research analysis.

Pure and Applied Research?

The kind of division proposed may seem like the common classification of research into "pure" and "applied." This is not exactly the case; rather, it is a matter of the level of abstraction at which it is necessary to attempt solutions to problems that are equally "applied" or "relevant." It is clear that there is a need for fundamental research and that some of the questions which it may be appropriate for such kinds of research to address emerge from operations research. And operations research requires a very close cooperative effort between the research workers and the decision makers at the level that has characterized this project. It may be that we are now beginning to see rather more clearly the roles that may be played by the different forms of research strategies.

Information Overload: Peace or War with the Computer[a]

Will intelligent computers ever be able to make better decisions than judges, parole boards, probation officers, and others concerned with the offender? Can

[a]Adapted in part from L.T. Wilkins, "Information Overload: Peace or War with the Computer," *Journal of Criminal Law and Criminology*, vol. 64, no. 2 (Baltimore: Williams & Wilkins, 1973). Reprinted with permission.

the provision of information by rapid retrieval systems connected to large-scale computers or information machines assist the courts? Should we look for the takeover of the human decision activities by automatic processes, or for some form of cooperation between the human decision maker and the computer? Will computers cooperate? Will decision makers cooperate?

The obvious answer is that human intelligence will always have an essential part to play in decision making, no matter to what extent computers can be designed to facilitate the processes of information retrieval and analysis. Currently, many criminal justice procedures and decisions could be assisted by the further utilization of computers, but, in order to cooperate, both the decision makers and the computers must learn to communicate. Computers can certainly be programmed to learn, but they must learn from somebody. Considerable problems exist in organizing material so that optimal use can be made of the computer and the particular strengths of human intelligence.[7]

This discussion is divided into three parts. The first section considers certain general issues and some questions that are somewhat abstract if not "philosophical." (Often the relevance of specific issues can only be discovered by taking an abstract viewpoint.) The second part reports in summary form a number of recently conducted experiments relating to parole and probation decisions. Apparatus that simulates the operations possible on an up-to-date computer is used to examine the interaction between the decision maker and the machine. Finally, an attempt is made to draw together the experimental evidence and the moral and philosophical questions while focusing on the present state of knowledge and process, and to suggest means of improvement.

More Information or Less?

Most decision makers believe that if they are given sufficient and correct facts they can make the decision required of them. Many believe that if their decision is somehow proved to be incorrect, the information was insufficient, or inaccurate. Seldom does the thought occur that the decision might have been a poor one because there was too much information for human intelligence to cope with. The decision-making machinery within the human skull can be overloaded just as any other piece of machinery, and when it is overloaded it fails to function as well as it might. A car indicates by groans and wheezes when it is overloaded, but no indicator seems to exist that advises the human intelligence that it is attempting to handle too much information at once. Only under experimental conditions can it be shown that the human intellect, no matter how intelligent the individual, can process only very small quantities of information.

Computer salesmen, not unexpectedly, fail to stress these findings when attempting to sell equipment. Speed and quantity of information retrieval are their watchwords. But rapid retrieval may or may not be an asset of an information system. Whatever goes into the computer has to be put there, and whatever comes out has to be interpreted by the human decision maker. The computer can tell neither whether a decision is correct nor whether it is morally acceptable. We may define *correctness* in terms of certain operations which the computer can carry out, but it is humans determining the logic who decide whether a computer-made decision is "correct" (consistent) or incorrect.

Kinds of Decisions

We have difficulty discussing issues of this kind because our language is extremely imprecise. It is impossible, even with the most appropriate choice of words, to express any complex concept in such a way as to avoid the danger of ambiguity. We talk about decisions and decision processes as though all decisions were similar—a decision is a decision. But consider just two examples of decisions: the first, the president decides to go to war; the second, I decide to wear a pink shirt. Clearly, these are two very different things. But different as the things are, we use the word *decision* to cover both instances. If we use the same word, we must infer that there is some sense in which the thing is the same. If the thing were totally different, surely a different word would have been used.

Anthropologists tell us that people who live in the Arctic have many different words that we would translate as *snow*. They have these different words because it is necessary for them to discriminate large flake snow from small powder and so on. In their experience, the various qualities of snow are so different that their language has evolved different words. In our language of decisions we have not found it necessary to discriminate decisions with serious consequences from decisions with trivial consequences in terms of the noun that describes the activity we call decision making.

Is it possible to assume that the processes of "coming to a decision" are sufficiently similar whether the decision relates to trivial or extremely serious matters? Is the difference in the two decisions merely a matter of degree or magnitude? Can we assume that any knowledge of the process relating to the one kind of decision can be applied to the other? Before we can consider these important questions, we must break down the decision process into some more useful categories of operations.[8]

Is Decision-Making a Process?

We have many words by which we refer to the idea of a decision. We talk about "coming to" a decision, using the analogy of a journey. There are other such descriptive words: we may "cut off discussion" and "force a decision"; we may weigh the evidence"; we may "make" (the analogy of building or construction) a decision; and so on. Some of the terms we use suggest that "making a decision" is itself a process, while other terms suggest that the making of a decision is not a process at all, but rather the termination of a prior process of information search, retrieval, and analysis. We say we have "decided" when we no longer wish to seek for more information. It is odd that our language is so imprecise in describing a matter of such importance. We have a very poor collection of analogues or metaphors to describe the decision act or process or termination of a process, and we do not discriminate, by our term *decision,* the very different classes of the act.

Despite such lack of precision in our language, we generally assume that *information* is related to *decision.* Perhaps our language is not much better at describing what constitutes information, but it is possible to utilize the operational definitions of Shannon and others[9] where necessary. Other concepts are closely related to the idea of decision. We must examine some of these before we can settle more precisely upon a description of a decision, and consider cooperation with the computer in the decision situation. However, let us first take the idea of information. We generally assume that a quantity of information exists, in our minds or elsewhere, which is relevant to the decision we are to make. This information may be formally stored in records, or we may make direct observations (for example, the color of the shirt) and think about possible situations (for example, meetings we may attend that day). We also have a strategy of search for information; we may call for files or merely stop and think (recall and make projections). Having obtained the information, or while obtaining it, we will begin to "process" it, relating one item to another and attaching certain significance to each.

No one would assume that similar kinds of information were of common utility in the case of the decision to go to war and the case of the pink shirt. But this does not imply that the strategy of search for information used in the two cases might not be similar, nor does it follow that the methods whereby the different kinds and qualities of information are processed by human intelligence are dissimilar. Do we "search for facts" (what are "facts"?) in exactly the same ways whatever the nature of the decision to be made? Is the idea of the seriousness of a decision a different consideration from the idea of the decision itself? If we are to discuss the seriousness of a decision, it is obvious that we shall need information as to the likely consequences of the decision. But is this not absurd? If we know only the consequences of making any one decision, we still have no information by which to discuss its consequences or its seriousness since we have to assume that the consequences of deciding something different or even deciding-not-to-decide may be either more or less serious. Thus the idea of the seriousness of the consequences of a decision usually implies some alternatives are possible and that these can be compared.

Leaving aside the idea of the seriousness or triviality of the consequences of some decisions, we may note a further related consideration in the decision process or act. We may say that we are quite confident that a decision is correct, or we may lack confidence in a decision. In some cases, we may be prepared to make a decision even though our level of confidence is low, while in other cases we would make strong efforts to increase our level of confidence before deciding. It is reasonable to suppose that for those decisions which we regard as trivial (say, the pink shirt case), we would be prepared to act at a low level of confidence, whereas in more serious cases we would want a much higher degree of assurance before deciding. Thus, it appears that there is a relationship between the degree of confidence we require in a decision and our assessment of the consequences of the decision. We require higher degrees of assurance where large differences in alternative outcomes rest upon our decisions. Thus, we arrive at the issue of probable outcomes, where the emphasis is on the word *probable*. The idea of probability and the idea of degrees of assurance or confidence may be taken as an identity.[10] Thus, we may relate the perceived difference between alternative probable outcomes to the degree of confidence required before making a decision.

If the decision maker wishes to increase the level of confidence, he may do more-of-the-same or perhaps try something different. In either event, it seems reasonable to assume that to increase a level of confidence more work will be required in some form.

It is unlikely that less activity on the part of the decision maker would result in a feeling of greater confidence. It makes sense to view the decision as a termination of a process of information search. We cannot reasonably argue that a person has reached a decision if he persists in seeking further information with regard to the act he must make or fail to make. It is, of course, possible to terminate the search for information while the level of confidence in the decision is still low, but the degree of confidence is a quality of a different order from the decision. Unless I am particularly fastidious, the decision to wear a pink shirt or another one may be one where I do not require much information, because I am satisfied with a low level of confidence in the decision. I may be satisfied with a low level of confidence because I cannot ascribe any serious consequences to making the wrong decision. However, there are circumstances where a person who is not fastidious with regard to dress may require a higher level of confidence in a decision regarding dress; for example, when going for an important interview. The level of confidence required is, in the first instance, related to the qualities of or in the decision maker and in the second case, related to the predicted likely consequences of his act within the external situation.

The preceding analysis does not throw any light on the processes of information search. In order to increase our level of confidence, we may do more of the same. If, however, we assert that the process of information search adopted in the trivial case must be different from that of the serious case, then the question arises as to how many different strategies of search the human intelligence can apply and what determines the adoption of one rather than the other. Common speech does not identify different strategies unless we assume that these are implied in the analogies to which we referred earlier. Moreover, whether there is one strategy or many for information search, there is still the further problem of the nature of information processing within the human intellect. Are there different forms of "information processing" which we adopt depending upon (1) the seriousness of the decision or (2) the strategy of information search or (3) both? How does human intelligence utilize the information it collects and manage to distill it into a decision? What is the process of distillation? Does it closely follow procedures that we can simulate by computer or formalize in other ways?

Decisions about Things and Persons

In the judicial process there are many decision branching points; few are trivial. At each point where a decision is required, information is available to the decision maker in a stored form. Often persons in the legal or correctional fields discuss "making decisions about individuals." Actually, a decision cannot be made about an individual, but only about information concerning that individual. The individual is moved into one channel or another according to the nature of the decision, but the decision maker cannot deal with more of the individual's characteristics than he can ascertain by whatever means are available to him. What happens to an individual is determined not by his actual individual characteristics, but rather by the characteristics of the information sought about him and processed in the mind of the decision maker. This may seem obvious, but the consequences are seldom recognized. We often claim that offenders are dealt with in terms of their individual needs, that each person is unique and must be so considered in parole and sentencing procedures, or that there is a necessity on the part of the decision maker to consider the whole of the information about the offender. These statements are not consistent with the earlier statement which was said to be "obvious." How can any unique event guide decisions when we emphasize its uniqueness?"[11] A unique event may guide our decisions if we are prepared to examine the similarities between that event and others. If we continue accumulating data before making a decision, we shall not reach a decision; hence we cannot obtain "all" the information.

Decisions are made by reference to information that is considered relevant, and the individual who is seen as unique is seen also as similar to other unique individuals. Accordingly, persons are dealt with in terms of the information that the decision maker thinks is relevant and in terms of the similarities between individuals and not in terms of all the information, nor in terms of "uniqueness." The process by which decision makers seek out information which they consider relevant is important in assessing their decisions. The means whereby decision makers process that information into similarities and differences is equally important.

The statement "each individual is unique," may be useful as a moral statement in the form, "every individual should be treated as a unique person"—individuality should be respected. By extension, statements of this order can be related to some of the basic concepts in the quality of life that we often refer to as "freedom." However, the statement that each individual is unique may better serve to indicate the limitations of our knowledge and the restrictions on our decision-making power rather than as a basis for the dispensation of justice. The idea of justice is another moral concept related to the idea of fairness. While the idea of justice seems to refer to some external standard, the idea of fairness is essentially a comparative assessment. This suggests a dilemma: we should proceed as though each individual were unique, and yet we should be "fair." However, we cannot know what is fair unless we are prepared to compare one individual with another and to discuss similarities rather than differences. Perhaps it is possible to approach the judicial decision-making problems from the phenomenological existentialist reference and avoid some of these difficulties which may pertain more to words than to processes.

Some Experimental Results

It is quite impossible to watch the process whereby a person recalls his past experiences and uses these in making up his mind. It is possible, however, to study the decision process when the relevant information is retrieved from a storehouse outside the individual. There are many decisions that fall within the second class. Perhaps the more important decisions we make are those in which information is sought by reference to external records or other external sources. We may decide which shirt to wear without asking for advice, without statistical data as to the frequency of the wearing of pink shirts, or even without the second opinion of a wife. But we will tend to search for data about yields before investing our money, we will consider a few different vacancies before accepting a particular job, and we will refer to newspapers before voting in an election. Judicial decisions are related to documents and to written sources of information.

There are very sound reasons for studying the judicial decision processes at this time. It has been projected that the use of conventional paper files will shortly be replaced by more efficient means. Some claim that computer storage and retrieval systems could now replace and improve upon all conventional filing, storage, and retrieval systems. Decision makers in the parole and related processes are well accustomed to searching through case papers for information which they consider relevant to their decisions. Often the material found in the files is checked or supplemented by information obtained by interviewing the petitioner. An investigation of the possible consequences of changing from files to computer-retrieved parole information display (on a cathode ray tube) was undertaken as part of the Parole Decision-Making project.

It is possible to simulate the computer of the future by the use of variable access slide projection equipment. This equipment can deal with only a few cases, whereas a computer file would store many thousands of records. Also, the slide projector is much slower in the recovery of any item of information. Nonetheless, the decision maker may sit at a small console and call up information at will which is displayed a second or two later on a screen. The fully computerized system would have access to any file and any item of information in microseconds. Normally, however, one decision is made about one case at any one time, and the limitations of the slide projector in recovering information only in respect of the case that is loaded in the slide file is not a serious mismatch with the projected computerized system. Using such apparatus, it has been possible to ascertain certain preferences which decision makers have regarding the display of case materials and the kinds of decisions they are likely to make under different conditions of display.[12]

Observation of the parole decision-making task suggests that different decision makers go about the process of their task in different ways. For example, the pattern of search for information appears to differ among parole board members as attempts are made to digest the case file, identifying aspects of the life history thought significant. In a given case or in general, a specific bit of information may be regarded as highly significant by one member but thought to be unimportant by another. Some members may prefer a reliance upon the objective features of the case file, while others may place more emphasis upon a subjective assessment. Some may approach the task with a prominent set toward evaluation of the offender in terms of the risk of new offenses or parole violation; others may emphasize concerns for equity in time served by persons in comparable circumstances, for issues of deterrence, for institutional adjustment, or for the potential impact of the decision upon the correctional system as a whole.

If these observations are correct, then it may be possible to describe the different processes used and to indicate that there may be very significant consequences deriving from these differing processes.

Decision makers differ not only in the decisions they make, but also in the methods they use for seeking information. For example, persons who are inclined to grant parole are likely to select different kinds of information from those who are more inclined to deny parole. In experimental conditions, decision makers seem to prefer considerable redundancy in the statements presented to them. Where the information was presented in the form of correct English sentence construction (this person is 23 years of age), decision makers were more satisfied with the material than where the same information was presented without the redundancy of ordinary English construction (age 23). Furthermore, where the information was presented in the shorter form, decision makers tended to deny parole to the petitioner more frequently. These data derive from simulated parole decision-making conditions, but there seems to be little doubt that the same kinds of results would apply in actual cases. It is possible that part of the difference in the decision preference is due to parole boards' greater familiarity with the narrative style of report than with coded data. Thus, one might suggest that if the shorter form of coded data were presented for any period of time, a learning curve might derive which would tend towards reduction of the differences in the kinds of decisions under the two conditions. Unfortunately, this seems unlikely. Similar tests were made where the decision makers were persons very familiar with coded information and similar differences in decision outcomes by method of codification were noted.

Experiments with groups have revealed very little agreement as to which items in a case file are most useful to consider first when there is pressure to make a decision as soon as possible. Members of the experimental group were asked to vote for the information they would require. The first item to be called up on the screen (file) received a favorable vote by between one-quarter and one-third of the persons present. The second item showed less agreement, and usually progressively fewer and fewer persons agreed as the number of items increased. After the first three or four items have been selected by a group, hardly better than random frequencies can be attached to any of the remaining items in a total file of just over fifty items. However, if members of a group vote for the information they require and the four items most often chosen are displayed,[13] decision makers have no difficulty in making an interim decision whether or not to parole the petitioner. On the basis of the four items presented, it is then possible to divide the decision makers into two groups: those who decided to grant parole and those who decided against parole. The two groups may then be asked to vote separately for the next four items of information which they would want to see displayed on any computerized file. In such experiments, little overlap has been found between the items selected to be seen by the two different groups. Persons who do select items also chosen by the other group are very likely to change their decision regarding parole.

In a majority of the experiments, subjects have been asked to rate both their confidence in the decision when initially made (after four items) and at each change thereafter. They have also been asked to assess the difficulty of the decision-making task at each point in the sequence. In light of the earlier theoretical discussion, the results are extremely interesting. We postulated that the level of confidence a decision maker would require would depend upon the consequences he assessed for the decision—the more serious the probable consequences, the higher the level of confidence required. Furthermore, we thought that a low level of confidence might be easily achieved by examining only a few items of information, whereas a higher level of confidence would require more activity and the processing of more information, and hence could be said to be the more difficult decision. All of the subjects in the entire series of experiments to date, consisting of parole board members, students in elementary statistical classes, graduate students in research methods and criminology, and others, provided ratings which express a completely inverse relationship between confidence and difficulty. As expected, they claim that their confidence in the decision they make increases as the amount of information they have seen increases. Although free to select as much information as they desire, decision makers do not claim that the more they see the more difficult the decision becomes; instead, they claim that it becomes easier in a direct relationship to their assessment of their confidence.[14] By stating that a decision in which they are confident is "easy" to reach, they seem to be saying that a decision in which they have confidence is one with which they are "at ease," relating the subjective feeling of being at ease to the subjective rating of easiness as the opposite pole to difficulty. The individual decision maker is not aware of the fact that he is performing much more work as he attempts to process more and more information. Rather he believes, without exception, that such processing makes decision making easier. If one were to simulate the human decision-making process on a computer, the greater the level of confidence required, the harder the computer would have to work. We might reasonably say that the computer would find this more difficult.

Our task in the Parole Decision-Making project was to improve parole decision making. The term *improve* is a difficult one to translate into specific methodologies; it seems clear, however, that a greater clarity and awareness of issues, procedures, decision outcomes, and consequences is relevant to the general task.

In attempts to improve decisions, it has become a common practice to utilize methods of information feedback. However, if the decision processes used differ among decision makers, the feedback of information derived from one form of decision processing to a group or persons who utilize a different form may not be helpful.

Decisions are made with reference to information about offenders; and there are, of course, varying qualities, types, and quantities of information to be explored. But it is now clear to us (from discussion with parole board members, from the questionnaire data obtained, and from the exercises described elsewhere in this book) that decision makers have preferences for certain kinds of information and methods of presentation. It is clear also that their decision outcomes are not independent of the methods of presentation, and are associated with the qualities of the information itself—and, further, with the ways in which the information is processed by decision makers.

Decisions and Information Use

We do not know exactly what constitutes a decision. In retrospect, we can say whether we have or have not yet decided, but we are usually unaware of the exact point at which the decision was made. In some cases we may add to our information in a sequential input and with each item of information adjust our assessment of a probability, or our beliefs; in other cases, we may seek out a pattern by acceptance of information that "fits" and rejection of items that do not. In some cases we may regard items of information as interchangeable, so that one piece of information which indicates a positive decision may, when it is not present, be substituted by another and different item, but one having the same influences upon our decision-making.

It does not seem that these considerations may be dismissed as trivial nor irrelevant to the parole decision making of board members, nor indeed of other decision makers in the criminal justice system. If we are to discover ways whereby decisions may be assisted by computer processes, obviously the software is the critical problem. Its appropriate design clearly depends upon the requirements of the user of the terminals and the manner in which they (the terminals) deliver information will become critical. In order to discuss the appropriate form of delivery of information to the decision makers, we need to know how they want the information delivered. However, the user is not able to tell us this directly, since it is now clear that people do not know that they use different mental processes of information retrieval and storage. Moreover, once the intake of information is in process, it is related to other concepts in different ways by different people.

Various experiments were, therefore conducted; and some are reported here. The purpose of these experiments is, in the end, to indicate ways in which the parole decision may be improved. There are several stages on the road to this goal, which, we conclude, cannot be arrived at by any more direct means. Part of the experiments may be seen as simulating the computer of the future. We constructed presentations of data that it would be feasible to make available to parole board members and other decision makers in this area when the software has been developed. We saw no point in rushing into the preparation of complex software which might prove useless.

A Typology of Decision-Makers? A Theoretical and Speculative Contribution

Apart from differences in personality factors (usually considered in terms of attitudes and abilities), it seems likely that there are important differences in modalities of problem-solving behavior. It is possible that these differences, as they relate to information search strategies, are of importance in relation to the planning of computer-assisted decision analysis.

Everybody makes decisions. Everybody can say about any specific matter about which he may be questioned, whether he has at that time made a decision or not. We are aware of having made or of not having made a decision, but we can say very little about our process of making decisions. It is as though the decision process were a one-way screen—when we are looking toward it we know without any doubt that we have not passed through it; but when we look backwards, while we know we have passed through, the time, method, or occasion of passing through usually avoids us. Once we have made a decision, we are sure of this fact; but we cannot say which item swung our vote in one direction or another. The information piles up, as it were; the gradual process of coming to a decision suddenly reaches a critical level; and we decide. Our awareness of some aspects of this process is much clearer than of others. The process may differ in respect of different kinds of decisions, but most people would have considerable difficulty in saying what kinds of processes were associated with which kinds of decisions. Indeed, most people would find the idea of classification along these lines an unrealistic suggestion.

The linguistic conventions by which we describe the decision-making processes reveal much of the nature of our thinking about this human activity. We have many ways in which we can describe the uncertainty we have before deciding—"I have not yet made up my mind" (a construction analogy); "I am still in doubt" (a locational analogy); "I do not have sufficient facts" (perhaps an analogy with weighing as in scales); "I do not know which side to come down on" (perhaps a different analogy of scales); and, of course, many more similar phrases using different metaphors.

There is, perhaps, as rich a selection of phrases in which we can indicate that we have decided—"I have made up my mind," "On balance, I would say . . . ," and so on, with weighing and constructional analogies dominant. But consider the process of the act of deciding. We have no such phrases which refer to the decision-making operation as in the present. Diplomatic communiqués often say that "documents are being studied" of similar phrases, but the frank statement that "we have not yet made up our minds" or, "we are in the process of making up our minds" would be a refreshingly unusual news release. It seems that to maintain the image of competence, the delay in coming to a decision must be blamed upon the lack of information or some uncertainty regarding it, as distinct from the process time of making a decision. "Why," the public seems to be assumed to ask, "should the process of *decision making* take any time?" Getting the facts: that takes time. Getting the facts into order: that takes time. In fact, any acts that are external to the actual act of making the decision can, with respectability, be claimed to take time. But once the preliminaries are disposed of, the act of making the decision should not take time: at least this seems to be a reasonable inference from the balance of available conventions for describing these different sectors of decision behavior.

The Importance of Decision-Making Strategies of Search

The question of what characterizes a rational decision where there is a total lack of information has engaged some mathematicians and philosophers, but this case is trivial. It is difficult to imagine a decision situation where at least some small quantity of information is not available. The decision-making process and the information search and sorting activity are closely related. However, it is interesting and useful to ask some questions regarding the relationship between information and decision.

Does the decision-making process run concurrently with the information search? Is the process continuous, smoothly increasing toward a point where, on one side we say we have not decided, but on the other side and only one very small step later, we say that we have decided? Do we, as our intake of information increases, use the information to destroy our uncertainty about the choice, or is there a gap between our state prior to and after making the decision which is of a different order from a change in a continuous variable? If there is a continuous variation, could this be described as a continuum of degrees of certainty or degrees of belief and our assessment of probabilities? Can we relate uncertainty to the concept of risk, and, if so, is the relationship a direct one? And, if we can do this, can we relate the concept of risk to the concept of probability? Can all uncertainty in relation to human decision making be seen as a matter of probabilities, even if we have also to add that we may be uncertain as to the probabilities? Perhaps some of these questions are irrelevant to any design of computer-assisted decision analysis which could be of use to any parole board. It does, however, seem necessary to ask how information is used in the parole decision process. If decision makers are, as a continuous function, modifying their uncertainty (whether to grant parole or probability of an outcome), *then the computer systems should, presumably, fit in with this human preference pattern.* If uncertainty assessment is continuously modified, does the step from uncertainty to decision take place quickly? If not, how can the interim state be described? If uncertainty can be taken in terms of probability, at what level of probability do we usually regard the balance as sufficiently weighted to state that we have moved from being undecided to being decided? How is the dichotomy (decided/undecided) related to the continuous variable of changing estimates of probability, or our reducing level of uncertainty?

If we are to work toward computer-assisted decision making in any sophisticated form, it is critical that we obtain some understanding of the preferences of decision makers (members of parole boards) for certain possible forms of information search and processing. It is, of course, possible to approach these problems from a purely theoretical angle. Much has been written about statistical decision theory. If we can accept certain basic concepts as relevant, and the idea of probability as central, we can fit together a large body of mathematical ideas. Whether these ideas and the related models are of use to any particular decision maker may depend both upon the preferences of the decision makers and the kinds of decisions with which he is concerned.

If we are concerned with preferences for forms of presentation of information, then it might be thought that we could find out what to do merely by asking decision makers how they go about their task. It would certainly be simpler if it were reasonable to assume that this approach would suffice. It is, perhaps, because all persons are decision makers at various levels of complexity, continuously and all their lives, that introspection is unsuccessful in uncovering the nature of the process. We also find it impossible to give an account of how we breathe. Decision making at certain levels is a learned process which becomes automatic. If one person should ask another, "How do you think about that?" the respondent will express his opinion about the content area under discussion; he will not describe his thought processes. Obviously, if somebody thinks "in the same way," we mean that his opinions are similar, not that his methods for deriving his opinions are similar to ours. Thus, the ways in which we talk about decision making do not seem satisfactory from the viewpoint of understanding the process in sufficient detail to be able to talk about the provision of assistance through technology. Some other methods must be worked out and put into effect.

The theoretical approach on its own will not suffice. But let us return for a moment to the issue that was raised when the idea of theoretical decision theory was introduced, namely, the relationship between uncertainty, risk, and probability. Suppose we were to ask those readers who are married, "Exactly when did you decide to marry your wife?" Leaving aside the reply, "I did not decide; she did!" we might try to follow up by asking, "What was the most important piece of information which led you to this decision?" The decision to marry is clearly an important decision of relatively low frequency, and hence one about which we might expect good recollection. However, even the unmarried, who may miss some of the significance of this example, will appreciate that these kinds of questions about this decision are really rather silly. But in the example, the decision had been made, and we have previously argued a major distinction between the before and after in the decision process. Let us then suppose that we asked the unmarried, "Have you decided to get married, not to get married, or are you in the process of coming to a decision about marriage?" This kind of logical format is used frequently by opinion polls, and we might expect people to respond in such ways that interviewers could fit their replies into the categories provided. We should certainly be able to give percentage figures as cross-analyzed by other data such as age, religion, type of home, income, occupation, and the like. We might consider it reasonably safe to use these data to work out the characteristics of an insurance policy which we could sell to cover the risks of getting married or other attendant risks, or the risk of not getting married. We would be poor businessmen if we could not make a profit out of treating the decision to get married as a risk and calculating probabilities associated with it. Thus, we can say that for the observer of the decision process, the idea of probability in relation to the idea of uncertainty makes sense—if only because it can be used to make a profit. But does the same model make sense also to the decision maker himself?

Viewed from different perspectives, a phenomenon may appear in different forms, as is well illustrated by the familiar story of the three blind men and the elephant. But if a particular explanation of a decision process makes sense for the observer, then it might be argued that a model based on this form of explanation should also provide a rational model for the observer. In other words, the observer should be able to utilize the model he has of the situation to make further deductions as to the decision-making process which he can check by observation. If this is not the case, then we would expect that there was some fault in the model or the explanation which the observer considered from his viewpoint to be satisfactory. But perhaps the critical issue is that there are different kinds of decisions and different kinds of decision processes. The ways in which the decision maker searches for information may depend upon how he sees the decision he is required to make. Or, alternatively (or in addition), different decision makers may utilize different processes of information search for a common decision. If rational decisions refer to experience, then clearly— since the backgrounds of decision makers will vary—we must expect variation in the rational decision processes. But will this variation in relation to background be as great as the differences in experience or personality? Is a process of classification likely to be possible? Perhaps a classification may be possible if the kinds of decisions are restricted. In this research, our concern is with the decisions regarding parole. This is a decision of the same kind, no matter who is the decision maker or the situation in which the decision is made.

In the parole decision, much of the information is formalized, and each decision maker has potential access to exactly the same information. If the individual to be decided about should appear in person, then the decision maker may ask questions; and while in theory he might ask an infinity of questions, in practice he will not do so. Thus, there are boundary conditions with respect to the information. Further, all decision makers except those who are newly appointed to boards will have considerable experience of making many decisions within the same kinds of boundary conditions. In many cases there is an added complexity in that the parole decision is a shared one in which the view of colleagues may be required. The added complexity may assist in the examination of the problems because the sharing of the process requires communication among the participants. Thus, what could be unexpressed and even vaguely formulated in the individual decision case must, insofar as it is considered to be relevant, be overtly expressed in a shared decision situation.

The research worker may take up a position similar to that of the colleague of the decision maker. Or, it may be possible externally to observe the information search strategy which decision makers prefer, because the information is external in the form of files.

But files do not provide an easy base for observation because many kinds of information may be displayed together on the same page and the observer would find it difficult without interference with the process to ascertain which items were being sought by the decision maker. Any change from the usual procedure is, of course, likely to introduce new variables, and inferences that might be made in the changed environment of decision making may not apply to the original setting. However, it was considered that the separation of items of information by a means that provided easy access, but to only one item at a time, would not do too much violence to the usual setting of parole decisions. Two methods have been used to try to see how parole board members prefer to search for information about the offender. One used small index cards, an item on each, set out in similar form to that of the files with which board members were familiar.[15] The other used slides (35mm) and a random access projector. The results of the latter experiments are reported in appendix A.

In this section we are concerned with more general speculation and our basis of data does not come from the operations requested or performed by board members, but by an analysis of the comments made during the latter experiment. With which kinds of data were board members most satisfied? Was there any general strategy which would indicate ways in which computers should be programmed in order to facilitate the decision-making process?

An Initial Suggestion for a Taxonomy of Parole Decision Makers

In the experiment using the random access slide projector, decision makers could request any item of data about the subject upon whom they were expected to make a decision, but only one item at a time. They had before them an indication of the contents of the file (the slides and the content) in terms of the topic, but without any information specific to the offender. The selection of the order of items to be viewed was a group choice, made after discussion. These discussions led to the setting up of the theory to be described.

It was clear that among different persons the types of information most strongly desired, the search strategy, and the weights given to items of information differed very considerably. As a part of the experiment, decision makers were asked to make an interim decision after searching for only a small number of items. The first major suggestion of a typology of decision makers begins to appear in this area. Some considered the request to make an interim decision a quite realistic question and, since they were permitted to indicate a low degree of confidence in any early decisions, they found the procedure acceptable. Others did not consider the making of a decision as a possibility until they had sufficient information. The majority of the parole board members was in the first category.

One method for obtaining prediction tables, termed *step-wise regression*, first finds the most powerful predictor and then searches for others, adding information and increasing the power of prediction as a sequential process. It seems that many decision makers work along similar lines when they are presented with the need to make a decision and a body of data to assist them in arriving at a rational conclusion. The individual does not have any prior knowledge of which item has the greater power to discriminate in relation to factors of his decision, but he has experience and a personal viewpoint which leads him to prefer a particular order in which the information is presented to him. He does not want to be cluttered up with items he would consider irrelevancies at the first stage: quite the contrary. His order of search may be related to some recent experience, or to a more general experience. But, by whatever means the information priorities are determined, a priority exists. The particular priority tends to be characteristic of the decision maker. (For this result, we have to rely upon collateral research, since in this particular parole decision study we had only one sample.) The important thing about this type of decision maker is that he fits a model which starts with a probability (a degree of uncertainty), which is modified as further data emerge. Each item may make a change in the assessment until the time when there is considered to be no point in further search—the series has "tailed off" as in the calculation of the value of (e), if a mathematical analogy may be used. It is not surprising that these decision makers can, at any time during their search, give an interim estimate; this reflects their own procedure. We may call these kinds of decision makers "sequentialists."

Another type may be named the "ah, yes!" type of decision maker. Quite often, these persons will terminate their information search by exclaiming, "Ah, yes, this is the typical . . ." It is as though these decision makers are searching for *patterns* in the data, and until they have fitted a pattern, they do not feel that they have any real information. Although, of course, they have to look at information in a sequence, they do not appear to handle it internally in a sequential manner, but rather place it in storage until it "clicks." There are statistical and other methods which deal with pattern recognition problems, but computers are not very good at handling these tasks, unless the pattern is a simple one.

Persons who use one type of strategy cannot, it seems, understand how the others operate. This seems to be similar to the differences between visualizers and verbalizers, which used to be discussed in some areas of psychology. The differences do not seem to be derived from the same kind of function, and it is quite probable that there are sequentialists who are verbalizers and there are doubtless some who are visualizers. It is not known whether this particular taxonomy makes sense only in regard to parole decisions (and perhaps to similar decisions meeting similar conditions of data, environment, and the like) nor whether this is a learned behavior in the parole decision-making situation. Experienced parole board members do acquire a large repertoire of typical cases, and there have been many published offender typologies which could provide the template against which the information could be matched. Similarly, other board members may store information regarding single items of information which relate to performance on parole and hence to their decisions. Some persons, in order to deal mentally with an abstract situation, will visualize a stage, fill it with actors, imagine their speeches and acts, and "play through" the dramatic representation of the problem. Others, instead of a stage, may use a geometric space as a vehicle to project an abstract problem. There are many analogies and perhaps as many preferences.

Another type of decision maker may be termed the "simplifier." He may be typified on the one extreme as a person who starts his observations from the viewpoint, "Anything known against this man?" At the other extreme is the person who searches for mitigating factors: "Anything known in favor of this man?" The attempt here is to reduce the complex problem to the simplest form, preferably the one most important item, and this item may be chosen in a large variety of ways. This is the kind of decision making that might be termed prejudiced. An initial set, whether strongly punitive or strongly sympathetic, tends to dominate the strategy. These two, albeit apparently contrasting viewpoints, tend to show the same logical and informational search strategies. Often, this approach is thought to represent a search for the "real cause" of the man's trouble.

The last of the four types is really a nondecision maker: he is the "ratifier," or, as he has been termed colloquially, the "I'll go along" decision maker. His search strategy is to try to find what has been said by some person with whose views he can associate—the psychiatrist, warden, or the probation officer. (There is evidence that judges in the sentencing decision tend to be ratifiers and that the probation officers, in operational terms, perform much of the sentencing function.[16]) All decision makers find themselves from time to time in the ratifer role, because of the decision-making environment, usually in the form of administrative procedures. Ratification is also often a safe procedure in delicate situations. Nonetheless, and without gainsaying that this may be a rational procedure, the frequency with which it is employed seems to vary from person to person, as well as from situation to situation. The central idea here is an appeal to "authority."

Implications of Suggested Taxonomy

It seems probable that if a model can be established which is inherently satisfying to the sequentialists, the pattern searchers will find it unsatisfactory to interact with it. Thus the dialogue between the decision maker and the computer to which he looks for assistance may not be a standard form. To provide the facilities that are sufficiently differentiated that the varieties of decision makers' preferences can be met is a challenge which we now face. There are further implications of this theory in terms of training for decision making. Feedback methods are used extensively in institutes for judges and many other decision makers in the criminal justice area. It might appear that feedback of models which imply the sequential method of problem solving will not be effective except in regard to those persons who intrapsychically use this method of information search and assessment; and, of course, similarly, there will be difficulties for sequentialists in appreciating the meaning of any pattern-searching model.

Some Inferences from Experiments

The experiments with the simulated computer of the future have shown that different decision makers, given the facilities of an immediate-access, on-line information retrieval system geared to individual case material, would use the facility in very different ways. It is also clear that the method of presentation of the information (design of the software of such systems) could have a considerable impact upon the nature and style of decision making. Almost any item in a case file is likely to be requested in almost any sequence and at any point in the decision-making process by different decision makers. Even if constraints are imposed, so that all decision makers see the same information about the same case in exactly the same form, different decisions will be given. Moreover, despite the very different strategies for information search and retrieval utilized by different decision makers, these different approaches can result in the same conclusions. Different routes can lead to the same end, and the same route can lead to different ends.

Are Decision Makers as Good as They Think They Are?

The decision makers' claim that they find the processing of much data to be easier than the processing of little is one of the most disturbing findings. There may, however, be some general relationship between the human performance of any task and the assessment of its ease or difficulty, and subjective feelings of how well the task is done. It is well known that persons who drive after an intake of alcohol feel that they are driving better than they usually do. We are aware of doing badly on a particular task when the situation, material, or information becomes disorganized,[17] but so long as a state of subjective organization remains, there may be little relation between actual performance and the subjective evaluation of the performance by the individual performer. Feedback that conveys the message that the performer is "not doing well" is necessary, in some form, before the performer will acknowledge this as a fact. Thus, it seems likely that we may assess our performance as improving the more work we are doing (otherwise, we would be unlikely to invest the further effort), and we will continue to believe in this improvement until we obtain feedback by information that the effort is not paying off. There are interesting and important problems with the decision-making process that are not directly related to the quantity or quality of information, but rather to the subjective processing of the data. The processing may be expected to differ according to the different forms of retrieval (for example, sequence) and styles of presentation (for example, degree of codification).

An important question was raised at the outset of this chapter. How much information can be presented to the decision maker without overloading him and deteriorating his performance in the decision-making process? It seems from the results of the experiments that we may see the decision as the termination of an information procurement and processing operation. If this form of explanation is preferred, it seems that the termination of a process is also a process, but of a different order than that terminated. The decision to seek no further information is a decision about information, not a decision about the subject to which the information relates.[18] Thus, I may terminate the process of information search when I conclude that no further useful information will be obtained, or I may decide to make an interim decision or decide not to decide. A decision to make an interim decision is a decision of low confidence in the subject of the decision, but a decision of higher confidence in the need for more information. It follows that information which will lead me to a satisfactory conclusion as to whether it is worthwhile to seek more information is information relating to information, and not information relating to the subject matter.

The problem of reconciling the subjective assessments of ease/difficulty and confidence make sense if this interpretation of the decision-making operation is used. Decision makers found it easier to "make a decision" (that is, to seek no further information) when they had already referred to a fairly large number of items. Decision making (or information search and analysis) is a process that becomes easier to stop when a respectable amount of work has been done, and it is difficult to stop when only a few items have been seen. Although this explanation makes sense of the rating of subjects in the decision-making experiments, it does not help us to regard human decision making as any more rational a process. If we accept the idea of a decision as the stopping of a process, then it seems reasonable to ask about the stopping rules, and to relate the stopping procedures to the search procedures, since persons stop with very different accumulations of information and acquire it in very different sequences. Furthermore, it seems improbable that in the information search strategies of most decision makers there is any conscious effort to collect information-about-information as well as about the subject of the decision. More experimentation is required to throw light on these kinds of problems. The importance of information-about-information will be quickly apparent to anyone who is familiar with any forms of statistical multivariate analysis. The problem of the overlap of information is well recognized and dealt with in various kinds of statistical solutions. However, it seems unlikely that human information processing considers the correlations between items of information, and correlated rather than uncorrelated items sometimes may be preferred.

Experiments have shown that the sequence in which information is presented to decision makers, as well as the form of its presentation, is likely to influence the decisions, irrespective of the content of the information. It has been shown that probation officer decision makers will continue to examine items of information well beyond the point at which it is possible to remember them or utilize them in a decision.[19] It seems that where the option is open, decision makers will continue to examine information until they reach a point where they perceive that their organization of the material has broken down—that is, the first point at which there is feedback to the performer that his functioning has deteriorated.

Where individuals are permitted to seek any information they wish, in any order they wish, and to continue as long as they wish (the usual condition for judicial decision making) some persons will change their decisions after a large number of items have been examined. However, although many cases have been studied, no person has yet stopped the search and settled for a decision at any later time which was different from that decided before the eighth item of information was seen.

It is apparent that decision makers who believe that they can consider all the relevant information are deceiving themselves. It is also clear that computer salesmen who try to persuade managers that "if only they could have the information at their fingertips their problems would be solved," have too simplistic an idea of information search and utilization in decision making. Much is unknown regarding the relationship between the human user and the computer. Computer information systems present us with a new set of problems in man-machine relationships, and these relationships are of a different order from prior man-machine relationships.

As the visitor enters Cranfield Aeronautical College, he may see a large mural. It shows a vaguely human-looking beast operating a center lathe; one arm is longer than the other, the trunk and legs are of extraordinary proportions, and the impression is of a humanesque monster of grotesque physique. The caption under the drawing states that for many years members of the college had tried to persuade the manufacturer of center lathes to design a lathe suitable for human operation, but, having become disillusioned, had taken up a different project—designing an operator suited to the machine! Are we going to have as much trouble with the design of machines which assist us in our logical functions as we have had, and still have, in the design of machinery to assist in our physical operations? Man may more readily adapt his mind to the information machines than his body to the physical machines. There is no danger of "the machines taking over," but there are dangers from machine designers exerting much more influence than even they themselves are aware.

Notes

1. Susan M. Singer and D.M. Gottfredson, *Development of a Data Base for Parole Decision-Making*, Parole Decision-Making Project, Report 1 (Davis, Calif.: National Council on Crime and Delinquency Research Center, June 1973).

2. G.E.P. Box and K.B. Wilson, "Experimental Attainment of Optimal Conditions," *Journal of the Royal Statistical Society*, Series (B), 1951, pp. 1-45.

3. This term refers to cybernetic theory, not big game hunting!

4. D.M. Gottfredson, L.T. Wilkins, P.B. Hoffman, *Summarizing Experience for Parole Decision-Making*, Parole Decision-Making Project, Report 5 (Davis, Calif.: National Council on Crime and Delinquency Research Center, February 1972 [draft]).

5. M. Metfessel and C. Lovel, "Recent Literature on Individual Correlates of Crime," *Psychological Bulletin* 39 (1942):133-164.

6. P.E. Meehl, *Clinical vs. Statistical Prediction* (Minneapolis: University of Minnesota Press, 1954).

7. This is by no means a new idea. The possibility of cooperation between man and computer in relation to decision making has been discussed for more than a decade.

8. The ideas of utility, probability, and risky or riskless decisions, which have been developed in the field of decision research, do not help very much at this point. The consequences for the decision maker of the president's decision to go to war may be less than the wearing of a pink shirt by a job applicant, and it is not very meaningful to ask whether the president would prefer to go to war or to wear a pink shirt!

9. See C. Shannon and W. Weaver, *The Mathematical Theory of Communication* (Urbana: University of Illinois Press, 1949).

10. In everyday language persons often say, "I believe that . . . ," meaning "I think it is probable that . . ." However, a more formal association between degrees of belief and probability is discussed in many texts on theoretical statistics. See I. Good, *Probability and the Weighing of Evidence* (New York: Hafner, 1950; and London: Griffin, 1950).

11. For a more extended discussion of uniqueness as it applies to decisions about offenders, see L.T. Wilkins, "Problems in Prediction Methods: The Unique Individual," in M.E. Wolfgang, L. Savitz and N. Johnston, *The Sociology of Crime and Delinquency* (New York, N.Y.: John Wiley and Sons, 1962).

12. In the first experiments, decisions were made after reference to cards. A pilot study concerning probation decisions is reported in L.T. Wilkins, *Social Deviance* (Engelwood Cliffs, N.J.: Prentice-Hall, 1964), p. 294.

13. It will be noted that it is unlikely that any one member of the group will obtain exactly the four items which he personally desired.

14. See Wilkins, *Social Deviance*.

15. L.T. Wilkins, D.M. Gottfredson, J.O. Robison, and C.A. Sadowsky,

Information Selection and Use in Parole Decision Making, Parole Decision-Making Project, Report 5 (Davis, Calif.: National Council on Crime and Delinquency Research Center, 1973).

16. See L.T. Wilkins and Ann Chandler, "Confidence and Competence in Decision-Making," *British Journal of Criminology*, 5 (January 1965):1; and J.D. Lohman, A. Wall, and R.M. Carter, "Decision-Making and the Probation Officer," *San Francisco Project Research Report Seven* (Berkeley: School of Criminology, University of California, June 1966).

17. The perception of organization and disorganization is another intriguing issue of persons and situations which cannot now be developed.

18. The argument at this point is closely related to the well-known "paradox of the liar," believed to have been devised by Eubulides about 350 B.C. For example, if I say, "What I am now saying is a lie," can I be said to be speaking truly or falsely? If I say the statement is true, then as it states, it is false; if I say that it is false, then, as it states, it is true. There are, of course, many statements of this kind, such as "What this sentence says cannot be proved." All these classes of statements cannot be proved or disproved "within the limits of the language" in which each is stated. K. Popper (*The Open Society and Its Enemies* (Princeton: Princeton University Press, 1963)) discusses this paradox and relates it to similar problems such as that of the paradox of freedom and the paradoxes of sovereignty.

19. It is possible for the average person to remember only some seven or eight numbers that may be dictated to him. However, if a process, such as addition or subtraction, is specified, he can continue to *process* numbers according to the rules of combination well beyond the number of items he can remember. The rules of addition or subtraction are methods for disposing of information as it arrives in a sequential form. If information is processed according to some sequential process or another, then clearly much information can be processed; however, it can only be processed if a rule is stated that enables the sequential disposal of the information to be put into effect. Thus it seems important to know the rules of procedure that decision makers use in the processing of information by means of their own mental faculties. It may be that in addition to some sequential processes for disposal of information the human intelligence can turn items into patterns and deal with materials in that form. Thus we may be able to sum a series of numbers and remember at each stage only the cumulative sum to that point. Many persons will remember playing with typewriter characters to form patterns by superimposition of characters such as: /(,),/,*,-, and will know that a line of these superimposed forms looks like a row of soldiers, and may be remembered as such. When it may be required to recall the characters we might work out the items from the remembered pattern. However, in the superimposition rule we have lost the sequence information. Rules that enable the recapture or use of more than a few items of information, while facilitating recall, in some regards results in a loss of some information; the kind of loss is

related to the rule. Thus, in the examples, the rule of addition results in the loss of items as individual digits, their sequence, and frequency; the rule of superimposition to achieve pattern results in the loss of sequence.

6

Implications for Sentencing: An Argument for Explicit Sentencing Standards

Introduction

The concern of disparate sentencing, a traditional issue in criminal justice literature, recently has received increased attention.[1] More properly termed unwarranted sentencing variation, this problem results from the unguided and almost unlimited discretion given to judges in sentencing criminal offenders in the United States. Under American law, a judge's discretion at sentencing is generally, for all practical purposes, unreviewable as long as his decision is within the limits permitted by statute.[2] Combined with the doctrine of individualization (punishment/treatment to fit the offender rather than merely the offense), the effective result has been that a sentencing judge is free to do whatever he thinks appropriate in any given case, with no standards to guide or limit his discretion other than his own conscience and the attitudes he brings with him or develops on the bench. It is little wonder that present sentencing practices have been described as "...so arbitrary, discriminatory, and unprincipled that it is impossible to build a rational and humane prison system on them."[3]

Unwarranted sentence variation, it has been argued, produces a number of negative consequences. It is morally offensive both to defendants and to the citizenry, leading to disrespect for the judicial process and potentially for the law itself.[4] It is particularly dysfunctional for prison rehabilitative efforts.[5] From the standpoint of judicial administration, it may cause delays in the orderly scheduling of cases, as attorneys jockey for hearings before judges perceived as lenient.[6] Moreover, appellate courts, which generally are not permitted to review sentences directly, may tend to distort substantive law to provide relief from sentences deemed grossly excessive.[7]

In spite of its potential for abuse, it is generally agreed that a certain amount of discretion at sentencing is essential.

While absolute uniformity is neither desirable nor attainable, it is imperative that a greater similarity of treatment be attained than now prevails. Individual treatment of offenders must inevitably lead to differences in sentences, but this does not account for the flagrant disparities which occur in cases where the only differentiating factors are the geographical situs of the offense or the proclivities of the sentencing judge.[8]

Adapted from P.B. Hoffman and L.K. DeGostin, "An Argument for Self-Imposed Explicit Judicial Sentencing Standards," *Journal of Criminal Justice*, vol. 3, no. 3, (Elmsford, N.Y.: Pergamon Press, 1975). Reprinted with permission.

That is, equality in sentencing does not necessarily mean that the same punishment should be applied to all offenders, but rather that there should be justifiable reasons for variations in punishment. Uniform sentences for each statutory offense may lead to results as unfair and unjust as does presently unguided discretion.[9] This is not to say, however, that revision of legislative codes which provide excessive or disproportionate penalties would not be a useful or desirable first step.[10] Moreover, as various critics have pointed out, legislatures obviously could provide considerably more guidance as to the appropriate goals of sentencing and the factors to be considered.[11] Nonetheless, it appears doubtful that any legislature could specify in advance and in sufficient detail the panoply of factors and circumstances that may be appropriately considered as aggravating or mitigating conditions and substantially limit judicial discretion without substituting excessive rigidity. Furthermore, there is serious question as to whether attempting to limit judicial discretion by legislative action in the form of mandatory penalties would not merely shift the exercise of this discretion to an earlier stage in the system (for example, charging or plea bargaining) where it would be even less visible and less subject to control.

Consequently, it is postulated that the most appropriate remedy for the problem of unwarranted sentencing variation is not to attempt to eliminate judicial discretion, but rather to develop methods to utilize discretionary power more appropriately:

... to eliminate unnecessary discretionary power, and to discover more successful ways to confine, to structure, and to check necessary discretionary power.[12]

... to provide a technique whereby discretion should be allowed ample creative scope and yet be subjected to rational external discipline or self-discipline.[13]

Control of Discretion

Various techniques to control sentencing discretion have been proposed, and in some jurisdictions certain of the techniques have actually been implemented. These include sentencing institutes, sentencing councils, appellate review of sentencing, providing written reasons for sentences, and the formulation of explicit sentencing policy. Articulation of sentencing criteria and the formulation of sentencing policy will be the major thrust of this chapter. However, a brief discussion of these other proposals and their limitations is required to present a proper perspective.

Sentencing institutes—meetings of judges in which sentencing objectives, procedures, and sample cases are discussed—have been conducted in the federal system since 1959.[14] Unfortunately, while these institutes may lead to some accord in sentencing principles, there is little evidence that they have greatly altered the attitudes or sentencing practices of judges.[15] Furthermore, the potential of this technique is inherently somewhat restricted due to the limited possible frequency and duration of such meetings.[16]

Sentencing councils—multijudge advisory sentencing panels—have been tried in several jurisdictions with apparently satisfactory results.[17] Under this procedure, several judges meet at designated times to review and discuss presentence investigations concerning cases about to be sentenced. However, the feasibility of this practice for widespread usage also appears to be restricted in terms of time, expense, and geographical limitations involved.[18] Moreover, while it seems reasonable that such panels tend to reduce extremes in disparity among individual panel members, it is problematic as to how much disparity among panels—or within panels from time to time—remains. It is to be noted that parole boards have traditionally utilized some form of panel arrangement, yet unwarranted variation in paroling decisions has remained a viable criticism.[19]

Appellate review is a third technique proposed for controlling sentencing discretion. Proponents argue that even the possibility of appellate review would tend to make judges reflect more carefully on their sentences. Opponents argue that appellate review would merely open a floodgate of frivolous appeals, further burden appellate courts, and cause even more delays in the celerity of punishment.[20] Experience in several jurisdictions in which appellate review has been available seems to indicate that it has achieved, at best, only a small reduction in the most excessive sentences.[21] A primary factor limiting the utility of appellate review of sentences appears to be the same factor responsible for the disparity in the first place—the lack of articulated sentencing criteria and sentencing standards.

While the adoption of sound legislation providing for some form of appellate review of criminal sentences is sorely needed, most of the common problems of sentencing equality, uniformity, and individuality relate to the initial question of the appropriate method by which a more enlightened sentencing policy can be achieved.[22]

Without such standards, as well as a written record as to the factors considered and the weights given to them, there is little for appellate judges to measure a sentence against except their own notions of propriety,[23] leading to the argument that the exercise of sentencing power is merely being moved an additional step away from the presence of the defendant and the community.

A fourth proposed technique, related to the articulation of sentencing policy but by no means synonymous with it, involves providing written reasons for sentences. As with appellate review, proponents argue that through the provision of written reasons, sentences will be more thoroughly considered. Opponents argue that such a practice will only become an additional burden for the court.[24] There appears to be some evidence that, where used, the mere statement of reasons has not had a great impact on disparity, and that the reasons given are usually pro forma or brief rationalizations of the sentence after the fact.[25]

It is our argument that providing reasons for sentences is a necessary but not sufficient condition for structuring and controlling discretionary power. Examination of the following example should convince even the most skeptical that without an explicit sentencing policy, even relatively detailed reasons will not ensure the consistency desired, although such reasons may be useful for identifying impermissible sentencing considerations (for example, race) or incorrect sentencing information. Let us consider provision of the following reason in the case of an armed bank robber sentenced to a prison term:

You have committed an armed robbery in which lives were potentially endangered. You are not a suitable candidate for probation because of the seriousness of your offense, combined with your prior record of two convictions during the past year. In addition, you were on probation at the time of the present offense and have a history of severe heroin usage.

Many would agree that this is a substantial narrative reason for Judge Lenient's imposition of a two-year prison term. However, when one agrees that it appears to be an equally good reason for Judge Moderate's imposition of a five-year prison term or Judge Severe's imposition of a ten-year prison term, it should be readily apparent that even the articulation of the criteria used without the weights given to them is not likely to produce the desired effect.

While it might be argued that the provision of such reasons combined with appellate review of sentences would over the years (or centuries) establish case law producing sentencing guidelines, there appears to be a more straightforward, convenient, and certainly speedier method: the purposeful formulation of an explicit sentencing policy identifying the major factors to be considered and the weights to be given to them.

Explicit Sentencing Policy

The question of whether judges can continue to operate without articulated criteria in light of due process and equal protection requirements is a troublesome one.

Unless the defendant can know in advance what information the trial judge will deem particularly relevant, in a very real sense he has little notice of the issues to be determined at sentencing. Thus, if due process requires notice and hearing at sentencing . . . , it may well require concomitantly that standards be enunciated.[26]

Formulation of an explicit sentencing policy by identification of the primary factors considered and the customary weight to be given to each would appear to have several significant benefits. It would provide an explicit policy or sentencing calculus which would indicate the customary sentence or sentence range to be imposed for each combination of primary factors. The effect would be to guide and structure an individual judge's discretion, but such discretion would not be rigidly limited or removed. That is, if a judge desired to impose a sentence outside the limits indicated by the sentencing calculus in a particular case, he would not be prohibited from doing so, he would merely be required to state his reasons for departure from customary policy. For cases within the policy ranges, brief formulaic reasons would be sufficient.[27] Thus, more detailed reasons would be required only for departures from customary sentencing policy. In this manner, not only would discretion be guided and structured, but an explicit basis for meaningful review would be provided. Moreover, since policy would be set by the judiciary itself rather than imposed legislatively, it would be more amenable to refinement and change as circumstances may indicate.

It is important to note that to provide an explicit sentencing policy, not all sentencing items would have to be catalogued and weighted, but only the most important. Utilizing a decision board game developed by Wilkins,[28] a study of sentencing recommendations by federal probation officers found that they were generally formulated and maintained after consideration of relatively few items.[29] In a related area, a study of federal parole decisions indicated that three dimensions of focal concerns (offense severity, parole prognosis, and institutional discipline) were primary.[30] From this latter study, explicit policy guidelines for parole decision making were developed and implemented by the United States Board of Parole.[31]

Thus, it is hypothesized that a workable explicit sentencing policy or sentencing calculus could be developed using a relatively small number of elements or focal concerns (from two to eight). The simplified hypothetical example of a sentencing calculus, shown in table 6-1, utilizes two focal concerns—offense seriousness (severity) and prognosis (likelihood of nonrecidivism). More dimensions or focal concerns could be readily added, merely requiring additional or more sophisticated charts.

In the hypothetical sentencing calculus shown, the customary disposition for an offender with a low severity offense and a good prognosis (low likelihood of recidivism) would be a suspended sentence and/or fine. For an offender with a high severity offense and a poor prognosis, the customary disposition would be a sentence of three to five years incarceration. To implement this type of sentencing calculus, the judge would complete an evaluation form containing the desired scales for each case about to be sentenced. (A hypothetical seven-scale evaluation form is given in table 6-2.) He would then refer to the appropriate sentencing calculus table to find the customary or normal sentencing range. If he wishes to make a decision outside of this range (either more or less severe) he would be required to indicate the particular factors that warrant this decision. Decisions within the normal policy range would, as noted, not require additional specification.

Table 6-1
Hypothetical Sentencing Calculus (Simplified)
Severity/Prognosis

		Prognosis (Likelihood of Nonrecidivism)				
		Very Good	Good	Fair	Poor	Very Poor
Severity of Present Offense	Low	Suspended sentence	Suspended sentence +/or fine	Fine +/or probation (up to 1 year)		
	Low Moderate	Suspended sentence +/or fine				
	Moderate	Fine +/or probation (up to 1 year)	Fine +/or probation (1-2 years)	Probation (1-3 yrs) +/or incarceration (up to 6 months)	Incarceration (6 months-1 year)	
	High Moderate			Incarceration (6 months-18 months)		
	High				Incarceration (3-5 years)	Incarceration (4-7 years)
	Very High					
	Most Heinous					

Note: As this sentencing calculus table is hypothetical, no attempt has been made to complete all of the cells.

Initially, the scalar dimensions or focal concerns could simply be subjective. As time passes, more objective categories might be substituted for certain of these scales. For example, with the federal parole guidelines cited, a nine-item actuarial device was developed to aid in determining the prognosis classification.[32] This actuarial device is completed for each case by the board's hearing examiners. If the hearing examiners disagree with the actuarial parole prognosis estimate, they may use their clinical judgment to override this predictive aid. However, their reasons for doing so must be stated. A list of objective definitions of common offense behaviors was also developed[33] and is used in a similar manner to assist in applying the board's severity scale. In this way, objective factors are utilized not to remove discretion, but rather to guide and structure it.

Table 6-2
Hypothetical Sentencing Evaluation Form

Name of Defendant _____ Docket # _____

(1) Offense Severity
    (Low)   (Low Moderate)   (Moderate)   (High Moderate)
      (High)   (Very High)   (Most Heinous)

(2) Prognosis (Likelihood of Nonrecidivism)
    (Very Good)   (Good)   (Fair)   (Poor)   (Very Poor)

(3) Prior Record
    (None)   (Minor)   (Moderate)   (Serious)
               (Very Serious/Extensive)

(4) Assaultive Potential
    (None)   (Low)   (Moderate)   (High)

(5) Social Stability (e.g., employment, drugs, alcohol)
    (Very Low)   (Marginal)   (Adequate)   (Very High)

(6) Age
    (16-20)   (21-25)   (26-30)   (31-40)   (41 or over)

(7) Community Resources
    (None)   (Marginal)   (Adequate)   (Very Good)

Special Factors (if applicable) _____

_____

Sentencing Decision _____

_____

Note: The dimensions noted are those commonly thought to be considered by sentencing judges. As this form is hypothetical, no attempt to include all possible relevant dimensions has been made.

Control of Plea Bargaining

An explicit sentencing calculus might also be used to bring greater judicial control to plea bargaining. Assuming that a determination is made that the practice of plea bargaining is to be retained,[34] the limits of an appropriate bargain might be one of the factors specified by explicit policy. That is, each guideline category could contain a sentencing range for conviction by plea as well as a sentencing range for conviction by trial[35] (see figure 6-1). In this manner, the acceptable range of leniency for a guilty plea for any particular category in the sentencing calculus could be specified in advance.

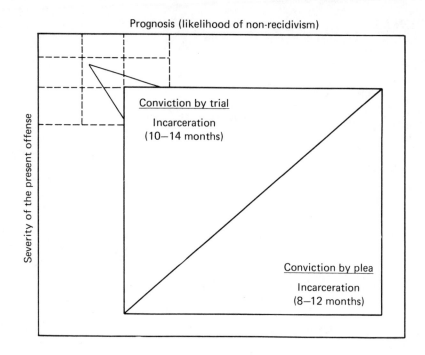

Figure 6-1. Hypothetical Sentencing Calculus: Severity/Prognosis/Plea

In addition to increasing sentencing consistency, such explicit policy could be used to define and prohibit improper (overly coercive) bargains. In fact, if the only reasons the practice of plea negotiation is tolerated is the necessity to secure a given proportion of guilty pleas,[36] the differences between the sentencing ranges for conviction by plea and conviction by trial could, with empirical experience, be adjusted to attain the smallest (least coercive) range that would produce the necessary results. This is not to argue that plea bargaining ought to continue, but rather that if it does continue such steps might be taken to minimize its negative effects.

Facilitating the Articulation of Sentencing Policy

While it might be possible for each individual judge to establish and articulate his own sentencing calculus (as one might conclude is presently done internally), this would not necessarily reduce the problem of unwarranted sentencing variation among judges, although it would likely produce greater consistency for any particular judge from case to case. Obviously, it would be desirable for a sentencing calculus to be developed on some jurisdictional basis (such as a district or circuit basis). Possibly, the presently available concept of regional sentencing institutes could be utilized to provide a body to consider the adoption, monitoring, and revision of such standards.

As an aid in determining the feasibility of establishing such sentencing guidelines, the following exercise could be used. Participating judges would complete an evaluation form (such as that shown) prior to sentencing each case over a given period of time.[37] The time period would be directly related to the need to collect a certain number of cases (preferably several thousand); obviously, those jurisdictions with a heavier work load would require a shorter period of study. The actual decision made in each case would also be recorded. Analysis of the relationships between the factors (or focal concerns) recorded and actual decisions would then be relatively straightforward. That is, one would be able to identify the degree to which implicit policy presently exists for the various factor combinations (even the most severe critics of sentencing disparity would probably concede that some rudimentary, although implicit, policy exists). By identification of this presently implicit policy, the judiciary would have a starting point for determining whether such policy is appropriate and should continue to exist, or how such policy should be amended or refined. The resultant policy could then be adopted to form the sentencing calculus. Objective guides or aids could then be added, where possible, to supplement the subjective scales. To avoid rigidity, it would also be important for some method to be established by which policy could be considered periodically for revision, with input from the individual judges concerned.

Conclusion

Establishment of explicit sentencing policy would to some measure shift the locus of discretionary power in regard to general policy from the individual judge to a larger body of judicial peers. Any such proposal would be likely to meet at least some judicial resistance. Nevertheless, it is felt that the establishment of self-developed and self-imposed policy guidelines could provide sufficient consistency to minimize the obvious injustices of presently existing unwarranted sentencing variation without creating the rigidity of legislatively attempted discretionary control (mandatory sentences), and thus is superior to either the presently unguided and unbridled use of discretion or those proposals calling for the substantial reduction or abolition of judicial sentencing discretion by legislatively mandated sentences.

Notes

1. See, for example M.E. Frankel, *Criminal Sentences: Law Without Order* (New York: Hill and Wang, 1973); W. Gaylin, *Partial Justice* (New York: Alfred

A. Knopf, 1974); A Partridge and W. Eldridge, "The Second Circuit Sentencing Study, A Report to the Judges of the Second Circuit," Federal Judicial Center, Washington, D.C., 1974.

2. "In the federal courts and in some two-thirds of the states, there is in practical effect no appeal from the trial judge's sentence." Frankel, *Criminal Sentences*, p. 75.

3. N. Morris, *The Future of Imprisonment* (Chicago: University of Chicago Press, 1974), p. 45.

4. U.S., Congress, House, Committee on the Judiciary, *Improving the Administration of Justice by Authorizing the Judicial Conference of the United States to Establish Institutes and Joint Councils on Sentencing, to Provide Additional Methods of Sentencing* House Report 1946, 8th Cong., 2d sess., 1958.

5. President's Commission on Law Enforcement and Administration of Justice, *Task Force Report: The Courts* (Washington, D.C.: Government Printing Office, 1967), pp. 14-26; see also J. Bennett, "Of Prisons and Justice," Senate Document No. 70, 88th Cong., 2d sess., 1964.

6. President's Commission, *The Courts*.

7. U.S. Court of Appeals, "Appelate Review of Sentences, A Symposium at the Judicial Conference of the U.S. Court of Appeals for the Second Circuit," *F.R.D.* 32 (1962):249, 271 (Remarks of Chief Judge Sobeloff, U.S. Court of Appeals, Fourth Circuit); see also Frankel, *Criminal Sentences*, p. 82.

8. W. Byrne, "Federal Sentencing Procedures: Need for Reform," *Los Angeles Bar Bulletin* 42 (1967):563-64.

9. For a discussion of this issue as well as the role of the legislature in confining and guiding discretion, see National Advisory Commission on Criminal Justice Standards and Goals, *Report of the Task Force on Corrections* (Washington, D.C.: Government Printing Office, 1973), pp. 539-543.

10. President's Commission, *The Courts*.

11. Frankel, *Criminal Sentences*; National Advisory Commission, *Report on Corrections*; American Law Institute, *Model Penal Code* (Philadelphia, 1962).

12. K.C. Davis, *Discretionary Justice* (Baton Rouge: Louisiana State University Press, 1969), p. 42.

13. S. Glueck, "Predictive Devices and the Individualization of Justice," *Law and Contemporary Problems* 23 (1958):461, 466.

14. L. Youngdahl, "Development and Accomplishments of Sentencing Institutes in the Federal Judicial System," *Nebraska Law Review* 45 (1966):513.

15. S. Rubin, "Disparity and Equality of Sentence—A Constitutional Challenge," *F.R.D.* 40 (1966):55, 57; see also, Frankel, *Criminal Justice*, pp. 61-68.

16. M. Frankel, "Lawlessness in Sentencing," *University of Cincinnati Law Review* 41 (1972):1, 19.

17. C. Hosner, "Group Procedures in Sentencing: A Decade of Practice,"

Federal Probation 34 (December 1970):18; see also T. Smith, "The Sentencing Council and the Problems of Disproportionate Sentences," *Federal Probation* 27 (June 1963):5.

18. See Rubin, "Disparity and Equality of Sentence," p. 58.

19. See Davis, *Discretionary Justice*, pp. 126-33.

20. See D. Thomas, "Appellate Review of Sentences and the Development of Sentencing Policy: The English Experience," *Alabama Law Review* 20 (1968):193; see also Byrne, "Federal Sentencing Procedures," p. 565; and J.D'Esposito, "Sentencing Disparity: Causes and Cures," *Journal of Criminal Law, Criminology and Police Science* 60 (June 1969):182.

21. "Appellate Review of Primary Sentencing Decisions," *Yale Law Journal* 69 (1960):1453, 1461.

22. F. DeCosta, "Disparity and Inequality of Criminal Sentences: Constitutional and Legislative Approaches to Appellate Review and Reallocation of the Sentencing Function," *Howard Law Journal* 14 (1968):54.

23. "Appelability of a Criminal Sentence—Sentence Modified on Appeal," *Rutgers Law Review* 16 (1961):186.

24. See D. Thomas, "Sentencing—The Case for Reasoned Decisions," *Criminal Law Review* (1963):243; see also S. Frankel, "The Sentencing Morass and a Suggestion for Reform," *Criminal Law Bulletin* 3 (1967):365.

25. Rubin, "Disparity and Equality of Sentence."

26. A. Pugh and M. Carver, "Due Process and Sentencing: From Mapp to Mempa to McGautha," *Texas Law Review* 49 (1970):25, 41.

27. For example, in reference to table 6-1, the following reason might be given: Your offense has been rated as *high* severity; your prognosis has been rated as *poor*. Guidelines established by this court (Circuit) indicate a sentence of *three to five years' incarceration.* After careful consideration of your case, this court finds no factors sufficient to warrant a decision outside this guideline range.

28. L. Wilkins, *Social Deviance* (Englewood Cliffs, N.J.: Prentice-Hall, 1964), pp. 294-304.

29. R. Carter, "The Presentence Report and the Decision-Making Process," *Journal of Research in Crime and Delinquency* 4 (1967):203.

30. See appendix B.

31. See chapter 2.

32. See chapter 3.

33. See chapter 4.

34. Abolition of the practice of rewarding guilty pleas has been recommended by the National Advisory Commission of Criminal Justice Standards and Goals (Washington, D.C.: Government Printing Office, 1973), p. 168. ("Sentencing courts should immediately adopt a policy that the court in imposing sentence should not consider, as a mitigating factor, that the defendant pleaded guilty or, as an aggravating factor, that the defendant sought the protections of

the right to trial assured him by the Constitution.") See also American Bar Association Project on Minimum Standards for Criminal Justice, *Standards Relating to Pleas of Guilty*, approved draft (Chicago: American Bar Association, 1970).

35. The sentencing range established for conviction by trial would be deemed the normal range; the sentencing range for conviction by plea would be deemed the lenient range. Thus, it may be argued that persons who plead guilty receive leniency and that those convicted by trial receive only what they deserve. Of course, an argument can be made equally well that rewarding pleas of guilty has the effect of enhancing punishment for those who exercise their right to trial, regardless of the semantics used.

36. The Supreme Court decision in *Brady v. U.S.*, 397 U.S. 742 (1970) upholding the practice of plea bargaining appears to rest upon the assumption that this practice is necessary to keep the criminal justice system going.

37. A similar exercise has been suggested by Frankel, *Criminal Sentences*, p. 111.

Looking Back

The completion of the research concerning the decision making of the United States Parole Commission has, with the cooperation of that commission, led to a very different process from that which previously characterized the parole determinations. It is not for the research staff to say whether the new system, facilitated by the research work, is better than that of the past. The commissioners believe it is—otherwise, they would not have changed their previous procedures. The courts have, on several occasions, indicated their approval and the Congress has incorporated the guideline concept into statute. Also, this concept has appeared in various proposals for legislative changes relating to sentencing. Various state paroling authorities have developed and implemented similar guidelines systems; and the concept has been applied also to sentencing by courts. That rather good record for a research operation became possible only because the commissioners were so willing to work closely with the research staff. This was not research *for* the customer, but *with* the customer—cooperation (indeed, collaboration) at all stages and at all levels.

Is it sufficient that we can claim with some justification (at least with support from data!) that the project was successful? Is it to be left to run without challenge? Perhaps the parole commissioners deserve a period of quiet after the continuous criticisms they faced before adoption of the modified procedures. Perhaps—but the research workers deserve no such respite. What could we, as research workers, do now if we had our chance over again, that we did not do the first time? How do we see the procedures changing? What are the unsolved problems that we were able to identify as we went along the road toward the "product" of this particular project? We will attempt to discuss some of these issues in this chapter. We realize that we are perhaps too close to our own work to be its best critics. That is one of the reasons for publication of the preceding chapters—we have told what we did so that we may be criticized and so that others may advance new models.

What Were the Long-Term Results?

The changed procedures are one aspect of the research and its application, but research should lead to more fundamental concerns than procedural change, no matter how sound and good that might be. We make our own claims, but realize that again others may disagree. Perhaps we can claim three points of concern

that the research addressed and that have, as we see it, substantial impact beyond this particular project. These three areas are:

1. The procedures for the granting of parole have changed from a closed to an open system. The philosophy from which the paroling decision is made is now spelled out in clear and quite specific terms and, indeed, in relation to quantified data. Nonetheless, the system retains flexibility.
2. The procedures have a built-in method for continuous modification, rather like a self-homing missile. Policy may be informed by information that the environment has changed and can change its direction accordingly to retain focus upon the target (goals/ethics/legislative directives).
3. A general method has been discovered that can reduce disparity in any decision field where considerable discretion obtains. The general problem of disparity extends beyond the area touched upon in this study; but the methods used provide a new dimension enabling a much more thorough investigation of this problem. The disparity issue is found at each step in the criminal justice process, wherever discretion in decision making occurs. Further, this general method has various implications for ways of addressing certain moral issues in the criminal justice field.

We shall discuss these claims first and then consider our own dissatisfactions with the model. Later, we will examine the probable future research strategies that seem necessary or desirable.

From Closed to Open Parole Decision Policy

Why parole? Are not many of the progressive thinkers in the field of criminal justice claiming that parole should be abolished? Is the system, developed with the aid of the research, not propping up a procedure that should be abandoned rather than modified and made more presentable? Of course, to a degree, all reforms militate against the revolution! That, as we see it, is a fact of life with which research workers, as others, must come to terms in their own ways. It may be that the open system of parole decision making is more likely to survive the test of time than the prior system. We believe that an open system is to be preferred. We claim, therefore, that the fact that the research was (at least partially) responsible for the move toward a system which all those concerned, including the offenders, could understand is one of the achievements of the project of which we can be proud.

The change in the decision process does not make much change in the nature of parole as experienced by the released offender; it does make a considerable difference to the determination of his period of incarceration. Decisions regarding the time offenders, once incarcerated, are to be held in prison will always need to be made by some authority, even if the use of paroling authorities as they now are structured is abandoned. Offenders may be discharged to unconditional freedom; they may be offered voluntary assistance or aftercare; or they may be required to submit to conditions that, if breached, would result in their return to a further period in prison. These are matters that are not investigated nor commented upon in the research reported here. They are quite different issues from those of the determination of the "time to be served" which was the focus of our inquiry and recommendations.

It is likely that there will be considerable continuing debate as to the most appropriate machinery for determination of the time to be served. It may be observed that almost all the information now used by the United States Parole Commission in its setting of time (granting of parole) is known at the time of commitment. Some may ask, then, should not the sentencing judge, using guidelines, set a fixed sentence, rather than having a parole board do so later? This kind of question, and others like it, now may be asked *because* the system is specific and open. When the decisions were hidden in mysticism, suggestions of this kind could not be made. Thus, one consequence of the open system is that the interconnectedness with other sectors of the general processes of criminal justice become more clear.

The greater degree of clarity of the process and its better understanding by those concerned provides an external possibility of challenge to the procedures, thus providing a means of stimulation for still further change. This is an important facet of the model, since it provides a necessary flexibility and stimulus to an evoluntionary system. Any new system, even one that was the best possible at any point in time, could soon become a poor system if it were to ossify. The environment in which the penal system is embedded will change and the penal system will change in adaptation. No system of decision making can be sound for long unless it has built into it, *as an integral part of the system,* a means to adapt to change.

Flexibility

It should be noted, particularly in reading the research materials, that the model is not "fitted" to the observations as closely as might be possible. It would seem to be possible to provide an equation that could explain over 90 percent of the decisions of a parole board. We would strongly recommend that a finer "tuning" of the guidelines *not* be attempted in the future. An 80 percent precision is quite adequate, and indeed guidelines that fitted more than 95 percent of the cases would become dysfunctional. The task of the decision maker is to identify those cases where the policy indicated in the guidelines *should not* apply. If his expectation of finding such cases were to drop too low (because the guidelines were "improved" in their fitting) he would soon begin to miss the cases where he

should depart from policy. The probability of finding a proper case for departure must not be too small nor, of course, too large. We have arbitrarily set this not-too-large-not-too-small at 85 percent as probably the best level of fitting to be sought.

Flexibility is preserved mainly through the mechanism of the departures from the guidelines determinations. In such cases, specific reasons for departure must be given. The collection and collation of the reasons accompanying departures from the guidelines provide the basic statistical data for examination of the question of possible need for change in the policy. The commission, meeting *en banc* at regular intervals, reviews the reasons for the verified departures from the policy. If the departures indicate the accommodation of individual idiosyncracies in the case decided, then there is no need to make any changes in policy. If, however, there is a trend toward a setting aside of guidelines for a category of case (a collective of reasons for decisions), then it may seem reasonable to investigate the possible change of the guidelines to accommodate the trend. Further, the individual decision makers may represent to the commission, meeting *en banc,* their objections to any policy indicated in the guidelines. They may not properly modify the guidelines in any particular case they may decide in terms of their individual view of policy. Policy change (guideline modification) is a matter for the whole board and not for any individual member. This is most important. Perhaps an example may indicate how this should work out in practice. It is possible that different decision makers have different views of the seriousness of certain kinds of offenses. It will be remembered, however, that the decision as to the level of seriousness of the offenses is a policy matter and is set by the whole board. Thus the fact that, say, one commissioner has a strong opinion of the seriousness of tax evasion does not allow him to set back the time of any tax evader, departing from the guideline for this category of offense. He expresses his views (correctly) to the commission, but he does not express his views on this matter by means of his decision about the parole applicant. This characteristic of the system must be preserved in the future. *Policy decisions must be dealt with differently and separately from case-by-case decisions.*

The Terms of the Equation

Policy may be expressed in general terms—and usually is. With the guidelines, however, each item of data used in the expression of policy is clearly stated. We not only say that the decision is made in accordance with the seriousness of the offense as one of the factors, but the ranked listing of offenses is made public. Not only is there a salient factor score that consists mainly of an expression of the prior criminal record, but the weight given to each single item of information about that record is specified and known to anybody interested. It may be expected that the details of the means for so assessing the seriousness of the offense and the previous record will, occasionally, come to be challenged. It may be agreed by some critics that seriousness is an important consideration, but the rank order for some offenses is not, in their view, correct. Presumably such opinions might be tested in court, although it would seem that the court could only add its support to the categories worked out by the parole commission. Since the commission is a properly constituted body for this purpose the mere substitution of one individual's opinion for the collective assessment based on discussion and analyses does not seem to offer any improvement.

The items in the salient factor score may be more open to challenge. At present, it can be shown that any and all of the items are predictive of future offending, but it cannot be claimed that each item is the optimal selection from all items that might be predictive. There are, thus, two considerations. It might be considered that more powerful predictive equations could be found if different items were included or different methods of combinations of items were carried out. The parole authorities might take the view that it is quite reasonable for them to provide information (provided that the security of the information could be guaranteed and protection provided for individuals in accord with legal and ethical requirements) to any research body that wished to attempt to improve predictive power from the data base. If such research did turn up more powerful predictive equations, it would be for the commission to consider whether they should use the new equations to substitute for the current salient factor score.

It seems unlikely that more powerful predictive equations will be found by any methods based upon the current data base. It might happen that a new predictive equation could be found to be more powerful, but it might use information items that would be suspect, or seem to be undesirable to include in the determination of parole policy. The general point of whether the correct equation to use is that which is the most powerful in predictive terms is also arguable. If the best is that which is the most predictive, then at what level of improved prediction and with what degree of confidence would substitution take place? It would seem to be undesirable to continuously change the equation system, even though a new equation might be found which was marginally more powerful.

The Predictive Basis as a Dimension of Decision

It is possible to question the fundamental philosophy of the use of a predictive scale as any factor in the parole decision. One problem of the predictive basis is that it has been closely associated with the treatment or medical model for the disposition of offenders, as implied in the very word *corrections* now used to describe most prisons and related facilities, the rehabilitative aims of prisons

have been increasingly stressed in the past few decades. The treatment model is now very much under attack; the criticisms come from both left and right, from reformist as well as conservative opinion. New basic concepts are gaining ground. Punishment and deterrence are now discussed as prominent aims of the system. The isolation of the dangerous and potentially dangerous is advocated by both criminal justice scholars and political leaders, although this also implies a predictive element. A concept which avoids prediction (or seems to do so) is that of "just deserts."[1]

Whatever the dominant philosophy for the disposition of offenders is, or becomes, the fact that parole policy is explicit may be expected to lead to debates on grounds of morality, efficiency, and effectiveness. Some may argue that the United States Parole Commission should adopt a strict just-deserts approach, rather than a modified version including the predictive model described in the preceding chapters. It will be noted that in the current (1976) salient factor score there are three items which, while predictive, do not accord with the desert model. The majority seem to present no difficulty from either approach—they are predictive items and they would be possible items in a desert model as well.[2]

It seems that there may be little conflict between two apparently quite different options in model building. We know that the weightings and methods for deriving equations do not seem to make much difference to the power of the prediction. Indeed we have noted that simple weights of either unity or zero (applied to the individual items making the scores) generally provide results equal to more sophisticated methods. We know also that equations that have different sets of items included provide equally good predictive performance—there is no particular set of items or weights which is clearly optimal in terms of predictive power. Clearly, one of the reasons for this is that the predictive items are also correlated with each other. It is, therefore, highly probable that equations could be found that reflected only the just-deserts theory, and that, at the same time, proved equally as predictive of success or failure as did equations that utilized items that were not justified by this theory.[3] In operational terms, this could mean that the distinction between a predictive mode and a just-deserts mode could be moot! Despite the very different considerations and highly significant theoretical and philosophical differences, the application could converge in one equation! For those who argue in favor of a strict desert model, this may be a philosophically *tidy* solution. Clearly, those who would advocate the just-deserts approach could not find any reasonable grounds to reject a set of guidelines merely because the means for quantifying the prior criminal record happened to be predictive.

Comparative Model Building

The general type of model described in the foregoing chapters is characterized by the concept of two or more dimensions (such as seriousness of offense, and probability of reconviction or seriousness of prior record). The idea of dimensions of policy is central. Individual items in the scores take a secondary place to concerns about the basic concepts. Adjustments of a minor nature in the individual items included may be made, but the argument in support of any such adjustments must be that the amended form represents the base concept more appropriately or more efficiently.

In the studies we have carried out to date, we have developed the models for the guidelines from experience in the field. Descriptive models, if they were found to predict decisions by board members, came to be adopted as prescriptive. We did not decide upon a theory as to what ought to be done or seek to set up an ideal scheme for parole decisions. We ascertained the existing practice, codified it into a model, and submitted our findings to the board members concerned. It now seems desirable to explore other methods. It is, of course, possible to approach model building in a variety of ways. It would be possible to develop models that were tailored to particular theories of decision making and to test these against practice, rather than letting practice decide the initial shape and content of the model.

It is possible to develop decision-making models that deal with information quite differently from that involved in the dimensional concept. It may be that attempts to use the concept of dimensions to explain the decisions of other parole boards or judicial decision makers in the future will not work. Data may be collected, submitted to analysis as in the previous studies, and it might be found that the models did not fit no matter what system of weights was applied. Such a failure of a type of model to fit might mean that the particular board concerned had no policy, or it might mean that the dimensional model *as a type of model* did not apply. In the dimensional models, it is necessary to find indicators (items of information) that add up to a score or otherwise permit classification of the person on each specific dimension. The addition of information items means that the individual may trade off any one good indicator against any one bad indicator, and provided that they were weighted equally, he would still attain the same level of score. Hence, quite different personal profiles (and score patterns) may add to the same score total. Since it is the score total that determines the action in the dimensional model, offenders with quite different profiles of informational detail will be treated similarly. This is, of course, exactly what would be expected with the concept of dimension as the controlling datum.

It might be expected that some persons would question this somewhat sophisticated approach on grounds of equity. It might be pointed out that two offenders, each possessing the same characteristic (for example, type of offense), have been treated differently. It is possible to argue that such an example would represent inequity if, and only if, the characteristic selected as the reference were regarded as the only one worthy of consideration in the decision, or all other things were equal. In our suggestion that different types of models should be examined, we are not limiting our thinking to simplifications of the model by leaving out all considerations except one single dimension, such as seriousness of

offense. Rather, we have in mind quite different structures of models and strategies for developing them. We will give some examples in general terms.

Moral Values and Models

It is possible to postulate moral concerns in regard to both the items considered in arriving at a parole decision and the process itself—issues of both content and operation (procedures). The relation between the model and the process may seem the major difficulty. Parole decisions have a moral content because human beings are processed by the decisions. We have strong views as to items of information which it would be unjust to consider in relation to an individual determination, such as religion and race, and we specifically outlaw such considerations. Thus, we state that any value other than zero given to these items is morally wrong. That is straightforward. But we are not so clear as to the processes of decision making and we do not rule out any particular procedure as immoral because, say, it inhibits risk-taking decisions.[4] In the past, questions relating to process styles have not attracted much attention, because the different kinds of structure were not clearly known or encoded.

We can now identify two kinds of issues, both of which raise moral value questions. These issues, however, are of quite different form. We have, in the past, discussed the moral concerns (in relation to parole decisions) in terms of the outcome of the decisions, such as whether the persons were detained too long or let out too soon with resulting risk to the community. These questions, of course, remain and are still the most significant. There is, however, the new question as to whether the process itself is justified. (This is not quite the same as the old ends/means questions.) Should decisions be made with respect to dimensions (as, say, seriousness) or should individual items of information discretely provide the basis for determination? Or should there be some constraints in terms of process as well as in (as already recognized) the use of certain factors as such? A still further question is whether the issues should not be resolved only in terms of outcome. Some may argue that the right (?) outcome is all that is required and any process that maximizes that end would be self-justified thereby. This could lead into a futile debate as to whether there can be two or more equally good or equally right ends obtained by quite different processes of decision making.

Processes of Modeling

A digression may now help to provide illustrations of some models that could represent different processes. Unfortunately, the kind of model and the kind of process are related and the probability of discovery of the processes may depend upon the strategy of the research operations. We must, then, take one further step backwards, and take a quick look at the research strategy. Although the models derived in the parole research to date have been invented through the study of ongoing decision making by parole boards, this is not the only method for model building. In some kinds of research, it is possible to state in advance the nature of the model that it would be reasonable to fit to the data and to ignore all others. The just-deserts model (suggested by the Committee for the Study of Incarceration[5]) was derived by thinking about what ought to be done, not by studying what was done. It is interesting that they emerged with a model very similar to that indicated by the guidelines of the United States Parole Commission.

Our attempt to find equations that explained parole board decision making was not devoid of all theoretical considerations. The use of theory was, however, somewhat weak.

It is possible to work instead with a strong use of theory. Models that represent the possible extreme positions may sometimes be designed. Such models may allow quite useful statements to be made without the support of any observation in the field. Such kinds of models are of considerable value in planning new forms of activity. Nagel provides an interesting example of this approach.[6] We may be concerned to estimate what might happen if modifications were made to the jury system such that six who were unanimous or a ten out of twelve majority were deemed adequate to provide the verdict. We may assume one extreme condition is that every juror will vote independently of every other member of the jury. As the other extreme condition, we may suppose that, as in a game of bowling, if the kingpin goes down the remainder will follow with a very high degree of probability. We thus have a model for independence (one extreme) and for interdependence (the other extreme). We may attach various mathematical assumptions to these models and see how they behave with varying assumed states. We may safely assume that whatever may happen in practice will lie between the two conditions.

Neither extreme model will apply as a fit to the behavior of any real-life jury. The question of the precise form by which juries act in reality is not relevant if we can make our inferences from the two models. The model encompasses all possible situations and makes no statements as to which is better or worse. The model may assist us in assessing either the morality or the efficiency of the operations that it maps, or it may assist with both; but the model itself merely provides a language. Models may represent ongoing operations, express theories, illustrate limiting possibilities, or illustrate the average. The model is a tool of wide use, but it is little more than a tool. Models may be turned from a language or abstract tool into an actual operating mechanism—such as an analogue machine or certain kinds of instrumentation. Let us consider a different example of model building.

Cheese making is more of an art than a science. Until recently, cheeses were

assessed for quality and ripeness by expert subjective inspection.[7] An experienced worker would press the cheese with his thumb and assess the fight-back quality. It seemed desirable to try to replace the skill of the subjective assessors by instruments so that when the processes were automated or the skilled assessors became unavailable, the quality control could still continue. Accordingly, research work was undertaken to see if an instrument could be designed to replace "Joe's thumb"! This was by no means a trivial exercise, since much depends upon the quality of the product. In the cheese case, research methods somewhat similar to those reported in the preceding chapters in relation to parole decisions were used. The research worker's task was to try to find a model that could predict the subjective assessment of cheese quality. The criterion of success for the research was how well the instrumentation represented the human decision.

Let us consider one further example of model building of a yet different kind. The income distribution of households in cities is not usually available except for a small sample of towns where surveys are regularly carried out.[8] For all cities, however, there is a variety of data from the number of telephones to the infant mortality rate, and these data are available at frequent intervals. It seemed useful to attempt estimation of the income distribution of cities where these data were not available by using as proxy some weighted sums applied to the available data. This proved possible within very narrow limits. The substitution of a set of weighted knowns which had been demonstrated to fit the observations where available for the unknown variable has again much in common with the fitting of equations to parole board decisions. One set of information (details about the offender) is available in all cases where decisions are required and in some (observation) instances the decisions of the board are known. We seek to map the one into the other and identify a set of proxy data for the decision data.

Selecting a Strategy

While there are more similarities than differences in the kinds of mathematical analyses necessary to carry out the different projects noted, one major distinction must be stressed, namely, that between a priori model building and a postiori model building. In the case of the jury models we have an example of a priori modeling—the model could be set up without observing juries in action. In other cases, models may be designed to represent ideal types of behavior on the assumption that rational decisions should be expected. Such are the Bayesian models and other prescriptive models, of which perhaps the best known is that of "economic man." These latter forms involve the making of assumptions about the real world, which are unlikely to be true, such as the assumption of perfect information in regard to market behavior models.

Our position in regard to parole decision-making research is somewhat different from these examples in one respect. As perhaps the reader has grown tired of hearing, the federal parole guideline research began as an a postiori model based on observations and was completely descriptive. It is, however, clearly incorrect to talk of guidelines as descriptive, since the very term indicates prescription. This transition from descriptive to prescriptive is critical to our approach and it is a transition that we ourselves are not prepared to make. This must be the board's decision in each jurisdiction. This decision involves something like a prescription which says that the policies of the past (recent case decisions) reflect a policy that should be continued into the future. In other words, the descriptive model (if it is sufficiently powerful) provides guidelines for future decisons by systematically condensing the past decision behavior of the board concerned.

There is, of course, no constraint on the board to adopt the formalized method for preserving their past policy through guidelines. Without such a procedure, however, there is no guarantee that they will be able to maintain their past policies in the future. They may drift toward being more risk-accepting or more risk-aversive and not know that this is so. The board may, of course, take the view that they do not wish to continue as they have done in the past. This is tantamount to modifying or rejecting the model where the model is analogous with the cheese testing case noted above.

The descriptive model provides a language that clarifies the existing policy, enabling it to be studied critically in a manner and detail not previously available. For example, if it should be necessary to consider the item "race" in order to explain (describe) the board's past decisions, then this revelation might suggest that the descriptive equations should not be turned directly into guidelines.[9] The board might modify the equations by deleting "race" in the score and make use of the modified equation. This would ensure that "race" was not taken into consideration in the future. A mere declaration that it was not to be considered would not necessarily suffice. In such a case (should it exist) it is not a change of attitude on the part of the decision makers that is required, but a change in the decision reference. Individual members of boards are not charged with making policy in the course of their individual decision making: policy formulation is a matter for the board acting as a whole. The modification of policy through the medium of guidelines is a mixture of a priori and a postiori modeling.

All modeling methods have one important facility: they enable simulation methods to be applied to both moral and efficiency questions. Before modifying a policy through the medium of changing guidelines, it is possible (and desirable) to use the old and the proposed new equations in simulation on a sample of past cases. Information gained by this means would enable value choices to be made on better information than merely to work upon the abstraction of policy statements.

Kinds of Accountability

Perhaps the most revealing thing a person can tell another about his decision making is how he knows when he has made an incorrect decision. The failures of a process are often more informative as to its nature than its successes, particularly if the failures are recognized. In some way or another, all parole boards are concerned with the possibility of getting a decision wrong and with the consequences of any error or accusation of error. It is important to note that accusations of error made by others and self-recognized errors can be similar or may be quite different things. Parole boards tend to be unnoticed by the general public while everything is going well. The determination of "well" is not necessarily unbiased. If a dramatic incident occurs (for example, a paroled murderer commits another crime) then the board is held accountable and accused of making a serious error in its decision. There is seldom much clamor that a board is detaining inmates too long (although it is unreasonable to expect that all error will be made in one direction). There is little comment upon a parole board's action except in terms of dramatic incidents, and there is a tendency to generalize from the single incident and to attack board policy. Such possibilities must always be in the minds of board members, even though suppressed. "If this case fouls up, what can I say?" or perhaps, after an incident, "How can we avoid another one like that?", where "like that" refers to the total effects on the board of the facts of the case and the ways in which these were represented to the embarrassment of the board. If parole is granted at all, there is always a risk of cases arising with similar facts to those that caused problems for the board. It is not, therefore, unreasonable to concentrate upon the second part of the problem, namely, the ways in which the facts may be represented to the discomfort of the board or as a challenge to the general policy of parole.

There are two kinds of defensive strategies—perhaps more. These may be expected to be reflected in the models discovered by seeking descriptive equations. The defense of a decision may concentrate on the individual items of information in respect to the individual "foul-up" or it might concentrate on the correctness of the general policy and play down the individual details. Which strategy is the more likely to be effective depends upon the environment (political climate) in which it is applied. It is also possible that the form of the attack (whenever it comes and for whatever reason) may differ according to the environment. The *New York Times* may attack with one form, while the *San Francisco Chronicle* may use another style, and so on. Boards are, of course, quite correctly, sensitive to their environment; the survival of parole as a system depends upon its remaining acceptable to legislatures and the public, and the press has an influence upon both.

It is not suggested that different parole boards may select a different method of information search and decision making because they are prepared for different forms of possible attack. Rather, board members in any area reflect in themselves something of the qualities of the area. States do differ from each other! People who live in the different environments of different states, whether or not born there, are continuously breathing that air, living in that information setting, and reacting to that political climate. It may be that the boards of various states should reflect the essential elements of their political scenes. If that prescriptive statement is accepted, then we may make another—the guidelines should reflect state differences. This is the stance taken by the research workers in the parole research studies. The research, as it proceeds to be worked out in additional jurisdictions will, we expect, reveal differences between paroling policies of those states. The models will make quite clear these differences because they are stated in very precise language and not in generalizations as is more usual with policy statements.

The test, as we see it, is whether the model as fitted to the decisions (provided that such a model may be found) is acceptable to the board for its future guidance. (Note: It is not possible for a board to claim that a model does not describe their policies in the past, since this is a matter of demonstrated fact.) In the specific case, if a model is accepted, there are also provided means for adaptation of the model to changes with time, as well as a possibility of departure for a limited proportion of cases. The exception procedure is part of the total system and a most essential part.

It may be that the seriousness of crimes which may be of the same category will not be the same in different environments. As a judge put it to us recently, "Cutting a wire fence in rural Vermont is a different crime from cutting a wire fence in urban Denver." The crime, was, of course, of the same category but the different environments attached different qualities of seriousness to the consequences of the act and hence to the way in which the residents perceived the crime. Comparisons between forms of equations are difficult and can be made only approximately. We accept that the qualities of a crime (which are related to the nature of the dispositions of the courts and the decisions of parole boards) are determined by two or more (but at least two) factors, the crime and the environment in which the crime was committed. We lack the means for adequate description or classification of the later and the legal categories of crimes are not strictly comparable among states. Comparisons would, therefore, be a difficult task and require considerable further research. We hope that this will be borne in mind by readers of this book and that they will not rush into criticism of boards in other jurisdictions which may work to different styles and hence may develop or use differently constituted guidelines.

Other Possible Methods

If the guidelines had been derived from theoretical postulates rather than inductively from observation, the opportunity for different models to appear

would have been limited. If, for example, we had prepared a priori a just-deserts model (as did the Committee for the Study of Incarceration), we would have found some considerable degree of fit in the federal system and perhaps in some other jurisdictions. In others, we might have found a rather poor fit; and we would not have known whether this was due to a different policy or to the deserts policy poorly executed. Any a priori model building carries the danger of prescription edging out description and hence could become a vehicle for research workers to insert their own values into operational activities. For example, Adam Smith stated a theory of economic behavior in terms of an a priori model and this model later became value-laden and prescriptive. Governmental budget departments began to act as though the Adam Smith model was truth in fact. In that case, treating the model as though it were true did not make it come true! With parole decisions, belief that a model is true may lead to its becoming so—true, perhaps, but not necessarily desirable.

Simulation Methods and Moral Questions

Model building, whether or not developed into the operational use of guidelines, is one of the most powerful methods for assessing the import of our social decisions. It may even be said that we may begin to examine some quantification of moral judgments by these methods. This is a sweeping claim and needs justification. Perhaps an example will indicate a possible approach.

In the model used by the United States Parole Commission, there are two major dimensions that account for most of the variance—seriousness and the salient factor score (probability of recidivism, or a quantification of the prior record in a just-deserts model). Examination of the degree of increment in the time-to-be-served value as against these two dimensions reveals that the seriousness factor is the more important—the slope of the penalty is greater for seriousness class than for the salient factor score by a ratio of about 60:40. It would be an easy matter to hold constant the same average time (in two dimensions) but to modify the scales so that seriousness of offense and the salient factor score were equally weighted, or the weights might be reversed. In other words, the discovered model may now be modified to one of the a priori kind. It would then also be a simple matter to draw a sample of decisions about individual cases and to see what differences the change of scale would make in the outcomes. In one pile, we could put those cases that would be decided in exactly the same terms, in another those whose penalty would increase, and in another those for whom it would decrease. This could be done for any model we wished to imagine and were prepared to put to the test. Simulation of different sets of decision rules upon the same set of cases (federal compared with federal, for example) does not give rise to the problems of comparison noted earlier to apply to comparisons among different jursidictions.

It is difficult, in abstract, to answer questions as to whether justice requires that the seriousness of the offense be given the same, lesser, or greater weight than factors about the offender that relate to his degree of commitment to crime. We now know that the United States Parole Commission was acting as though the correct weight was slightly greater for the seriousness of the instant offense. (That seems to be a reasonable inference to be drawn from the relative slope of the penalty.) This is the codification of the wisdom of the board as it has developed over the years. We know of no reason for claiming that the ratios should be changed.

The important thing about modeling is that we do not have to make the actual changes or to put into effect an innovation in order to be able to study its probable consequences. And, of course, simulation is made possible through the use of the discovery of models which fit practice and which could, therefore, be represented to fit to changed practice. Simulation methods can be used to examine very many and highly varied and controversial issues. Indeed, the number and types of simulations that can be researched appear to be limitless—only the time available and the imagination may restrict their number. There are very good reasons: simulation costs little, does not involve any real risk, is not politically embarrassing, and is less time-consuming. Some of the qualities which are usually assumed to involve moral value choices may be simulated and the input varied. Justice (a moral concept) involves concerns as to the equity and possible influence of prejudice on decisions. It is known that the kinds of decisions people make are related to the ways in which they search for information. It is also known that it is possible to change the probability of decisions of particular kinds where the decision makers are presented with information in varying orders. That is, the type and content of the information are identical, the decision makers are the same persons, but the different order of information made available leads to different decisions. This is particularly true where the decisions involve risk. It is also known that the medium of presentation influences the nature of the decisions. Redundant information (correct, but unnecessary information) also modifies decisions. These modifications can all occur whether the decision involves moral value choices or merely economic welfare (for example, investment) decisions. We are now able to study these phenomena because we can, as it were, take apart the complex processes which previously hid the same kinds of effects, although most were intuited by experienced decision makers.

Some Research Priorities

We know that the data base throughout the criminal justice system is of poor quality. Some have called for very large investments to improve the information both in terms of quality and in its handling. Is the cost of improvements justified in terms of improved decision making? Improvements for their own sake are not

justified. We already have investigated techniques for data handling and analysis in relation to decisions and data quality. Some methods can withstand more noise in the data set than can others, and they prove equally as efficient as guides to decisions. It would seem to be a good strategy to ensure that the improvements in the quality of the material are matched with improvements in our ability to use it. An expensive cloth and a cheap tailor will not produce the best suit! Perhaps we should devote a little time to these meta-questions?

At the end of the research projects reported in this work, we (the research staff, and perhaps others) are like children with a new Tinker Toy. We can see all the things that it is possible to examine by setting up models and by simulation and data analyses. As research workers we find some of the questions more intriguing than others, but we do not consider ourselves alone to be the authorities on the priorities that should be given to the questions. We want some persons concerned with other aspects of the criminal justice processes to look over our shoulders, as it were, as we go through the manual of things that can be built and to say from time to time, "Why don't we build that and see how it works?" In short, we need guidance as to the priorities that should be given to questions that are amendable to analysis with the new techniques.

There is a more fundamental question that has to be faced (or avoided, which will amount to the same thing!). Continuing the analogue of the Tinker Toy, the question is, "What size basic kit should we invest in?" It is possible to imagine very sophisticated sets which involve computer data bases and man-machine interaction with automatic recording of simulated decisions within various constraints. The paper file is already obsolescent; and perhaps we need to know how decisions may be reached when the medium of presentation is changed.

It is possible that those decisions that we now regard as moral choices will be modified by the mere change of the medium of presentation of information. We already have research findings which strongly indicate that this will be so. We can simulate the computer of the future at this time and be ready to meet the new problems it will bring. We can leave matters as they are and rely upon reactive measures. That is the major value choice now to be made by action or by default.

The Climate for Change

The environment in which this research began was one of challenge and hence of potential for change; it was a climate conducive to research. There had been, for some considerable time, two related influences toward the kinds of change that were facilitated by the research. There was criticism of many aspects of secretive activity in the government bureaucracy—in the press particularly, but also in other mass media. In the Congress of the United States, considerable attention was given to similar criticisms. Furthermore, the courts were beginning to take jurisdiction where previously they had not interfered with the administration of the penal system. Some judges had both commented in court and written critically of the parole processes. The modification of the parole decision process, with explication of specific policy, was, therefore, a child of the times—perhaps a little precocious, but not wholly premature. Accordingly, this child survived and even prospered. With this setting, can we make some guesses as to the future opportunities which research workers may be able (and some may wish) to grasp?

It would assist if we could find a concept that will dominate criminal justice philosophy in the next few years. It seems quite obvious that the concept of treatment in terms of the medical model will not be the dominating theme that it has been in recent times. The treatment model is closely related to the efficiency concept and the demand for cost-effectiveness in the operations of the criminal justice system. The demand for efficiency spawned much research in the evaluation of the correctional processes. Indeed, it was the fact that the idea of treatment led to claims of benefits which enabled the concept to be discredited.[10]

Opportunities for research arise from time to time, but seldom are these created by the research workers themselves. Value choices have to be made, implicitly or explicitly, as to whether a particular research opportunity is to be taken up or not. Opportunities are likely to be noticed when the area concerned is attracting some publicity—which is to say that research workers, like others, read the newspapers! There are doubtless many and varied stimuli to the research workers' minds, but in most instances it seems unlikely that the stimulus is purely internal. Like others, research workers have great difficulty in attaining great heights by pulling on their bootstraps! Thus in considering where research is likely to go in the future, we would take the view that the determinants will be much as they have been in the past. The climate (environment) in which research is contemplated influences the nature of that investigation. Whether the results of research are implemented or not is also very much related to factors external to the quality of or characteristics in the research investigations themselves.

Will Parole Continue in the Future?

It is possible that the demise of the dominance of treatment theory will have considerable impact upon the nature of parole. There has, of course, always been some conflict of the perceived goals of parole supervision—it combined help to the ex-inmate with surveillance, case work with compulsion; or so it was claimed. Some doubted that this mixture could be therapeutic and others that it was even possible of achievement. This debate will harden, but whatever the

outcome there will be a need for some authority to make decisions regarding the length of time an offender, once incarcerated, shall be detained. If penalties are more finely graduated, then decisions as to when an offender may be moved from one level of restriction to another will also be required. Thus, whether parole (meaning supervision and surveillance of the discharged offender) is necessary or not, some decisions closely akin to those now made by parole boards will be needed. Offenders so dealt with may be discharged to complete freedom or offered voluntary assistance without conditions or whatever; but the length of time served will remain as a question to be decided by somebody according to some decision rules. The necessary body might be constituted in a variety of forms and consist of many kinds of persons in various mixtures. The decision about time cannot, it seems, be avoided.

Mandatory Sentences?

Some have taken the view that discretion by parole boards and even the judiciary should be eliminated. They propose to do this by having the legislatures fix penalties for each offense. A person found guilty of a specific offense would, in this system, be given a definite term penalty determined by statute. Others take the view that no attempt to destroy discretion will be effective; that if discretion is squeezed out at one point it will appear somewhere else in the system. If judges cannot vary penalties, then the juries or judges may be reluctant to convict where the penalties are seen as too severe; or the prosecution will vary the nature of the charge upward or downward as related to current practice, and so on. There is plenty of scope for the exercise of discretion without its being too obvious. Mandatory penalties may only make the exercise of discretion less obvious to the public. If this is true, then it may be considered to be undesirable to seek to eliminate discretion, but, perhaps more reasonable to seek to structure it. Rather than set up a system that would result in the exercise of discretion becoming hidden, we might set up machinery that would result in its exercise being obvious. Discretion may not be undesirable as a feature of the criminal justice decision process. The stance taken in the research described here fits this latter view. Moreover, it is clear that with a mandatory model the penalty can be varied only in precise accord with the category as described in the mandate. This seems to provide a straitjacket of limited categories into which all offenders will somehow or another be fitted (or compressed!). No lawmakers can, in our view, imagine in advance all possible varieties of criminal behavior, and if they could, they could not record and classify them adequately, relating each category to a morally justified penalty.

The Just-Deserts Theory

We have already referred to the deliberations the "Blue Ribbon" Committee under the chairmanship of Charles E. Goodell which proposed the idea of just deserts as the basis for the disposition of offenders found guilty before the courts.[11] Their system would not only fit the penalty to the instant offense but would take account of the prior criminal record.

So far as the major dimensions of the proposed just-deserts sentencing procedure is concerned, the prescription is very similar indeed to that of the United States Parole Commission. The Goodell committee specifically rejected any predictive basis for their sentence determination; but, of course the fact that they wished to take into account the prior record of the offender, in fact, provided a predictive dimension. There is no suggestion that their thinking was influenced by the research noted earlier in this work nor by the policy of the United States Parole Commission. It is interesting, however, that they should devise a priori a model for sentencing which was quite similar to that developed from our research. There is, however, a difference of considerable importance.

The committee's suggestions did not include any procedure for the continual review and change of the system once established. This, we believe, is critical. No system, no matter how refined, can be expected to remain at a high level of efficiency under conditions of a changing environment. Furthermore, societal values are also changing and what is seen as justified now may not seem so justified in a few years time. The environment of criminal justice will change and sentencing policies must also change to accommodate the new environments. If a process for change does not exist as part of the general structure, then the system will ossify and end up no better than the one that it replaced. A system that can, as it were, redesign itself in accord with general principles seems to us more desirable than one that must be suspended and redesigned by an external authority at such intervals as seem necessary. The fact that the guidelines of the United States Parole Commission are designed to be reviewed periodically is the major factor distinguishing our approach from that of the Committee on Incarceration. It distinguishes it also from the prominent sentencing reform model of presumptive sentencing in the Twentieth Century Fund report.[12]

Notes

1. A. von Hirsch, *Doing Justice: Report of the Committee for the Study of Incarceration* (New York: Hill and Wang, 1976).

2. Since this chapter was written, the commission has indeed substituted a revised salient factor score method that deletes two of the three items.

3. Generally, it will be possible to identify indicators that are merely consequences of acts or characteristics. Such items may be excellent proxies for the real thing, and there is no point in discarding powerful information because it is merely an indicator—counting the consequences rather than the event. Some proxy items may, however, look rather odd as items, and given rise to criticism by persons who are not accustomed to data of this kind. Given that items of data are correlated with each other and with the criterion, we have an information-rich field from which to select the data items. There is a very large

possible array of indicators of undesirable qualities and proxies for such measures (all of which are singly predictive of recidivism), and we cannot go on adding them together without limit. Any reasonably sized sample of indicators, with a reasonably sized data base, will give us a measure of predictability. A very large number of samples must be assumed to exist, and many of these possible samples of items and weights could give predictions of approximately equal power. The power level does not provide us with a criterion for selection of an optimal equation from the large number of possible equations. Some equations may be so weak that they would be rejected, but it seems likely that an equation could be found that rejected all information not supported by the desert philosophy, but which was equally as predictive as any other equation.

4. It may not be immediately apparent that process is of a quite different order from rules of inclusion or exclusion. An example of a process, as used here, would be the requirement of unanimity or the acceptance of a majority of any specified ratio in jury verdicts. Items of information that are exactly the same in content may be presented in a number of different orders and it is known that the *order* of presentation (without any change whatsoever in the content or form of any item) will influence the nature of the decision made. The order of presentation would be a process variable in our terminology.

5. Von Hirsch, *Doing Justice.*

6. S. Nagel and M. Neef, "Operational Research Methods Applied to Political Science and the Legal Process," in *Quantitative Applications to the Social Sciences.* Seen in draft by author.

7. G.W. Scott-Blair and J.M. Burgess, *Deformation and Flow* (Amsterdam: North Holland, 1952), p. 22.

8. L.T. Wilkins, "Estimating the Social Class of Larger Towns," *Applied Statistics* 1, 1 (1952).

9. No such case has been found in our research to date where "race" has been a factor, and this is given as an example where there would be little or no disagreement as to the undesirability of the transition from descriptive to prescriptive equations (guidelines) without some modification.

10. For a discussion of this issue, see, for example, L.T. Wilkins, "Current Aspects of Penology," *Proceedings of the American Philosophical Society* 118, 3 (1974):235-47.

11. Von Hirsch, *Doing Justice.*

12. Report of the Twentieth Century Fund Task Force on Criminal Sentencing, *Fair and Certain Punishment* (New York: McGraw-Hill, 1976).

8   Looking Ahead

The Generality of the Guidelines Method

Many kinds of decisions made by a variety of organizations can be usefully regarded as falling into two parts; these are the *policy* element and the *individual case* element. Where such decisions relate to moral values there is a case for the consideration of a *guideline* approach to ensure equity. Two examples may serve to indicate the generality of the model building and related procedures to other kinds of problems. Although we choose only two examples[1] for this purpose, it may be noted that many other decisions in juvenile and criminal justice could serve as well. These include, but are not limited to, decisions in the juvenile justice system such as: whether or not a child, on referral to a juvenile court's probation department is to be detained before adjudication or not; whether or not the jurisdiction of the juvenile court is to be waived, with referral to the criminal courts for disposition; and, of course, dispositions following adjudication by the juvenile court. The determination of custody of children in divorce cases may also seem a possible area of application. The decisions in criminal cases are many and varied; all include the exercise of discretion and may be suggested as areas for guideline model development and application. These include police decisions such as whether to arrest, release, cite, or issue warrants; prosecutor decisions such as whether to prosecute or not (and the allocation of resources related to the vigor of prosecution, for example, investigation time) and the general area of plea bargaining; probation officer decisions as to violation recommendations; prison administrator decisions about institutional assignments and dispositions of disciplinary hearings. We will consider as examples the decision whether to grant bail to an accused (where such a decision is permitted by law), and the decision to recommend certain individual patients for allocation of scarce resources such as kidney transplants.

Determination of Bail

In many jurisdictions bail may be granted or refused by the court. The amount of security is often set with the expectation that the defendant will not "make" the sum and will be detained in default. In the United States, outright "preventive detention" is permitted by law in some jurisdictions, not in others. Views as to the legal and moral issues of preventive detention by refusal of bail are strongly held and widely divergent. Our model would not, of course, determine any value position; rather it would make any implicit value position clear. The clarity would emerge from the very form of the model which reflected the determinations currently being made in the relevant jurisdiction. If it is desired to hide the basis for decisions, guidelines and the related models would be rejected. The willingness to advocate a guideline model implies a value choice in favor of the concepts of open government and, with that, a high level of accountability on the part of decision makers.

Many readers will be familiar with the VERA system for release on recognizance decisions and will recognize that the points score used in that system is closely related to the guidelines methods described in this report. There are, however, some major differences of importance both in terms of policy and techniques, which may be:

1. The VERA score is a single dimension, whereas the federal parole guidelines are two-dimensional.
2. The VERA scores were derived a priori whereas the federal model requires the derivation of guidelines from discovery of implicit policy as previously practiced through the application of prediction methodology. (Prediction, that is, of the decisions that are probable in individual cases in accord with a general policy.)
3. The VERA system does not have a continuous feedback procedure for review and modification in accord with experience of the operation of the system.

Initial Considerations

It must be noted that in approaching the idea of the development of guideline models, there are several elements to be dealt with before work may begin. Besides research matters, there are administrative and legal or jurisprudential concerns. It is necessary for any organization thinking about guidelines to know the existing system and to be able to note both facts and values regarding it. A data base indicating the decisions made in the recent past is a basic requirement. Alternatively, a data base must be set up as the first step. Some of the issues in regard to bail decisions are:

1. Has bail often been "granted" but the individual unable to raise the sum required as surety?
2. What are the presumptions regarding bail? Are there any statutory limitations or limitations derived from precedent?
3. How much is the problem regarded as related to extremely rare events? Often the issue of bail lies dormant until a particularly dramatic event

awakens the public consciousness. How do decision makers see this problem?

4. Is the concern about bail really limited to the possibility (probability?) of failure to appear? Or, is the probability that the accused may not appear at his trial weighted by the nature of the crime charged?

5. What is known about those who fail to appear? What precisely is the definition of "not appear"? (Note: Some offenders have been known to go to the right building but to get lost while genuinely trying to find the court.)

6. Are there figures for the cost of issuing of warrants for those who do not appear? What is the effectiveness of such process?

7. What would be the rules of procedure for the implementation of any guidelines which might be developed? Will new machinery be necessary?

8. What is the nature of delays in trials? How do delays relate to failures to appear?

The preceding list is not exhaustive, but rather is intended to serve as an indication of the background information desired before a model-building exercise is attempted. The major issue is, of course, that of the criterion. That is, it is necessary to define most clearly what the system is intended to do. The development of guidelines is not necessarily involved in any restructuring of the purpose of the system, but it does require most explicit statements of that purpose. Continuing with the bail example, we might find in some jurisdiction that the granting of bail is perceived to be contraindicated where:

1. The defendant has previously jumped bail;

2. There is a reasonable probability that the accused would not appear at the trial;

3. The alleged offense is rated as extremely serious;

4. A prior offense is proved and is rated as of a very serious nature;

5. There is a probability that witnesses might be interfered with or endangered;

6. There is a probability that a (new) offense will be committed while on bail;

7. There is evidence that the accused had a long prior record (but not as provided for in [4]).

This list is perhaps not exhaustive. Also, it might be thought by some to contain items that should not count against the granting of bail. It might be possible to work through such a list and to obtain subjectively assigned weights to the various criteria on the part of officials concerned in the criminal justice process. If a ranking of weights is not possible it may still be possible to divide the list into three parts—very serious consideration; medium weight; little or no weight. Each sampled person could assign from a list provided and add his own considerations if these were not included. Armed with this list, appropriately weighted, we may begin to consider the basic research design.

Given that the purposes can be stated in a suitable form, we might look next to the administrative background data. These issues in the case of bail would turn upon the manner in which the procedure of bonds, sureties, or other guarantees would be taken into account. Is there any evidence that bonds of various kinds result in a higher or lower probability of the accused to appear in court? If there are no data, what is the considered opinion? Is there any suspicion that high bonds generate thefts to raise funds? What are the other desirable and undesirable contingencies associated with the possible varieties of procedures?

Clearly the fixing of a sum that cannot be raised by the accused is operationally equal to the refusal of bail. It is probable that sufficient data will not be forthcoming to decide many questions empirically. Where there are no data there will be beliefs, and there may even be some concordance of beliefs. In order to continue the illustration we will assume that there are available three categories of decisions: (1) release on own recognizance (no bond required); (2) bail granted provided that a satisfactory bond can be posted (or similar sureties found); (3) bail refused.

The central category (2) is the most difficult to fit with existing theory and facts. Analysis could enable a model that might provisionally be set up to be modified, and data should particularly be examined in respect of the center category.

An Outline Model of Guidelines for Bail

We will take the necessary assumptions in order to present an outline model for guidelines for the determination of bail. We assume that there are three major criteria and that these are (more or less) uncorrelated, namely, (a) the probability of appearing at the trial (b) the seriousness of the offense charged, and (c) the seriousness of the prior record of offenses. A fourth factor seems to be included as a correlate and it could be so accommodated, namely, the probability of committing (another?) offense while on bail. (Obviously a person not granted bail will both appear and not commit offenses—he has no opportunity of either.) The table of figure 8-1 shows in outline a model fitting these considerations.

The advantage of the two-dimensional structure of the guideline table becomes apparent immediately. Each of the two dimensions needs only to be specified to a few levels or categories to provide a considerable degree of discrimination. For example, in the table we show only six levels of offense and five levels of probability, and hence obtain ($6 \times 5 = 30$) thirty categories of individuals. This is considerably greater precision than that of a single score.

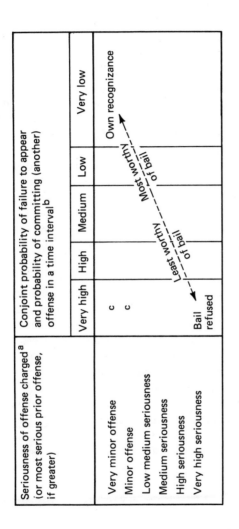

Figure 8-1. Example of the General Form of a Guideline Table for Bail Decision Making

[a]A rating scale for a typical set of offense categories would be required. The numbers and types of examples in each category should relate to the legal code(s) which apply.

[b]To be determined from past experience by research. For an illustration of the application of prediction methods to this problem, see M.R. Gottfredson, "An Empirical Analysis of Pre-trial Release Decisions," *Journal of Criminal Justice*, 2, 4 (1974).

[c]Entries in cells would be "Own Recognizance"; "Bail on Bond"; "Bail Refused" or similar options. The ratio of refused to granted bail would initially be set to accord with current practice as the general constraint. An equation (using the categories) would provide the necessary smoothing and relative weights to the two dimensions.

156

The Prediction Problem (Again!)

In the parole decision we saw that it is possible to avoid the problems associated with the prediction of likely future behavior by resorting to the just-deserts philosophy. In the case of bail decisions they cannot be avoided. In any predictive statement (whether explicit and coded into mathematical models or implicit in terms of subjective assessments) there are always two kinds of errors. These errors are usually known as "false positives" and "false negatives," or in other fields, as "consumer risk" and "producer risk." Some persons will be incorrectly predicted to appear for trial if granted bail and will not do so; others will be predicted not to appear but (if given the opportunity) would do so without being detained. These are the risks of incorrect decisions to the suspect on the one hand and to society on the other. Which type of error is called the "false *positive*" is a matter of point of view!

Although the term, *reasonable probability* is often used in the law, it rarely is defined. There clearly are jurisprudential issues in the acceptance of given probabilities, which are necessarily associated with the risks of false classifications, in any system of rules for decisions. Perhaps it is a fundamental human right that no person should be treated as a "false positive" (no person should be detained in custody without bail if an element of uncertainty exists).

Uncertainty, however, is a fact of life. It is possible to sustain an argument that this right may be eroded by particular forms of behavior. The principle of derogation of rights is recognized in law and it could be extended to relate to this problem. Persons in prison or on parole or probation lose certain civil rights, as, say, the right to vote. It might be argued that the "right not to be treated as a false positive" by a predictive statement about the likelihood of appearing for trial is both measurable and modifiable. For example, a person who previously had been granted bail and failed to appear might be expected to lose much of this right. Perhaps to a lesser degree the rights of persons who had been previously convicted should be diminished in proportion to the seriousness of their prior criminal records. Prediction of specific forms of criminality are of low validity, but prediction of general criminality is more powerful. A person granted bail might be expected to avoid all forms of crime, and not only crimes against persons, while awaiting his trial.

Policy and Case Decisions

Central to the guidelines approach is the separation of the machinery whereby policy and case decisions are made. The application of guidelines to bail decisions would facilitate the division of labor and the separation of these different levels of decision. It would, for example, be possible for the judiciary to delegate the determination of eligibility for bail, if this was desired, to hearing officers or to its probation staff within the guidelines determined by a representative body of judges in the court concerned. The court could then hear only cases where the staff wished to depart from the guidelines or other forms of appeal from the decision. A policymaking body of judiciary would, of course, be a requirement. If, however, the judiciary were prepared to exercise control over policy they could be relieved of much of the work of individual case decisions.

Figure 8-2 illustrates the nature of a system that may be envisioned. The self-regulating information feedback and the ways in which this relates to the idea of accountability should be noted. It is, we think, also necessary to consider three levels of operation and relevant information; namely, that which is relevant to the particular case, that relevant to the determination and modification of policy, and that which relates to our concepts of democracy and public accountability. The guidelines approach makes it possible for justice to be seen to be done because an accountability system has been provided.

The method of guidelines not only separates the policy considerations from the case-by-case decisions and seeks to provide information appropriate to each level, but it also makes clear the difference between professional responsibility and political/societal accountability. For example, whether a fingerprint is or is not correctly (efficiently) lifted from the scene of a crime is a matter for professional judgment by fingerprint experts. Whether fingerprints should or should not be lifted from certain scenes is a matter of social accountability. Social accountability takes as a given that professional expertise is exercised, but is concerned with where and how that is done. The highest level of accountability is that indicated in the first box in the diagram over the heading of "external environment." It is necessary to be as clear as possible as to the appropriate level of accountability and to ensure that all levels are covered. We might, for example, take the view that whether an item is or is not predictive is a matter of "fact" (expert/professional determination) but whether predictive measures should be used is a matter outside professional expertise and in the area of public accountability.

A Medical Ethics Application of Guidelines

In order to stress the possible generality of the application of the principles proposed, an example outside the realm of criminal justice decision making may be discussed. Most hospitals in most countries are faced with the problem of the allocation of scarce resources among the claimants to treatment. The question is particularly acute where human spare parts are involved such as in organ transplants or where the apparatus is extremely costly and in short supply. Decisions for the allocation of these resources among possible beneficiaries usually are made by committees which may include a variety of professional persons. In general, the public is not informed as to the principles that govern

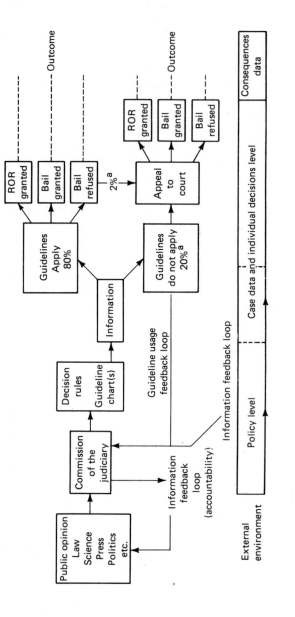

Figure 8-2. The Logic of a Bail Guidelines Scheme

aIndications of possible magnitudes

these decisions; and, indeed, it would be possible to make a case for secrecy. It should be remembered, however, that the United States Parole Commission used to maintain "almost as a matter of pride," that the reasons for a judgment whether or when a prisoner would be released were unknowable.[2] That stance came to be indefensible.

It should be possible to obtain data on past decisions by medical committees with regard to allocation of resources. These data could be used to see whether it is possible to predict with reasonable validity the decisions from the case data. This would be precisely analogous to the method used in the parole research. If prediction of decisions were possible, then we might conclude that a latent policy had been discovered. An illustration of the general method is given in the diagram of figure 8-3.

If the discovered policy could not be faulted, it might be used as a guideline model by the committee or committees. Cases could be studied, either by single decision makers, subcommittees, or committees of the whole with a view to ascertaining whether there were any good reasons for departure from policy (precedent). The reasons could be noted and considered as such by the same body, or an augmented body, at regular intervals. By this means the process could develop as an evolutionary system and the authorities responsible could be better informed of and learn from their own experience.

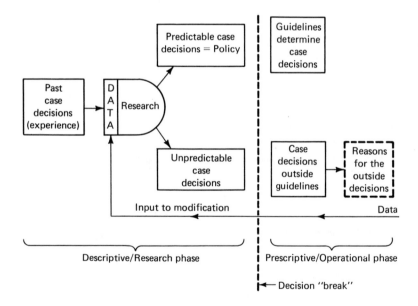

Figure 8-3. The Logic of Guidelines Development and Implementation as an Evolutionary System

A more elaborate model could include an appeals procedure and a method for policy control independent of the individual case decision-making system (or it could consist of the same persons acting in a different role). This system is illustrated in general terms in the diagram of figure 8-4.

The General Issue of Value Choice

The guideline method is not required where the determination can be made in terms of cost-effectiveness and only in those terms. In many cases, however, there is an ethical question as to whether it is morally defensible for cost-effectiveness to be the exclusive consideration. Furthermore, the concept of cost is not a simple cash accounting term in most decisions concerning human welfare. The guideline method has much to commend it where the received wisdom of a collective conscience is sought in the decision process.

The assumption that the scientific method can be value-free is perhaps not tenable at the present time in most scientific or technological inquiry; it is certainly untenable in the social sciences. Whether a problem should be given the

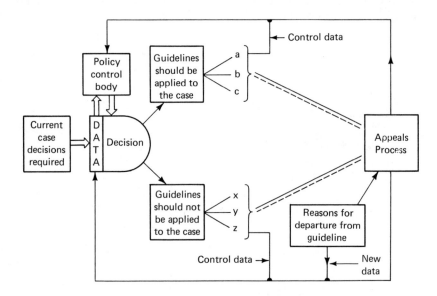

Notes:

a, b, c, – – – – – – = Dispositions made by guideline model

x, y, z, – – – – – – = Dispositions made by individual decision maker.

Figure 8-4. Operational Feedback Loop for Guideline Usage with an Appeals Process

attention of research workers or not involves value choices by the research workers themselves, those who provide the funds, and those who use the research results. There are, perhaps, many questions in the field of education, social welfare, economics, politics, and medicine where public accountability could be considered to be desirable and where professional ethics alone should not decide the issue. The application of the guideline methods to legal matters is, perhaps, easier to appreciate and to organize because law recognizes that moral value choices are involved in decisions implementing it. In other fields the value choices may be less obvious; but there are few where they can be said to be irrelevant.

The general concept of guideline development to provide a self-regulating, evolutionary system for decision policy control may profitably be considered in other fields. Decisions are made that determine the future of individuals in business as well as in fields of social control. Committees often decide whether to offer employment to candidates on the basis of subjective assessment, and sometimes not without prejudice. Is the policy to which such committees work always clear to the members? Can the policy be spelled out in precise terms such as could be afforded by a guidelines model? Is it not true that selection committees are concerned with policy as well as with case decisions? Do they have feedback of information which would enable them to monitor their decisions and perhaps to improve upon them? Can information relating to policy be identified and processed in policy decisions, or is policy made willy-nilly through series of case decisions?

Selection by education committees provides another example of discretion where policy control models may be useful. For example, admission to college or to graduate study is not a matter of hard data and rational decision alone. Would a guideline procedure not add credibility to the decision process? Would it not assist to know exactly upon what basis decisions were being made and to be able to have a form of policy control for such decisions? There is clearly an assessment of probability in the selection process decision; there are consumer (student) and producer (taxpayer/teacher) risks in such decisions. Are there not similar problems and decision processes involved in decisions as to faculty hiring and tenure considerations?

Future Issues and Problems

The major problems faced today in criminal justice and other social fields, and likely to become more pressing in the near future, are not those of technological development. The main issues are—and will continue to be—moral, political, and organizational. There is a need for behavioral scientists and other research workers to become more aware of ethical issues in relation both to the methods they use and the consequences of their work. It is possible for a research worker to become so fascinated by the technical issues and the challenge to his inventiveness which they offer that he loses sight of the probable consequences of his research. There is a still greater difficulty in assessing side effects and "unexpected consequences." Many of the latter are unexpected only because they are given less than adequate consideration.

A delight in one's science may easily lead to proposals that are written in salesmanship terms; the product may become a stronger concern than the concern for ethical constraints. The research worker is all too often in the role of salesman whether he likes it or not; and usually he does not like it. Nonetheless, he does not control his own funds and must convince others. He must sell his "product," namely, his expertise and methodology. The "customer" for such products will be able to select from several competing procedures of research, but may not fully understand the nature of the competition that is providing him with alternatives. This is perhaps particularly true when the research relates to operational and management problems, rather than to research of a more fundamental nature of inquiry. The problem of ethical concern is exacerbated by the fact that frequently the managers of research organizations working in the human sector are not themselves research workers but come from management roles and have a management orientation regarding research activity as a production process. The word *product* has come to be adopted as a descriptor of the outcome of research effort.

Of course research workers should "produce," but the question arises as to the nature of control of that production. The concern for ethical standards must be married into management styles and research techniques in research organization administration. If not, the quality of the "product" will deteriorate with a probability of failure to observe the ethical constraints which are essential. To achieve this balance the research workers must have some information on the customer's (funding agency's) attitudes toward the product and also on *competing* products. This latter requirement is the main difficulty. It suggests that secrecy in research is so closely related to a danger to moral values that secrecy itself becomes a dangerous concept in research involving humans, either as subjects or as recipients of its product.

As research workers we have been most concerned in the research reported in the preceding chapters that we could defend our action in terms of moral values. Our value choices have, we hope, become clear from our reporting. We have little to guide us as to the quality of our moral choice at this time in history. We live in an age of uncertainty and value choices under uncertainty are very different from those of the past when it was believed that there were absolute values directly revealed. One could do what he believed to be right when his particular god was believed to have told him so. If there were different views, then these were clearly morally wrong. We are not now so sure, and indeed the very concept of certainty has been eroded. Research is needed into value choices under uncertainty. Value choices must be made in terms of false positives and false negatives. Value is a matter of trade-off; but, of course, even this assertion may be challenged. The field of criminal justice provides an interface between ethics and politics; it is an area of social action. Into this social action are encoded many moral value choices, and we need to understand these issues better and to find ways of studying them.

To establish the boundary conditions of ethical constraint it may be necessary to have more regulations and to support some of these with the force of law. When all other controls fail, this is a line of last resort. It is our frequent resort because we have such a small armory of other techniques. If the concern for ethical standards of research finds expression in law, then we should be aware of the contingent difficulties which will arise. It is very unlikely that the required constraints on the use of undesirable scientific methods could be well effected by law. More law may not result in more order! The fact that industrial production can be totally disrupted by workers who "work to rule" is well known. Proliferation of laws can be counterproductive in industry and perhaps research workers could be even more inventive! Styles of research management, worker group norms, informal control systems, and reference groups can help, and we need to know more about the impact of these systems on value choices. The law may protect its citizens from being subjects of research by the use of methods deemed unethical. However, it is known that certain research workers who wished to obtain data from human subjects by means banned by the law of the United States are now obtaining their data from countries where citizens are not so protected. Some balance between control by regulation, law, and sanctions on the one hand and informal self-regulation on the other seems to be required to deal with the issues of ethical and human values deriving from scientific investigations and technological development.

Criminological research is as open to malpractice as are any methods developed for the control of crime and criminals. In any police state (whatever that might mean) crime research will be likely to be pressed into service in support of those in power. At the extremes the ethical choices are easy for those outside the particular system. For those within, the perspective may not be so clear.

Policy control guidelines appear to work because they permit of deviation— it is the deviations that preserve the system as a learning process. It is, therefore, difficult to see how the methods might be misapplied, where by misapplication we mean application in ways damaging to the democratic principles of a society. An undemocratic (or closed) society would find it best to reject the concept of public accountability which the guideline method implies. Nonetheless it is possible that policy control guidelines could be used for ends of which the research team and the parole board members would disapprove. This is our greatest concern. It cannot be our concern alone. That is why we regard it as an integral part of the guideline system that the control afforded by public accountability is exercised through the democratic process in an open society. The preservation of an open society is the concern of all.

Notes

1. A guidelines model for sentencing has been tested and claimed to be feasible. L.T. Wilkins, J.M. Kress, D.M. Gottfredson, J.C. Calpin, and A.M. Gelman, *Sentencing Guidelines: Structuring Judicial Discretion,* Final Report of the Feasibility Study, prepared under Law Enforcement Assistance Administration Grant 74NI-99-0054, draft, October 1976.

2. M.E. Frankel, *Criminal Sentences: Law without Order* (New York: Hill and Wang, 1973).

Appendixes

Appendix A:
Information Selection in
Parole Decision Making

This investigation was designed to elicit material about decision makers' patterns of search for information to assist them in the prison release decision, the rationale employed by these decision makers for acquiring particular types of information at various stages in the search sequence, and the relationships between given sets of information, choice of disposition (grant or denial of release), and confidence in the appropriateness or correctness of the choice.

The technique employed by the investigators was adapted from the "information board" approach developed by Wilkins,[1] using a random access slide projector for information retrieval rather than cards as in the original method. Thus, an offender's case report was content-analyzed, and the information transferred to a set of slides with information from each content area assigned to a separate slide. Decision makers were provided with a list of content headings (for example, age, offense, job skill), and could be permitted to acquire the information from each category (for example, age: 21 years) in whatever sequence they preferred. At various points in their cumulative acquisition of information (after a given number of items), they were required to make a case decision on the basis of available information, and to indicate the confidence in their decision (on a scale ranging from very easy to very difficult). As further information was supplied, the decision makers revised their decisions and their confidence estimates.

In this study, the technique was modified to yield more information about the process of decision makers' search for information, their reasons for requesting a particular item, and the meaning or manner of influence of the information upon their interpretation and judgment of the case. This was accomplished by small groups discussing and agreeing about which information to acquire. Once agreement was reached, the experimenter presented the requested data, using the slide projector, called for a case decision, and encouraged discussion to select the next item. While the sequence of information acquisition was consequently identical for all members of a group, each member made private notations of his own decisions and confidence levels. The group sessions were tape-recorded for later review by the decision makers and research workers.

This appendix was adapted from a report section prepared by Don M. Gottfredson and James O. Robison, from L.T. Wilkins, D.M. Gottfredson, J.O. Robison, and C.A. Sodowsky, *Information Selection and Use in Decision-Making*, (Davis, Calif.: National Council on Crime and Delinquency Research Center, June 1973).

Results

A total of forty-one decision makers participated in the experiment. They were assembled in six separate groups containing from five to nine members each. The sample contained twenty-three state parole board members, three federal parole board members, and one hearing examiner—persons whose routine duties include responsibility for prison release decisions. The remainder of the sample included three corrections administrators, two corrections research professionals, one chief of parole services, two attorneys (a professor of law and a representative from an American Bar Association committee), a corrections executive secretary, an academic (presumably another university professor), a layman, and three persons who did not indicate their status. For purposes of some comparative analyses, the sample was divided into two subsamples—twenty-seven persons whose jobs were directly relevant to the experimental decision task and fourteen with more peripheral jobs. In each of the six groups, parole board members outnumbered other members of the group.

Only one case was presented in each group, and the same case was utilized for all six groups. This case was abstracted to yield fifty-one separate categories of information. The details of the case follow, arranged in sets which show how *often* the items were requested among the six groups and how *early* they were selected. The arrangement provides some perspective on the popularity and priority of given information elements in case decision making.

Because of limitations on the duration of the group sessions, and because of the different levels of discussion between items among the six groups, no group asked to see the full set of fifty[2] items, and the number of items used ranged from thirteen to thirty-eight among groups.

Each group was allowed to acquire four items of information before the members made their first decisions, and opportunity was then provided to revise decisions after each subsequent piece of information was acquired. Seven of the items (see table A-1, sec. G) were never requested by a group, and may then be considered relatively unimportant to these decision makers. It is possible either that the information itself was thought to be unimportant, or that other information already requested provided implicit answers about the contents of these slides. There were only three items (offense, age, and alcohol history) that were requested by every group. Offense and age were typically requested at an early point, presumably to establish some initial bearing about the amount of time the case should serve and, therefore, whether—unless later facts dictated otherwise—it was time to release the prisoner. Alcohol history, in contrast, was typically employed later (from ninth to twentieth in the search sequence) and was probably used for the purpose of corroborating or modifying a decision that was already essentially made.

It is interesting that only two of the six groups requested "time served prior to present hearing" among the first four items on which their initial decision would be made, and that two other groups never requested this item. These findings suggest that the penalty element of the release decision was being discounted by these decision makers (that is, the matter of whether the offender has yet been incarcerated for six months, or for three years) in favor of items they believed were prognostic of future adjustment. From this perspective, it would seem likely that two other items chosen early and often by the groups (table A-1, sec. A)—type of prior convictions and number of prior arrests—were obtained more for their prognostic implications than their penalty implications (as an indication of what sorts of behaviors to expect, rather than as an element for determining how much incarceration penalty the offender deserved). This interpretation is further supported by the fact that type of admission (information about whether the offender was serving the initial part of the sentence for his instant commitment offense, or whether he had completed this and been returned for a subsequent portion of the sentence because of a parole infraction) was never requested—a fact quite relevant to the issue of appropriate penalty and the decision to release. Decision makers did, however, display an interest in the general area of prior parole and probation revocations (requested by five groups, at points ranging from fifth to twelfth in the search sequence). In the particular case utilized, since the person had no revocations, the nature of the admission status could be derived from the revocation information.

In general, it might be expected that the type of information desired at any stage in the information search will be conditioned by the set of information already required, and that no rigid or consistent search sequence would be found over different cases processed by the same decision maker or the same case processed by different decision makers. Participants in the study expressed dissatisfaction with the one-piece-at-a-time conditions of the experiment and voiced a preference for a starting array of material, such as is found on a case summary sheet, from which to initiate their review. To some extent, these conditions were satisfied by the convention that four items could be accumulated before an initial decision was requested.

While there was some overlap among groups in the set of items employed for the initial decision, it seems less than one might expect (see table A-2). One item was called for by all six groups, and one by four groups, but of the remainder there were six items used by only one group each, and four items used by only two groups. As a consequence, the highest number of items shared by any pair of groups was three, and this extent of commonality was present in only two of the sixteen relationships. Actual similarity in search patterns is somewhat higher because roughly equivalent forms of information could appear under different content headings (for example, number of prior arrests and number of prior convictions). (See table A-3.)

The findings in table A-3 indicate that members of any given group tended to arrive at an identical decision on the basis of the first four items they acquired—Group 1 members were unanimously in favor of release; group 2, with

Table A-1
Popularity and Priority of Case Information among Decision Makers

Class	Number of Groups	Earliest Use	Information Category and Content
A. Early and Often (requested by at least four out of six groups, and selected among the first four items by at least one group)	6	1	*Instant Offense—Official Description:* "The subject voluntarily appeared at an FBI office and told them that he had stolen checks from a former employer and had negotiated several of them." (Item 30)
	6	1	*Age:* "Subject is 21 years old." (Item 1)
	5	2	*Type of Prior Convictions:* "Subject has been convicted for theft of over $50 and possession of forged instrument." (Item 25)
	5	2	*Mitigating Factors:* "The subject both turned himself in and pleaded guilty." (Item 35)
	5	3	*Number of Prior Arrests:* "Subject has been arrested twice prior to present offense." (Item 14)
	5	4	*Release Plan Living Arrangement:* "Subject plans to return to his parents' home in rural Ohio." (Item 48)
	4	1	*Base Expectancy:* "Subject's base expectancy based on a two-year follow up is 61%." (Item 51)

Time Served Prior to Present Hearing: "Subject has been incarcerated nine months for the instant offense." (Item 36)	3	4
Time Remaining to Mandatory Release: "Three years, three months remain until subject's mandatory release." (Item 38)	4	4
Alcohol Use: "There is no history of alcohol use." (Item 11)	9	6
Prior Parole and Probation Revocations: "There have been no prior parole or probation revocations." (Item 26)	5	5
Release Job Prospects: "Subject hopes to attend college, taking business administration." (Item 49)	7	5
Educational Level and Adjustment: "Subject is a high school graduate considered an average student." (Item 4)	7	5
Living Arrangement Prior to Incarceration: "Subject was living with his parents and younger brother in a seven-room, two-story frame house in rural Ohio." (Item 16)	9	5
Drug Use: "There is no history of drug use." (Item 10)	10	5

B. *Often, but Not Early* (requested by at least four groups, and by one or more groups among the first ten items, but never among the first four items)

172

Table A-1 (cont.)

Class	Number of Groups	Earliest Use	Information Category and Content
	4	6	*Recent Employment History:* "Subject has held a number of short-term jobs, mainly unskilled or clerical in nature. He seems able to secure employment without much difficulty and most of his employers like him." (Item 19)
	4	8	*Number and Type of Disciplinary Infractions:* "Subject has clear conduct record." (Item 44)
	4	9	*Academic Progress in Institution:* "Subject is not enrolled in the education program." (Item 41)
	4	10	*IQ Score:* "Subject has an IQ of 119." (Item 8)
C. *Often, but Late* (requested by at least four groups, but never among first ten items)	5	12	*Early Home Environment:* "Subject is the seventh of eight children raised by an intact family in a rural environment. Both parents worked on occasion, but they maintained a well supervised and controlled home. They enjoy a good reputation in the community." (Item 15)
	4	11	*Financial Resources:* "Subject has no known financial resources." (Item 50)

Item		
Changes in Attitude Noted: "No changes in attitude have been noted." (Item 46)	15	4
Homosexuality: "Subject is a homosexual." (Item 6)	15	4
Susceptibility to Influence: "There is no susceptibility to influence cited." (Item 13)	17	4

D. Early, but Not Often (requested by three or fewer groups, but by at least one group among first four items selected)

Item		
Number of Prior Convictions: "Subject has had one prior conviction." (Item 24)	3	3
Instant Offense—Inmate's Description: "The subject stated that he had a long history of involvement with bad checks from his employer and some credit cards from his brother-in-law." (Item 31)	3	3

E. Not Early and Not Often (requested by three or fewer groups, and selected by one or more groups among first ten items, but never among first four items)

Item		
Number of Prior Incarcerations: "Subject has been incarcerated once before." (Item 45)	4	1
Indications of "Nomadism": "Subject has moved often from Ohio to Texas, but he has relatives in both areas." (Item 12)	7	3
Vocational Training in Institution: "Subject has had no vocational training." (Item 42)	10	3
Institutional Work Experience: "Subject is assigned to industries as a clerk and has performed well." (Item 43)	8	2

Table A-1 (cont.)

Class	Number of Groups	Earliest Use	Information Category and Content
	2	9	*Job Skill:* "Subject has no job skill." (Item 18)
	2	10	*Contact with Family Members:* "Subject's case history implies that he has frequent contact with his family." (Item 17)
	1	5	*Time Remaining to Full-Term Expiration:* "Subject has five years, three months to serve until full-term expiration." (Item 37)
	1	6	*Longest Prior Incarceration:* "Subject was once incarcerated for 18 months." (Item 22)
	1	9	*Reason for First Arrest:* "Subject was first arrested for defrauding an innkeeper in a national park." (Item 28)
F. *Late and Not Often* (requested by three or fewer groups, and never among first ten items selected	3	15	*History of Mental Problems:* "There is no history of mental commitment or psychiatric treatment." (Item 7)
	3	18	*Detainers:* "Subject has no detainers." (Item 40)
	3	20	*Marital Status and Relationship:* "Subject is single." (Item 5)
	3	14	*Ethnic Group:* "Subject is white." (Item 2)
	2	19	*SAT Score:* "Subject has an SAT score of 11.7." (Item 9)

Item		
Longest Time in Community: "Subject has remained in the community for five months." (Item 23)	21	2
Reason for First Conviction: "Subject was first convicted for theft over $50 and possession of a forged instrument." (Item 29)	13	1
Codefendants: "There were no codefendants." (Item 33)	21	1
Letters and Visits from Family: "No letters or visits are noted." (Item 47)	28	1
G. Never Requested		
Type of Admission to System: "Subject is a new court commitment." (Item 3)	—	0
Number of Previous Convictions for Instant Offense: "Subject had one previous conviction for the same offense as the instant offense." (Item 34)	—	0
Use of Weapons: "There were no weapons used in the instant offense." (Item 32)	—	0
Escape History: "Subject has had no history of escapes." (Item 27)	—	0
Age at First Conviction: "Subject was first convicted at age 19." (Item 21)	—	0
Age at First Arrest: "Subject was 19 at first arrest." (Item 20)	—	0
Parole Eligibility: "Subject is eligible for parole at the board's discretion." (Item 39)	—	0

Table A-2
Four-Item Information Frame for Initial Decision

		Group 1	Group 2	Group 3	Group 4	Group 5	Group 6
S	1	Age	B.E. Score	Offense	Offense	Offense	Offense
e	2	Offense	Offense	Type Prior	Mitigating Factor	Type Prior	Inmate Version
q u e	3	Type Prior	Age	No. Prior Arrests	No. Prior Arrests	No. Prior Convictions	Time Served
n c e	4	B.E. Score	Release Living	Time Served	Type Prior	No. Prior Incarcerations	Time to Mandatory

Number Groups Using Item

Offense	6
Type Prior	4
No. Prior Arrests	2
Age	2
Time Served	2
Base Expectancy	2
Release Living	1
Mitigating Factor	1
No. Prior Convictions	1
No. Prior Incarcerations	1
Inmate Version	1
Time to Mandatory	1

Number of Items Shared by Pairs of Groups

	1	2	3	4	5	6
1.		3	2	2	2	1
2.			1	1	1	1
3.				3	2	2
4.					2	1
5.						1

exception of one member, favored release; groups 3, 4, and 6 favored denial, with one member dissenting in each group; group 5 was the most divided, with five members for denial and two for release. The two groups predominantly in favor of release (groups 1 and 2) shared two items of information not yet acquired by the remaining groups which favored denial—the fact that the offender was twenty-one years old, and the fact that his probability of success on parole was 61 percent. While we may speculate that youthfulness inclined these groups to leniency, and that the base expectancy inclined them to optimism, it is difficult to account for the initial decision difference between groups 1 and 2 (release) versus groups 3 and 6 (denial). One means of checking on the influence of these two information factors is to determine the frequency of mind changes among members of groups 3 and 6 when they later acquired these items. Twenty-five members of these groups were exposed to the age factor, and fifteen of these members were favoring denial at the point of acquisition. Only three of these fifteen respondents shifted from deny to release upon acquisition of the age information,[3] despite the fact that its exposure occurred relatively early (positions 7 and 11) in the search sequence. This

Table A-3
Initial Decision and Confidence Level

Member Number	Group 1		Group 2		Group 3		Group 4		Group 5		Group 6	
	Decision	Difficulty	Decision	Difficulty	Decision	Difficulty	Decision	Difficulty	Decision	Difficulty	Decision	Difficulty
1	Release	8	Release	6	Release	8	Deny	5	Deny	1	Deny	8
2	Release	4	Deny	3	Deny	1	Deny	2	Deny	1	Deny	3
3	Release	5	Release	2	Deny	3	Release	5	Deny	7	Deny	6
4	Release	3	Release	2	Deny	7	Deny	4	Deny	1	Deny	8
5	Release	6	Release	2	Deny	4	Deny	6	Release	8	Deny	8
6	Release	2	Release	6	Deny	1			Release	1	Deny	6
7	Release	5	Release	1					Deny	3	Release	7
8	Release		Release	1								
9	Release		Release	2								

finding suggests either that age was not a critical information factor, or that its impact was weakened by the prior receipt of other information elements. Base expectancy score was subsequently acquired by the thirteen members of groups 3 and 6, though at a late point (positions 20 and 37) in the search sequence. Seven of these members were in a state favoring denial at the point of base expectancy acquisition, and two of these shifted to "release" upon learning recidivism likelihood. Given the supposition that decision preference was likely to be fairly well stabilized at a late point in the search, base expectancy would appear to possess moderate power for changing minds (two shifts out of seven possible).

Twenty-one of the forty-one decision makers, or about one-half, were in a state favoring denial of parole after their receipt of the first four items of information. They indicated their level of confidence in decisions made at this point on a two-inch scale with the polar extremes labeled easy and difficult. Confidence scores are shown in table A-3, based on a division of the scale into eight quarter-inch intervals, with 8 representing greatest difficulty and 1 greatest ease. Confidence scores in each group were quite variable and, across all groups, ranged from one to eight for decision makers recommending either denial or release. Overall, the average level of confidence for twenty-one members in a release state was identical (4.2) to that for the 20 members in a deny state.

The initial decisions were compared with decisions at the close of the experiment, when all information acquired by each group was available (table A-4).

Shift in Decisions after Further Information

Fifty-one percent of the decision makers favored denial at the point of initial decision. By the close of the experiment, upon receipt of subsequent information, the balance had shifted to 88 percent favoring release. These findings indicate that initial decision biases were susceptible to modification, and that the bulk of case information was interpreted as neutral or favorable. Subdivision of the sample into twenty-seven parole board members and fourteen other

Table A-4
Decisions at the Start and Finish of the Experiment

		Finish		
		Deny	Release	All
S t a r t	Release	0	20	20
	Deny	5	16	21
	All	5	36	41

professionals revealed that the former were more inclined to make risk-aversive decisions (table A-5).

Inquiry was made into the relation between confidence in their initial decision on the case and tendency to change of mind upon presentation of subsequent information. Twenty of the members maintained the same decision throughout the course of the experiment. Twenty-one changed their minds at least one time, and one shifted his decision twelve times in response to further acquisition of information (table A-6).

All six of the decision makers who reversed their decision three or more times were parole board members, and three of these were participants in the same group (group 4). The total sample was split at the median on the initial confidence and decision shift variables, and comparison revealed a trend: those who were more confident in their initial decision were less likely to reverse that decision as further information was acquired (see table A-7).

Information categories were next examined to determine which items were associated with decision reversals. While findings from this inquiry might have some bearing on the issue of the amount of influence or impact a particular item—

Table A-5
Decisions by Board Members and Others to Deny Parole

	Decision to Deny Parole	
	Start	Finish
Parole Board Members (N = 27)	59%	19%
Other Professionals (N = 14)	36%	7%
Total Decisions	51%	12%

Table A-6
Changes from Initial Decisions

	Initial Decision	
Number of Decision Changes	Deny	Release
None	5	15
One	12	0
Two	0	3
Three	1	0
Six	0	1
Seven	1	0
Nine	1	0
Eleven	1	0
Twelve	0	1

Table A-7
Decision Changes and Initial Confidence

	Decision Shifts	
Initial Confidence	None	Any
More Difficult than Easy (Scores 5-8)	7	12
More Easy than Difficult (Scores 1-4)	13	9

held, one must keep in mind that such impact may occur without producing decision reversal—the decision maker may be in a preference state that the new item serves to strengthen, rather than overthrow. One indication of this latter type of influence would be an abrupt shift upward in the rated confidence level (see table A-8).

Items were included in table A-8 if either of two conditions were met: three or more decision makers changed their decision after the item was presented, or five or more persons' confidence was affected by at least 15 points (on an 80-point scale) upon presentation of the item. The purpose of these conventions was to shift for influential items and determine the contribution to the decision process. The results yielded by this procedure are somewhat confusing. Eight decision makers felt more confident of their decision to release upon learning that the offender had no disciplinary infractions, and three changed their decision from deny to release upon receipt of this information. Favorable information about institutional work experience and former jobs in the community also served to change decisions, but had no clear impact on confidence levels. Knowledge of the offender's above-average IQ increased decision maker confidence and changed some decisions. The facts that the offender had received no institutional vocational training and had shown no change in attitude affected decisions unfavorably despite absence of knowledge about whether his original attitude was unacceptable or whether the vocational training could be made available to him. Upon learning that the subject was a homosexual, five decision makers favoring release lowered their confidence in this decision, and two others changed their decisions from release to deny; another two members switched from deny to release in response to the same information. The fact of no prior revocations had no effect on changing decisions, but served to increase confidence in the decision to release. Strangely, however, this information led one decision maker to reduce his confidence in the release decision.

In general, the findings indicate an impact of the specified information factors on decision process, but these impacts are without particular focus, and the nature and direction of their influence are neither regular nor clear. It is evident from the findings that, as new pieces of information are acquired by decision makers, they may have the effect of reducing certainty rather than increasing it. That is, there is no steady increase in decision confidence as a function of increasing quantity of available information.

Table A-8
Information Impact on Decisions and Confidence

Changed Decision			Changed Confidence by at Least 15 Points			
			Upward		Downward	
Deny ↓ Release	Release ↓ Deny	Item	Release	Deny	Release	Deny
2		38–39 months until mandatory release	5	1		
		26–no prior parole or probation revocations	5		1	1
	4	46–no change in attitude	1	1	1	2
3		43–performed well as clerk in institution	1			
3		44–no disciplinary infractions	8			
	3	42–no vocational training	1		1	1
	2	50–no financial resources	2		2	1
1		49–hopes to attend college	3		2	
3	1	48–will live with parents in rural Ohio	3		1	1
3	1	1–21 years old			3	1
	1	15–from large family and well supervised home	2	1	2	1
		4–high school graduate, average student	1		1	3
2	2	6–homosexual		1	5	1
2		12–moved often to relatives in Ohio, Texas	3		2	1
4		8–IQ of 119	3			1
1	1	16–lived with parents	3	1	2	1
3		19–short-term clerical jobs obtained easily–liked by employers	2	1	3	
2		51–61% likelihood of success on parole	3			1

Discussion

The results of this experiment do not define any specific set of information as perceived by decision makers to be critical to the decision, although certain items are regularly thought to be important. Neither do they show that any particular sequence of information is regularly preferred by those whose task is decision making. Rather, they illustrate the complexity of the process, the individual differences in preferences and beliefs concerning information relevance, and perhaps different styles of decision making.

The behavior of participants during the sessions was similarly revealing of this complexity and of these individual differences. In one group session, for example, heated discussion ensued as one participant argued for selection of the item offense (meaning the description of the legal offense for which the person was sent to prison) and another urged that the inmate's version of the offense was equally or more important. In various groups, a general frustration with the piecemeal mode of information presentation was evident as group members appeared to struggle to obtain enough information to give them a feeling of satisfaction that they understood the person—who he was, how he came to prison, and his probable behavior if paroled. Different general sets toward the decision-making task seemed evident, too. For example, one participant marked a high degree of confidence in his decision—to deny parole—after only four items of information and exclaimed "I don't have enough information to parole him"; whereupon another participant remarked "I don't have enough information to keep him in prison."

From this exercise, together with other simulations conducted during the project, several general results stand out. Persons paroling, compared with persons not paroling, sought different information. Different items of information were generally considered important for different cases. The same decision often was made on entirely different bases; that is, different information was used by different people to arrive at the same conclusion. There is no unanimity among decision makers as to the relative importance of information available to the decision. Finally, information may *reduce* confidence in the decision as well as increase it.

Notes

1. L.T. Wilkins and A. Chandler, "Confidence and Competence in Decision-Making," *British Journal of Criminology* 5 (1965):1.

2. The experimenter revealed beforehand to each group that the case was eligible for parole, and there was thus no reason for a group to request that item.

3. One other member shifted from release to deny upon learning the offender's age.

Appendix B:
A Paroling Policy
Feedback Method

Parol board members make two kinds of decisions about parole. They make decisions about individual persons; also, they make paroling policy decisions which set the framework within which the individual case decisions are made. The paroling policies that guide individual case decisions may or may not be explicitly stated. Most often, parole selection policies are not explicitly articulated. When stated, they are likely to be put in very general terms (for example, there must be a reasonable probability that the prisoner, if paroled, will remain in the community without violating the law), although there may be certain explicit policies for very specific types of cases (for example, persons committed for armed robbery must serve at least three years in prison). Various norms are learned through interaction with other parole board members on individual case decisions and in other discussions, but these are rarely stated formally and are not uniformly adhered to by the members.

The lack of clearly articulated policy guidelines may lead to the problem of disparate decisions. If parole board members are following different guidelines concerning implicit policy, then different decisions for the same case will likely result. This is not to argue that parole board members should be continually of one mind. Especially in the formulation of parole selection policy guidelines, a broad range of opinion would appear useful. In the implementation of these guidelines by actual case decision making, however, a lack of consistency may be equated with a lack of fairness, since inconsistency would be expected when the idiosyncratic views of individual members play a larger role in the decision-making process.

This appendix reports the development of a feedback device for parole board members of the Youth Correction Division of the United States Board of Parole concerning the relationships between their evaluations of specific case factors (the severity of the subject's instant offense, institutional program participation, institutional discipline, and parole prognosis) and paroling decisions. Implicit paroling policies may be inferred and made explicit from these relationships, based upon a sample of case decisions.

Provision of feedback of this type can enable parole board members to test the congruence between actual and desired policies concerning the weights given to the various factors. For example, the parole board may find that it gives more (or less) weight than intended to institutional discipline. Once known, corrective action could be taken. Feedback based upon subsequent decisions would then provide a measure of whether the planned change had been effected.

Adapted from P.B. Hoffman, *Paroling Policy Feedback* Parole Decision Making Project, Report 8, (Davis, Calif.: National Council on Crime and Delinquency Research Center, June 1973).

183

Such a feedback measure can also serve a second purpose; it can make explicit presently implicit paroling policies and thereby reduce the criticism leveled against parole boards as having unfettered discretion. Davis[1] and Remington et al.[2] have argued that, while discretion in the administration of criminal justice is necessary, there must also exist effective checks on its arbitrary use. One method proposed for such checks is the articulation of the criteria upon which decisions are based. Providing a measure of the weights given to the primary factors in the parole selection decision may provide a step toward this objective.

A policy indicator may provide, at the same time, a measure of equity, alerting parole board members to recommendations or decisions that appear to vary substantially from established policies. Such indicators would not be intended to remove the individual parole board member's discretion. As Ohlin[3] has argued on another topic (in relation to the use of predictive devices), indicators should function merely as a stop sign to alert the parole board member to further specify his reasons for case decisions that appear to deviate from the usually expected decisions in similar cases.

Youth Corrections Act Decisions

Cases of federal offenders sentenced under the Youth Corrections Act[4] and appearing for original parole (not reparole) consideration were selected for this study. These persons have no minimum sentence and are eligible for parole at any time. Each person's case is reviewed initially by the parole board within three to six months after reception in prison. Although eligible for parole at the initial hearing, most cases are continued for an additional period determined by the board. Each offender's case is reviewed thereafter at least once every three years until he is paroled or released by mandatory parole. Mandatory parole occurs two years before an individual's maximum expiration date (with credit for jail time). Therefore, the paroling decision may be viewed as one of *when* rather than *whether* the offender is to be paroled. In most cases, the maximum sentence length is six years, providing a mandatory parole date at forty-eight months.

The actual parole selection decision (at the time of this study) was made in Washington, D.C., on the basis of the information in the case folder and hearing summary (or institutional progress report). After the first parole board member reviewed the case and rendered a decision, the case file (with decision attached) was transmitted to a second parole board member. If the second member agreed, the determination was final. If there was a disagreement which could not be resolved, the case folder was submitted to a third member who cast the deciding vote. Cases judged especially serious or notorious were reviewed by the full parole board (youth and adult division members sitting together) at *en banc* hearings.

Informal interviews with parole board members and hearing examiners indicated some difference of opinion as to the appropriate nature of the continuance at the initial hearing. The prevailing sentiment appeared to be that the initial continuance should be of a length sufficient to take into account the severity of the offense (reflecting the concern of accountability) and initial estimate of parole risk so that the person would be paroled at the second hearing if there had been satisfactory institutional adjustment. In serious cases (as armed bank robbery) this continuance was likely to be at least two years (the maximum continuance permitted at any one decision was thirty-six months). Other persons, however, found the concept of long continuances undesirable since the inmate is not given an opportunity to demonstrate more rapid improvement. Those with this view argued that a lengthy continuance may create feelings of negativism in the inmate and is in opposition to the rehabilitative intent of the Youth Corrections Act. Shorter continuances, however, also have disadvantages: the parole board may find itself in a position at the second hearing in which the inmate has demonstrated satisfactory institutional progress but is still unacceptable for release in view of the severity of the offense (or prior record) and the short amount of time served. It may be argued that giving another continuance at this point creates as much or more frustration for the inmate. The extent to which either policy was followed in practice is one subject of this study.

Research Design

The research plan called for an evaluation sheet containing a set of four scales to be completed by each parole board member after reviewing each case and prior to making his decision for a sample of parole consideration decisions. The evaluation sheet (see table B-1) requested each parole board member to place his or her evaluation of the severity of the offender's instant offense, participation in institutional programs, institutional discipline, and parole prognosis (probability of favorable parole outcome) on four scales and record the decision recommendation. The relationships between the variables, jail time, prison time served, and decision outcome (parole board member's recommended decision) could then be analyzed by multiple regression techniques and policy profiles (scattergrams with lines of best fit) plotted.

Parole board members of the Youth Correction Division of the United States Board of Parole agreed to complete evaluation forms for a 30 percent sample of case decisions beginning November 1, 1971. The sampling for this report was terminated May 30, 1972. Thus, a sample of 30 percent of all Youth Corrections Act cases considered by the parole board for original release (whether first or subsequent hearing)[5] was obtained. Each individual whose prison register (identification) number ended in one of three odd digits became a sample case; it was assumed that this procedure would approximate random selection.

Table B-1
Youth Corrections Act—Evaluation Sheet

Case Name _____   Register Number _____

FBI Number _____

Please complete this form, seal in the envelope provided and replace in the case folder. Remember, your best estimate is requested; it is not expected that you will provide exact answers to these questions.

1. *Offense Severity*

    Please circle the letter which most closely corresponds to your evaluation of the severity of the offense behavior for which the subject was committed.

    a. Among the least serious offenses
    b. Less serious than the average
    c. Slightly less serious than the average
    d. Slightly more serious
    e. More serious than the average
    f. Among the most serious offenses

2. *Participation in Programs*[a]

    Please circle the letter which most closely summarizes your evaluation of the subject's participation in institutional programs (since last review).

    a. Very Good
    b. Good
    c. Fair
    d. Poor
    e. Very Poor
    f. Not enough information available

3. *Institutional Discipline*

    Please circle the letter which most closely summarizes your evaluation of the subject's institutional discipline record (since last review).

    a. Very Good
    b. Good
    c. Fair
    d. Poor
    e. Very Poor
    f. Not enough information available

4. *Estimate of Likely Parole Outcome*

    The 100 at the right of the scale represents certainty of favorable parole outcome. The 0 at the left of the scale represents certainty of unfavorable parole outcome. The center of the scale represents the point at which either favorable or unfavorable outcome is equally likely. Please circle a number on the scale below or mark an X on the line to indicate your estimate for this subject.

    0   5   15   25   35   45   55   65   75   85   95   100

Certainty of   Certainty
unfavorable parole   of favorable
outcome   parole outcome

Table B-1 (cont.)

5. Your Decision Recommendation: Parole _____

   Number of months continued _____

6. Initials of Parole Board Member
   completing this instrument _____

---

aPrior to 2/3/72, the scales used for "Participation in Programs" and "Institutional Discipline" are shown below. At the suggestion of several parole board members, these were revised to produce a five-point scale with an additional choice for cases with insufficient information. For our analyses, the following transformations were made: Very Good = Very Good; Above Average = Good; Slightly Above or Slightly Below Average = Fair; Below Average = Poor; Very Poor = Very Poor. (Insufficient information choice cases were eliminated from computation; however, such cases were limited to initial hearings.)

Institutional Progress

Please circle the number which most closely summarizes your evaluation of the subject's participation in institutional programs.

1. Very Poor
2. Below Average
3. Slightly Below Average

4. Slightly Above Average
5. Above Average
6. Very Good

Institutional Discipline

Please circle the number which most closely summarizes your evaluation of the subject's institutional discipline record.

1. Very Poor
2. Below Average
3. Slightly Below Average

4. Slightly Above Average
5. Above Average
6. Very Good

Evaluation forms and envelopes were placed in the appropriate case folders by parole board clerical staff prior to decision consideration. As a minimum of two parole board members review each case, at least two evaluation forms for each were obtained.[6] Parole board members were instructed to complete the evaluation forms independently and seal them in the envelopes provided.[7] Therefore, while the second parole board member was aware of the first member's decision, he was not aware of the ratings given on the four scales. These evaluation forms were retrieved by project staff and additional information was recorded.

Parole board members were very cooperative in completing the evaluation forms. Before submission to the parole board, this experiment was reviewed and approved at a meeting of the project's Scientific Advisory Committee. The research design was then presented to the full parole board at their October 1971 business meeting. In addition, individual meetings were conducted with the parole board members who would be participating, to explain the research procedures in detail. These conferences resulted in several suggestions and amendments to the research design.

For example, one parole board member expressed discomfort with the use of numbers in the scale to be used to estimate likelihood of favorable parole outcome. However, a line scale to be checked was unacceptable to other parole board members. This led to the development of a scale consisting of both numbers and a line, which satisfied all parties and increased their comfort with (and probably interest in) the experiment. A second example concerns the number of scales used. Originally, only three scales had been proposed: severity, institutional discipline, and risk of parole violation. The number of scales had been limited in order to avoid imposing unduly upon the time of the parole board members. However, at their suggestion, a fourth scale (participation in institutional programs), representing a factor perceived important, but distinct from institutional discipline, was developed.

Predictor Variables

Four subjective factor ratings were selected for consideration as predictor variables. They were chosen to reflect four important and prevalent parole selection concerns cited by Dawson[8] and O'Leary.[9] The first factor (the severity of the present offense) relates to the concern known as accountability, sanctioning, or the service of a sufficient minimum time. The second and third factors (institutional program participation and discipline) relate to the concerns of system maintenance and encouragement of the constructive use of prison time. The fourth factor (chance of favorable parole outcome) relates to the concern of risk of parole violation. The concern of reducing sentencing disparity was not considered, owing to the nature of the data. Since Youth Corrections Act cases have no minimum sentences and the vast majority have maximum sentences of six years, the problem of disparate sentences does not appear.

An advantage of the use of subjective measures is that parole board members are making these types of judgments in actual case decisions and appear to have little difficulty in articulating them. As a first step, they can provide a measure of the implicit policy the parole board member is attempting to follow. If, at a later date, more objective indicators of these concerns are developed (for example, base expectancy or severity scale measures), the objective measures may be substituted in the predictive equations to indicate to the parole board member the appropriate course of action to better implement desired policy.

A disadvantage of subjective measures is that they may reflect rationalizations for decisions rather than determinants of them. For example, if a parole board member is examining a case and develops a subjective desire to parole, he may tend to credit the subject with better institutional progress or a higher chance of success than is, in fact, indicated. Nevertheless, the ability of parole board members to consider possible biased responses is likely to be improved if decision items (focal concerns) are examined separately.

Criterion Measures

In order to examine the relationships of these factors to paroling decisions, a number of criteria were selected. At the initial decision, the first criterion measure to be considered was the continuance recommended (in months) with parole treated as zero months. The second criterion measure used was the total time in custody recommended until decision number two (jail time plus time in prison until initial decision plus recommended continuance). At subsequent decisions, the criterion considered was the dichotomous parole/continue decision.

Results and Discussion

Stepwise multiple regression equations were calculated for the 378 responses concerning initial decisions. A random split half technique was used to provide construction ($N = 196$) and validation ($N = 182$) samples. It must be noted that three of the scales used (severity, progress, and discipline) were rather crude ordinal measures which were treated as interval measures for these computations. Nevertheless, the predictive power of these indicators was substantial. (Table B-2 displays the zero order correlations among the variables.) Using only the variables severity and prognosis (risk) as predictors, multiple Rs of 0.70 for the first criterion measure (recommended continuance) and 0.68 for the second criterion measure (recommended total time to be served before next review) were obtained on the construction sample. For the validation sample, these Rs were both 0.56. Neither discipline nor institutional progress, which were highly intercorrelated ($r = 0.90$), added significantly to the predictive equation, which is shown in table B-3.

In light of the substantial correlations found, it may be tentatively concluded that a fairly consistent (although implicit) youth parole selection policy was in effect. It is to be noted that two events occurred during the data collection phase which would have been expected to reduce the correlations found. One, the chairman of the youth division retired and was replaced by a member of the adult board. Two, the youth board decided to give credit for jail time uniformly in calculating time to be served. Previously, there had not been a consistent policy on this issue.

A Policy Profile

From equation 2, a table of the expected total number of months to be served before review may be calculated (see table B-4).

Table B-2
Zero Order Correlations among Variables in the Construction Sample

Variable	Offense Severity	Institutional Program Participation	Institutional Discipline	Prognosis (Parole Risk)	Recommended Continuance	Recommended Total Time to Be Served before Next Review
Offense Severity	1.00a (196)	0.13a (190)	0.10 (192)	−0.06 (196)	0.67a (196)	0.63a (196)
Institutional Program Participation		1.00a (190)	0.90a (190)	0.09 (190)	0.04 (190)	0.02 (190)
Institutional Discipline			1.00a (192)	0.16a (192)	0.04 (192)	0.02 (192)
Prognosis (Parole Risk)				1.00a (196)	−0.28a (196)	−0.29a (196)
Recommended Continuance					1.00a (196)	0.93a (196)
Recommended Total Time to Be Served before Next Review						1.00a (196)

Note: Number of observations is given in parentheses.
[a] Correlation coefficient is significant at $\alpha = 0.05$ (one-tailed).

Table B-3
Predictive Equations

Predicted recommended continuance from offense severity and parole prognosis (in months).

0.59 + 3.99 × Severity − 0.075 × Prognosis.

Predicted recommended total time served before next review (in months).

7.73 + 4.41 × Severity − 0.12 × Prognosis.

The expected time to be served for each combination of severity and prognosis (parole risk) is shown at the intersection of the appropriate row and column in table B-4. With a severity level of three (slightly below average severity) and a favorable parole outcome estimate of 50 percent, the expected total time to be served before review is 15.0 months. For a severity level of six (among the most serious cases) and a favorable parole outcome estimate of 70 percent, the expected time to be served is 25.9 months.

This type of matrix may be used to make explicit presently implicit paroling policies. It may be seen that the greatest weight is given to the factor of severity, while considerably less weight is given to the issue of parole risk. For example, it would appear that a difference of one level of severity shifts the decision 4.4 months, while a fifteen-point difference in parole risk estimate shifts the

Table B-4
Expected Total Number of Months to Be Served before Review

Prognosis (Parole Risk)	Severity					
	1	2	3	4	5	6
10	10.9	15.4	19.8	24.2	28.6	33.0
20	9.8	14.2	18.6	23.0	27.4	31.8
30	8.6	13.0	17.4	21.8	26.2	30.6
40	7.4	11.8	16.2	20.6	25.0	29.4
50	6.2	10.6	15.0	19.4	23.8	28.2
60	5.0	9.4	13.8	18.2	22.6	27.0
70	3.8	8.2	12.6	17.0	21.4	25.9
80	2.6	7.0	11.4	15.8	20.3	24.7
90	1.4	5.8	10.2	14.7	19.1	23.5
100	0.2	4.6	9.0	13.5	17.9	22.3

decision 1.8 months. Once the severity and parole risk estimates are taken into account, institutional discipline or progress does not significantly add to the prediction. It will be seen that at subsequent (review) decisions, institutional behavior becomes a strong predictor of decision outcome.

From the knowledge provided by this type of matrix, a parole board can test the congruence of actual and desired policy. They may be asked whether the values in the matrix conform to those they expect or desire and whether there are any particular values that they desire to change. Furthermore, the provision of this feedback on a regular basis would alert the board to apparent policy changes.

In individual case decision making, this measure could be used in the following manner. After reviewing a case, the parole board member would complete the rating scales and make his recommendation. He would then check his recommendation against the matrix provided. If he found that his recommendation varied from the expected decision by more than a given amount (for example, two months), he would be alerted to specify the considerations resulting in this difference or to reconsider his recommendation. For example, consider a case in which the parole board member recommends a continuance of four months and the expected continuance is nine months. The parole board member might point out that the subject's mother is extremely ill or that his institutional performance has been much above average. On the other hand, he might, upon reflection, find no exceptional factors and reconsider his recommendation. In either case, potential disparity would be reduced. Analysis of the reasons cited for deviation from the expected time held would provide insight into the incidence and importance of other factors in the parole selection decision and might be used to refine the policy model.

An Interval Severity Scale

As noted, the severity rating initially used was a rather crude ordinal scale. An attempt to transform this ordinal scale into an interval scale was made by substituting the median total time to be served before review (table B-5) for each severity level in place of the ordinal rating for the construction sample. Multiple regression equations were then recalculated using the prognosis and transformed severity ratings. Higher construction sample correlations ($R = 0.76$ and $R = 0.76$) were obtained for criterion 1 and 2 respectively.

Validation sample correlations were also higher ($R = 0.65$ and 0.68). Table B-6 displays these differences. Thus, it appears that a more refined severity scale increases the correlations noted. However, larger samples would be required to confirm this finding.

Table B-5
Median Total Time Served before Review for Each Severity Level

Severity	N	Median Total Time[a]
1	1	6.0
2	8	16.0
3	45	14.0
4	53	15.0
5	46	18.7
6	43	28.8

[a]The median time held for severity level two (16.0 months) is more than for severity levels three (14.0 months) and four (15.0 months). This may be a function of the small sample size for severity level two response forms ($N = 8$).

Nonlinear Relationships

The multiple regression methods used assume that the relationships among the variables are linear. In fact, nonlinear relationships may exist or there may be other interactions among the variables. Figure B-1 displays certain hypothetical relationships which would be masked by a multiple regression equation.

While each of the relationships described by figure B-1 has a perfect correlation, the correlation for low severity offenses is nonlinear. Furthermore, the relationships for medium and high severity offenses are linear, but they have different slopes. If a linear multiple regression equation were calculated for the total sample, the multiple correlation would be much reduced.

To examine for these possibilities, scattergrams (not shown) of parole prognosis versus expected total time held before review were plotted for each severity rating. No nonlinear relationships were apparent. The slopes of the best fit line (for each severity level) appeared similar, except for that of severity level five, which appeared much steeper. That is, comparatively less weight appeared to be given to prognosis for severity level five cases than for the other severity levels. Table B-7 displays these slopes.

Again, the small sample size limited further exploration. However, it appears that calculating the expected numbers of months to be served before review for each serverity level separately could be hypothesized to increase further the correlations noted.

Subsequent Decisions

Two alternative policy models had been articulated by the parole decision makers (hearing examiners and parole board members). One model proposed

Table B-6

Construction and Validation Correlations for Initial and Transformed Severity Scales

	Construction R	Validation R
Recommended continuance predicted from parole prognosis and initial severity scale	0.70	0.56
Compared to		
Recommended continuance predicted from parole prognosis and transformed severity scale	0.76	0.65
Recommended total time to be served before next review predicted from parole prognosis and initial severity scale	0.68	0.56
Compared to		
Recommended total time to be served before next review predicted from parole prognosis and transformed severity scale	0.76	0.68

that the initial decision should be of a length sufficient to take into account the severity of the offense and initial estimate of likely parole outcome, and that subsequent decisions should primarily consider institutional behavior. Under this model, the initial continuance would indicate to the inmate that he would be granted parole at the next review if he maintained a satisfactory institutional record. The second model proposed that shorter continuances be given to all subjects. Release would not necessarily follow good institutional adjustment at the next hearing, but could be granted for extremely good institutional progress.

In tables B-8 and B-9 the relation is shown between institutional discipline rating and the parole/continue dichotomy[10] for decisions two (number of response forms = 222) and three (number of response forms = 78).

It is apparent that the institutional discipline rating is a good predictor of the parole/continue decision ($\phi = 0.301$). At decision two a person with a fair or better discipline rating is very likely to be paroled (82.2 percent paroled). The relation between below-average discipline and parole/continue is not as strong (40.1 percent continued). It is possible that there is a mixture of the two policies in operation at this point.

For decision three, the institutional discipline rating proves to be a better predictor of the parole/continue decision ($\phi = 0.585$). The relation between

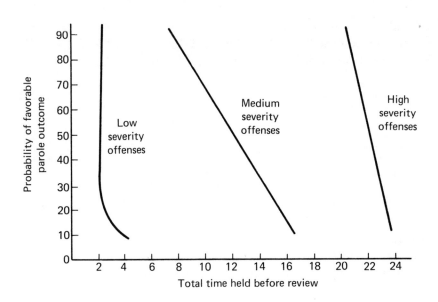

Figure B-1. Hypothetical Relationship between Parole Risk and Total Time Held
before Review

average or better discipline rating and parole is higher (88.0 percent paroled) as
is the relation between below average ratings and a decision to continue (55.6
percent continued). It would appear that at the third hearing a good institutional
discipline rating will result in parole.

Conclusions

From a set of four rating scales completed by parole board members for a
sample of cases at the time of decision making, a method of describing and
articulating presently implicit paroling policy is shown. This method might be
used by parole board members to examine the congruence of actual with desired
policy on a macroscopic level. At present, it appears that at initial hearings,
primary weight is given to the board member's estimation of the severity of the
instant offense. Secondary weight is given to estimate of risk of parole violation.
At subsequent hearings, institutional adjustment becomes a primary decision
determinant.

A set of expected decisions for given factor combinations may be determined through the use of multiple correlation techniques and graphical analyses.
In relation to individual case decision making, these expected values may provide

Table B-7

Regression Line Slope (Prognosis vs. Expected Months Served before Review) by Severity Level: Combined Construction and Validation Samples

Severity Level	Slope	Number
1	not calculated	1
2	−8.2	13
3	−9.4	78
4	−7.7	113
5	−50.8	99
6	−9.6	74

Table B-8

Relationship between Institutional Discipline Rating and Parole (Recommended Decision ≤ 4 Months) vs. Continue (for Decision Two)

	Institutional Discipline Ratings					
	Very Poor	Poor	Fair	Good	Very Good	Total
Number Paroled	8	30	43	61	21	163
Percentage	40.0	68.2	79.6	85.9	77.8	75.5
Number Not Paroled	12	14	11	10	6	53
Percentage	60.0	31.8	20.4	14.1	22.2	24.5
Total	20	44	54	71	27	216[a]

Note: $X^2 = 19.62, P < 0.001$
$\Phi = 0.301$

[a]Six subjects had a rating of 6 (not enough information).

an equity measure to alert hearing examiners and parole board members to potentially disparate decisions.

While the measures utilized in this research were subjective, more objective ones would be desired for implementation as a policy control and equity device. For example, an experience table might be substituted for the prognosis (risk) measure, and an objective scale, such as the one developed by Sellin and Wolfgang,[11] might be utilized for the severity measures.

Practical Applications

Several practical results appear to have been associated in some part with this research. As part of a pilot regionalization project, the parol board requested

Table B-9
Relationship between Institutional Discipline Rating and Parole (Recommended Decision ≤ 4 Months) vs. Continue (for Decision Three)

	Institutional Discipline Ratings					
	Very Poor	Poor	Fair	Good	Very Good	Total
Number Paroled	2	10	21	15	8	56
Percentage	18.2	62.5	77.8	100	100	72.7
Number Not Paroled	9	6	6	0	0	21
Percentage	81.8	37.5	22.2	0	0	27.3
Total	11	16	27	15	8	77[a]

Note: $X^2 = 26.32, P < 0.001$
$\Phi = 0.585$

[a]One subject had a rating of 6 (not enough information).

from the research team, and subsequently implemented, a policy/control/equity device similar to that described earlier (with separate guidelines for youth and adult offenders).[12] Furthermore, in this pilot regionalization project, the policy of considering severity and prognosis (risk) at the initial hearing and, with a few specific exceptions, considering institutional performance as the major determinant at subsequent hearings was adopted.

Notes

1. K.C. Davis, *Discretionary Justice* (Baton Rouge: Louisiana State University Press, 1969).

2. F. Remington et al., *Criminal Justice Administration* (Indianapolis: Bobbs-Merrill, 1969).

3. L.E. Ohlin, *Selection for Parole* (New York: Russell Sage, 1951).

4. For a description of the Youth Corrections Act and the structure and function of the United States Board of Parole, see *Rules of the United States Board of Parole* (Washington, D.C.: U.S. Department of Justice, 1971).

5. In order to reduce the demands on the parole board members' time, the sampling for subsequent decisions was terminated March 30, 1972.

6. This procedure resulted in 729 evaluation forms from approximately 340 cases. Unfortunately, sixty-five cases were omitted from the sample owing to the failure of the board clerical staff to place the required forms in the case folder prior to decision. However, as the clerical staff do not read the folders, and the folders are processed sequentially, this bias was assumed to be random.

7. In addition, there were forty-one instances in which a board member neglected to complete the evaluation form.

8. D. Dawson, "The Decision to Grant or Deny Parole," *Washington University Law Quarterly* 243 (1966):265-285.

9. V. O'Leary, "Parole Frame of Reference Inventory" (New York: National Council on Crime and Delinquency, 1969; mimeo).

10. Parole includes all decisions to parole or to continue four months or less (such continuances generally relate to parole program formulation).

11. T. Sellin and M. Wolfgang, *The Measurement of Delinquency* (New York: John Wiley, 1964).

12. See chapter 2.

Appendix C:
The Relationship between Mean Cost Rating and Kendall's Rank Correlation Coefficient

Leszek Lancucki and
Roger Tarling

Mean Cost Rating (MCR)[1] was first proposed by Duncan, Ohlin, Reiss and Stanton as an aid to making selection decisions.[2] Since then MCR has been employed in criminology to assess the power of prediction instruments. Its wider use, however, has been limited because its sampling distribution is not known. In this appendix, after briefly describing MCR, we prove that it is closely related to Kendall's rank correlation coefficient tau, τ, and show how the significance of the degree of association, of which MCR is a measure, can be tested. In addition, we give an example of its calculation.

In table C-1, offenders have been classified according to two criteria. The first criterion, (risk class) is usually an estimate of the offenders' risk of failing. This can be a score (often referred to in the literature on methods of prediction in criminology as a base expectancy score) or a probability of failure which is derived from a prediction instrument developed using background characteristics of the offender by some statistical technique (for example, multiple regression). The offenders are sorted into k ordered risk classes with t_i in each class. The second criterion is a dichotomous measure, success or failure, and a commonly used measure in criminology is whether an offender has been reconvicted within a given period of time, for example, after being released from prison. If he has not been reconvicted he is classified as a success but if he has he is classified as a failure. In the sample shown in table C-1 there are N_s successes and N_f failures.

In order to make comparisons of an instrument with others, to assess the usefulness of his prediction instrument, and to make the researcher require a measure of its ability to discriminate between successes and failures: he requires a measure of the predictive power of the instrument.

Mean Cost Rating (MCR)

MCR measures the power of a prediction instrument by contrasting the concepts of cost and utility.

MCR is defined as:

$$MCR = \sum_{i=1}^{k} C_i\, U_{i-1} - \sum_{i=1}^{k} C_{i-1}\, U_i$$

©*Social Science Research,* Academic Press, 1978. Reprinted by permission.

Table C-1
Criterion Categories by Risk Classes

Risk Class	Success	Failure	Total
1	s_1	f_1	t_1
2	s_2	f_2	t_2
3	s_3	f_3	t_3
.	.	.	.
.	.	.	.
.	.	.	.
.	.	.	.
k	s_k	f_k	t_k
Total	N_s	N_f	T

where k is the number of risk or score classes.

i is the risk class above which (i.e., for greater values of i) all cases are accepted (predicted as successes) and at or below which all cases are rejected (predicted as failures).

C_i is the cost at risk class i which is the proportion of total successes rejected by cutting the table just above risk class i. Cost, therefore, reflects the errors in prediction.

U_i is the utility at risk class i which is the proportion of total failures rejected by cutting the table just above risk class i. Utility, therefore, reflects correct predictions.

For table C-1:

$$C_i = (\frac{s_1}{N_s} + \frac{s_2}{N_s} + \ldots + \frac{s_i}{N_s})$$

$$U_i = (\frac{f_1}{N_f} + \frac{f_2}{N_f} + \ldots + \frac{f_i}{N_f})$$

MCR may lie between -1 and $+1$ but $|MCR|$ is usually quoted.

Kendall's Tau (τ)

Table C-1 is equivalent to a two-way $(2 \times k)$ contingency table with a dichotomous variable, measuring success or failure, and a polytomous variable, measuring the risk of failing, grouped into k rank order categories (members within the same risk class having equal rank). The degree of association between these two variables—the predictive power of the prior variable—can be measured by Kendall's rank correlation coefficient tau, τ.[3] Kendall's τ for a $2 \times k$ contingency table is defined as:

$$\tau = \frac{4S}{T^2}$$

where:

$$S = \sum_{i=1}^{k} s_i(f_{i+1} + f_{i+2} + \ldots + f_k) - \sum_{i=1}^{k} f_i(s_{i+1} + s_{i+2} + \ldots + s_k)$$

Like all correlation coefficients τ may lie between -1 and $+1$. (Strictly this is only true in certain circumstances—see Kendall, p. 47.) The variance of S is known and is equal to:

$$Var\ S = \frac{N_s N_f}{3T(T-1)} (T^3 - \sum_{i=1}^{k} t_i^3)$$

Thus knowing the variance of S provides us with a test of the significance of τ, or rather of S from which τ is derived. For samples greater than 10, $\dfrac{S - C}{\sqrt{Var\ S}}$ is approximately normally distributed. C is a correction for continuity and Kendall suggests as an estimate of C:

$$C = \frac{2T - t_1 - t_k}{2(k - 1)}$$

Relationship between MCR and τ

It can be shown that

$$MCR = \frac{-S}{N_s N_f}$$

The proof of this result is given in the last section of this appendix. As the absolute value of MCR is usually quoted, more generally

$$MCR = \frac{|S|}{N_s N_f}$$

202

Thus MCR is a function of S just as τ is a function of S and they are related in the following way:

$$MCR = |\tau|(\frac{T^2}{4N_s N_f})$$

(and when $N_s = N_f$ $MCR = \tau$).

The important statistic is S and the denominator of MCR and τ constrain them both to the range -1 to $+1$. The degree of association, of which MCR and τ are measures, can be tested by reference to S.

Example

To illustrate these points we calculate MCR and τ, and test their significance, for one of the prediction instruments developed by the Parole Decision-Making Project.[4] Background information was collected on 1,546 male prisoners released from the federal prison system during 1970 and from this a salient factor score was developed using a simple Burgess point scoring method. The relationship between this score and actual outcome is given in table C-2.

Table C-2
Parole Outcomes and Salient Factor Scores

Salient Factor Score	Success	Failure	Total
1	19	26	45
2	61	66	127
3	127	80	207
4	152	73	225
5	154	60	214
6	136	39	175
7	123	25	148
8	122	18	140
9	85	12	97
10	106	6	112
11	56	0	56
Total	1141	405	1546

$$MCR = \frac{|S|}{N_s N_f}$$

This formula provides an alternative means of calculating MCR to that suggested by Inciardi, Babst, and Koval.[5]

$S = 19(66 + 80 + \ldots + 6 + 0) + 61(80 + 73 + \ldots + 6 + 0)$

$\quad + \ldots + 85(6 + 0) + 106(0)$

$\quad - 26(61 + 127 + \ldots + 106 + 56) - 66(127 + 152 + \ldots + 106 + 56)$

$\quad - \ldots - 12(106 + 56) + 6(56)$

$S = -192788$

$$MCR = \frac{192788}{1141 \times 405}$$

$MCR = 0.42$

$$\tau = \frac{4S}{T^2}$$

$$\tau = \frac{4 \times (-192788)}{1546^2}$$

$\tau = -0.32$

$$Var\ S = \frac{N_s N_f}{3T(T-1)} (T^3 - \Sigma t_i^3)$$

$\Sigma t_i^3 = 45^3 + 127^3 + \ldots + 112^3 + 56^3$

$\Sigma t_i^3 = 46038604$

$$Var\ S = \frac{1141 \times 405}{3 \times 1546 \times 1545} (1546^3 - 46038604)$$

$Var\ S = 235323290$

$s.e.\ S = 15340$

$$C = \frac{2T - t_1 - t_k}{2(k - 1)}$$

$$C = \frac{2 \times 1546 - 45 - 56}{2 \times 10}$$

$$C = 150$$

$$Z = \frac{S - C}{\sqrt{Var\ S}}$$

$$Z = \frac{192788 - 150}{15340}$$

$$Z = 12.6$$

The probability that this is attained or exceeded in absolute value is $<.001$ and the value of S, and hence MCR and τ, is very highly significant.

Proof

Proof that $MCR = \dfrac{-S}{N_s N_f}$

$$S = \sum_{i=1}^{k} [s_i(f_{i+1} + f_{i+2} + \ldots + f_k)] - \sum_{i=1}^{k} [f_i(s_{i+1} + s_{i+2} + \ldots + s_k)]$$

$$MCR = \sum_{i=1}^{k} C_i U_{i-1} - \sum_{i=1}^{k} C_{i-1} U_i$$

where:

$$C_i = \left(\frac{s_1}{N_s} + \frac{s_2}{N_s} + \ldots + \frac{s_i}{N_s}\right) = \frac{1}{N_s}(N_s - s_{i+1} - s_{i+2} - \ldots - s_k)$$

$$U_i = \left(\frac{f_1}{N_f} + \frac{f_2}{N_f} + \ldots + \frac{f_i}{N_f}\right) = \frac{1}{N_f}(N_f - f_{i+1} - f_{i+2} - \ldots - f_k)$$

Summations throughout are over the range $i = 1$ to k and are henceforward omitted.

$$MCR = \frac{1}{N_s!} \sum_j (N_s - s_{i+1} - s_{i+2} - \ldots - s_k)(N_f - f_i - f_{i+1} - \ldots - f_k)$$

$$- \frac{1}{N_s N_f} \Sigma \, (N_s - s_i - s_{i+1} - \ldots - s_k)(N_f - f_{i+1} - f_{i+2} - \ldots - f_k)$$

$$MCR = \frac{1}{N_s N_f} \Sigma \, (N_s N_f - N_s f_i - N_s f_{i+1} - \ldots - N_s f_k - s_{i+1} N_f + s_{i+1} f_i + \ldots$$

$$+ s_{i+1} f_k \ldots - s_k N_f + s_k f_i + s_k f_{i+1} + \ldots + s_k f_k)$$

$$- \frac{1}{N_s N_f} \Sigma \, (N_s N_f - N_s f_{i+1} - N_s f_{i+2} - \ldots - N_s f_k - s_i N_f + s_i f_{i+1} + \ldots$$

$$+ s_i f_k \ldots - s_k N_f + s_k f_{i+1} + s_k f_{i+2} + \ldots + s_k f_k)$$

It can be seen that upon subtraction only terms in s_i and f_i remain.

$$MCR = \frac{1}{N_s N_f} \Sigma \, (- N_s f_i + s_{i+1} f_i + \ldots + s_k f_i)$$

$$- \frac{1}{N_s N_f} \Sigma \, (- N_f s_i + s_i f_{i+1} + \ldots + s_i f_k)$$

$$\frac{1}{N_s N_f} \Sigma \, N_s f_i = \frac{1}{N_s N_f} \Sigma \, N_f s_i = 1$$

$$MCR = \frac{1}{N_s N_f} \Sigma \, [f_i(s_{i+1} + \ldots + s_k)] - \frac{1}{N_s N_f} \Sigma \, [s_i(f_{i+1} + \ldots + f_k)]$$

$$MCR = \frac{-S}{N_s N_f}$$

Notes

1. The sampling distribution of the statistic *MCR* has not previously been known. Because of the extensive use of this statistic in parole prediction studies and related criminological research, we are especially grateful to the authors and to the British Home Department for permission to include this appendix here.

2. D.O. Dudley, L.E. Ohlin, A.J. Reiss, Jr., and H.R. Stanton, "Formal

Devices for Making Selection Decisions" *American Journal of Sociology* 58 (1953):573-584.

3. M.G. Kendall, *Rank Correlation Methods* (London: Charles Griffin, 1970).

4. J.L. Beck and P.B. Hoffman, "Time Served and Release Performance: A Research Note," *Journal of Research in Crime and Delinquency* 13, 2 (July 1976):127-132.

5. J.A. Inciardi, D.V. Babst and M. Koval, "Computing Mean Cost Rating (MCR)," *Journal of Research in Crime and Delinquency* 10 (1970):22-28.

Index

Index

Uniform Parole Reports program, 42
"Uniqueness" of individuals, 99-100
United States Board of Parole (Parole
  Commission), 2, 16, 18, 23, 41,
  44, 57, 69, 123, 131, 149
United States Department of Justice,
  44

Value systems, 91-92
Variance, 85-86, 88

VERA system, 152
Vold, G.B., 43

Warner, F.B., 43
Wilbanks and Hindelang study, 42
Williams and Lambert method, 46

Youth Correction cases, 15, 17, 23,
  44, 56, 151, 183-188

About the Authors

Don M. Gottfredson is dean and professor at the Rutgers University School of Criminal Justice. Formerly director of the Research Center of the National Council on Crime and Delinquency, Dr. Gottfredson is a Fellow of the National Center for Juvenile Justice, a member of the Advisory Council of the National Institute of Law Enforcement and Criminal Justice, and vice president of the American Society of Criminology. He has been a consultant or advisor to various national and state criminal justice planning bodies including recent membership on the Task Force on Research and Development, National Criminal Justice Standards and Goals and Chairmanship, New Jersey Correctional Master Plan Policy Council.

Leslie T. Wilkins, is a professor in the School of Criminal Justice at the State University of New York at Albany, and was previously acting dean of the School of Criminology, University of California at Berkeley. He has been a senior advisor to the United Nations Asia and Far East Institute, Tokyo, and U.N. Headquarters, Geneva and New York. Prior to this, he was director of research, British Civil Service, Home Department. Professor Wilkins was awarded the Francis Wood Memorial Prize of the Royal Statistical Society, of which he is a member of the Council, and was twice elected as chairman of the General Applications Section.

Peter B. Hoffman is director of research of the United States Parole Commission. He was previously a research associate of the Research Center of the National Council on Crime and Delinquency. Dr. Hoffman's prior experience includes work in both probation and parole supervision. He received the Ph.D. in Criminal Justice from the State University of New York at Albany and was a Guggenheim Visiting Fellow in Criminal Justice at the Yale University Law School.